FACTS, RESEARCH AND INTERVENTION IN GERIATRICS SERIE

HYDRATION AND AGING

Serdi Publisher
Springer Publishing Company
Paris - New York

Serdi Publisher, 320, Rue Saint-Honoré, F75001 Paris, France
Springer Publisher Company, 536 Broadway N-Y 10012-3955, USA

ISBN 2-909342-52-2

Serie : Facts, Research and Intervention in Geriatrics 1998

We wish to express our sincere thanks to

INSTITUT DE L'EAU

PERRIER VITTEL

for their support of this publication

(Facts and Research in Gerontology Contents are listed in : ISI/IST P&B online database, Current Book Contents - Current Contents / Life Sciences and Clinical Medicine Philadelphia, CNRS / Pascal, Paris, Current Literature on Aging, Washington, C.P.A: New Literature on Old Age and Age Info, London; CAB International, Biosis).

FACTS, RESEARCH AND INTERVENTION IN GERIATRICS 1998

HYDRATION AND AGING

Invited Editors
M. J. ARNAUD
R. BAUMGARTNER
J. E. MORLEY
I. ROSENBERG
S. TOSHIKAZU
(Vittel, Albuquerque, Saint-Louis, Boston, Tochigi-Ken)

Editors
B. VELLAS, J.L. ALBAREDE, P.J. GARRY
(Toulouse France, Albuquerque USA)

Serdi

320, Rue Saint-Honoré, F-75001 Paris
Fax : (33) 5 61 75 11 28 - E-mail : 100775.1315@CompuServe.com

Springer Publishing Company
536 Broadway N-Y 10012-3955, USA
Tel : 212 431 4370 - Fax : 212 941 7842

3

CONTENTS

CONTENTS

III - INTERVENTION

RECOMMENDATIONS TO AUTHORS

Manuscripts proposed to "Facts, Research and Intervention in Geriatrics" must be submitted in accordance with the standards established by the International Committee of Editors of Medical Journals, Annals of Internal Medicine, 1982, 96, part 1 : 766-771, summarized below:

* The text should be submitted in the following format : title page, abstract and key words, text, acknowledgements, references, tables, illustrations and captions. It should be typed with single spacing, on one side only on paper measuring 21 x 29,7 cm, leaving a left hand margin of 4 cm.

* The title page includes : 1) the title of the article ; 2) the authors' fornames and surnames ; 3) the names of departments and institutions to which the authors belong ; 4) the main author's name and complete address ; 5) the funding sources (donation award, grant etc...).

* The second page should include the abstract and the key words.

* The third page includes a very short title (less than 40 characters) as a header for each edited page.

* The text will be eventually divided into : introduction, material and methods, results, discussion and conclusion.

* References in the text should be cited by numbers, placed in line with the text and numbered in order of appearance. They should be listed in numerical order at the end of the paper in the form prescribed in the Uniform Requirements.

** Table : All tables must be written in the same version than the text **with maximum dimensions of : large = 115 mm and high = 183 mm**. Each table should be inserted in the text. It should have a title and, if desired, an explanation. Each table should be cited in the text and should be numbered according to the order of appearance.*

* Illustration for diagrams, original artwork : Black ink on white paper and glossy prints will usually be acceptable. All illustrations should bear author's name and the number of the illustration on the reverse side, also an indication in soft pencil if only part of the illustration is required.

*Captions should be typed on separate sheets. **All illustrations or figures must be cited and inserted in the text and in the disk**, and the space must be shown in the text. It is the responsibility of the author(s) to ensure that any requirements of copyright and courtesy are fulfilled in reproducing illustrations and appropriate acknowledgements included with the captions.*

* Copyright : Authors of accepted manuscripts must transfer copyright to "Facts, Research and Intervention in Geriatrics", which holds the copyright to all articles, comments, reviews and notes published in "Facts, Research and Intervention in Geriatrics".

* Submission of manuscripts : Contributions and correspondence should be sent to :
- Professor Bruno VELLAS, Centre de Gériatrie, C.H.U. Purpan-Casselardit - 31300 Toulouse (France) or Clinical Nutrition Program, UNM, Rm. 215 Surge Building, 2701 Frontier Place N.E., Albuquerque, NM 87131, USA.

* Two copies must be submitted. Submission of an article is taken to imply that its content has not previously been published and is not being considered for publication elsewhere.

* Manuscripts are sent to reviewers for recommendation and comment. Reviewers' comments are provided to authors.

The submission of electronic manuscripts is requested. Electronic manuscripts have the advantage that there is no need for rekeying of text, thereby avoiding the possibility of introducing errors and resulting in reliable and fast delivery of proofs. The desired storage medium is a 3 1/2 inch disk in Macintosh format, and the preferred Microsoft is "Word Version 4., 5. or 6.". Although the Microsoft "Word Perfect 5.1" is welcome in IBM PC Format. After final acceptance, your disk plus one final, printed and exactly matching version (as a printout) should be submitted together to the accepting editor. It is important that the file on disk and the printout are identical. Both will then forwarded by the editor. Please label the disk with your name, Microsoft used, and the name of the file to be processed.

THE JOURNAL OF NUTRITION, HEALTH & AGING

Edited by B.J. VELLAS, M.D., Ph.D.; Wm.C. CHUMLEA, Ph.D.; D. LANZMANN, M.D.

MISSION AND EDITORIAL POLICY

There is an increasing scientific and clinical interest in the interactions of nutrition and health as part of the aging process. This interest is due to the important role that nutrition plays throughout the life span. This role affects the growth and development of the body during childhood, affects the risk for acute and chronic diseases, the maintenance of physiological processes and the biological process of aging. A major aim of "The Journal of Nutrition, Health & Aging" is to contribute to the improvement of knowledge regarding the relationships between nutrition and the aging process from birth to old age.

1998 SUBSCRIPTIONS INFORMATION

❑ Institution: $120.00 per year in U.S. ; $140.00 per year elsewhere (for subscriptions outside North America, please add $20.00 for air freight)
❑ Individual: $80.00 per year in U.S. ; $ 95.00 per year elsewhere (for subscriptions outside North America, please add $20.00 for air freight)
❑ Check
❑ Charge my ❑ American Express ❑ VISA
❑ MasterCard 4-digit interbank # _____

Card # _____ Exp. date _____
Signature_____
Name (please print)_____
Address _____
_____

City/State/Zip/Country _____
Send order and payment to:
• For North America : Springer Publishing Company, 536 Broadway, New York, NY 10012-3955, USA. Fax: (212) 941 7842
• For Europe : Serdi Publishing Company, 320 Rue Saint-Honoré, 75001 Paris-France. Fax: (33) 5 61 75 11 28 • E-mail: 100775.1315@CompuServe.com

FOREWORD

M. J. ARNAUD

Institut de l'Eau Perrier Vittel, BP 101, F-88804 Vittel Cedex France. e-mail: instieau@worldnet.fr ; http//www.institut-eau.tm.fr

Aging has become an important issue because of the dramatic change in life expectancy. This increase in life expectancy due to the progress in sciences and in medicine is largely explained by the improvements in mortality in infancy and young adulthood. If we try to understand aging, it appears rapidly that the results of studies conducted in younger people cannot be extrapolated to older people. Because the aging population demands major changes in society and health care, more fundamental and clinical research is needed to understand impairments in cellular mechanisms or decline in physiological functions associated with aging. The final objective of this research is to maintain health and quality of life by reducing the number of years that people spend with diseases or disabled.

With environmental factors, including lifestyle and physical activity, nutrition has a key role in maintenance of health. In the elderly inadequate food intake or the poorer ability to synthesize vitamin D in the skin or to absorb nutrients from the gut are frequently mentioned in the recommendation of higher intakes of specific nutrients.

The importance of hydration and dehydration is also mentioned but early diagnosis of fluid and electrolyte disorders from physical signs may be absent or misleading in older patients. It is thus essential to understand why the elderly are at risk for dehydration and to define and quantify the prevalence of dehydration and borderline dehydration.

Among the factors leading to a decreased fluid intake and to increased fluid losses, the altered sensation of thirst, the modifications of kidney functions, hormonal and neurotransmitter changes are the most important ones. These physiological modifications are reinforced by behavioral attitudes such as the occurence of urinary incontinence and frequent immobility. Healthy elderly people and even more older people with a chronic illness whose occurence rises with advancing age are more likely to require drug treatments. Diuretics and laxatives increase the risk of dehydration. For other drugs, aging may impair the way the body handles drugs and to prevent the risk of iatrogen toxicity in the elderly, adequate water intake is also recommended. While it is well recognized that the maintenance of water balance is essential for human health, the tools for a rapid and accurate evaluation of hydration are not available and the consequences of borderline dehydration are not known.

It appears extremely important for the Perrier Vittel Water Institute to contact different scientists and research laboratories working on various aspects of the hydration of the elderly to update our knowledge on the changes in fluid and electrolyte homeostatic mechanisms that adversely affect the elderly and increase morbidity and mortality.

This special issue of "Facts, Research and Intervention in Geriatrics" dedicated to "Hydration & Aging" will fulfill our objective if it stimulates readers to initiate further research efforts in this new and multidisciplinary area.

HYDRATION AND AGING

I - FACTS

AGE-RELATED CHANGES IN BODY FLUID COMPARTMENTS AND THE ASSESSMENT OF DEHYDRATION IN OLD AGE

M. G.M. O. RIKKERT*, W. H.L. HOEFNAGELS*, P. DEURENBERG**

*Departments of Geriatric Medicine, University of Nijmegen, The Netherlands.** Department of Human Nutrition, Wageningen Agricultural University, The Netherlands. Grant support This work was supported by The Netherlands Programme for Research on Aging, NESTOR, funded by the Ministry of Education, Culture and Sciences, and the Ministry of Health, Welfare and Sports. Address correspondence to: M.G.M. Olde Rikkert, MD: Department of Geriatric Medicine, University Hospital Nijmegen, P.O. Box 9101, 6500 HB Nijmegen, The Netherlands. Telephone: 00-31-24-3616772; Fax: 00-31-24-3617408 E-mail address: M. Olde-Rikkert@czzoger.AZN.NL

Abstract : From the beginning of gerontology it has been recognized that the homeostasis of fluid balance is an important prerequisite for healthy aging. However, only since modern techniques of measuring body composition became available the effects of aging on body hydration could be studied scientifically. Following a summary of the historical notions on age-related changes in body hydration, this article reviews the recent findings concerning the effects of aging on the absolute and relative amount of total body water and its distribution over extra- and intracellular compartments. The high prevalence of disturbances of fluid balance in elderly patients and the difficulty of diagnosing early stages of dehydration triggered also clinical research on age- and disease-related changes in water homeostasis. Empirical findings on risk factors of dehydration, and on diagnostic strategies of detecting dehydration will be described subsequently. Although there has been made much progress in research on normal body hydration and the assessment of dehydration in the elderly, up till now no single measure proved to be the ideal watermark in the diagnosis of dehydration. It will be explained why the considerable between-subject variability in body hydration makes it highly unlikely that an initial assessment of dehydration in geriatric patients can ever be based on a single measure. Research efforts should rather be focussed on validating modern techniques of body composition analysis in elderly subjects.

Key Words : *Body composition, Body water compartments, Dehydration.*

INTRODUCTION

From the classic Greeks until now, theories, facts and research on body composition, especially with regard to body hydration, have played an important role in studying the aging process. The first concepts about the nature of aging, dating from the mid-fifth century B.C., attributed aging to the loss of heat and body water. This remained the central hypothesis of aging for a long time. Only in the seventeenth and eighteenth century A.D., advances in chemistry, anatomy, and physiology putted less weight on body fluids and their central role in the aging process. However, the new scientific methods provided evidence for the prescientific notion that body water is of ultimate importance for human life. Circulation, thermoregulation, nutrition and cell metabolism were partly unraveled and proved to be highly dependend on the homeostatic mechanisms that regulate water balance. Therefore, it remained important for modern gerontologists to study changes in body hydration, not as a cause but as a consequence of aging. Clinicians also became aware of the practical implications of body hydration in medicine by studying pharmacokinetics (i.e. the study of how the human body deals with drugs). Water plays a crucial part in absorption, distribution and elimination of drugs, especially in case of water soluble drugs. Consequently, knowledge about age-related changes in body hydration is an important issue in geriatric medicine. However, current procedures to assess the state of hydration are technically difficult to perform and require a lot of expertise. As greater numbers of people reach older ages, there is a growing need, both clinically and scientifically, for simple non-invasive techniques to measure body hydration in elderly subjects [1].

At the present, there is substantial evidence that aging causes changes in body composition. Moreover, renal function and thirst perception on average decline in the elderly [2-8]. Together these three factors explain for an important part why dehydration is common in the elderly population [9]. In 1991 6.7% of the hospitalized patients aged 65 and over were diagnosed as dehydrated and 1.4% had dehydration as the principal diagnosis [10]. Prospective studies in nursing homes showed that residents were dehydrated in 50% of the febrile episodes, and that 27% of the nursing home population that was referred to hospitals, was admitted because of dehydration [11]. Apart from the institutionalized population, dehydration proved to be very common in community-dwelling elderly [12]. Moreover, dehydration is not only a common, but also a very serious condition in geriatrics. Mortality of dehydration may exceed 50% if not treated adequately [13-15]. In terms of morbidity, Seymour et al. showed an association between high degrees of dehydration and poor mental function [16]. Others found that dehydration was a significant risk factor for developing thrombo-embolic complications, infectious diseases, kidney stones, and obstipation [17-21]. Altogether, these epidemiological findings clearly show the importance of an early diagnosis and adequate treatment of dehydration to reduce its serious effects on geriatric patients and health care expenditures. However, such an early diagnosis is often difficult because the classical signs of dehydration may be absent or misleading in an older patient.

This article reviews the most important methodological developments and the results of current research on assessing body hydration and dehydration in the elderly. Age-related risk factors are discussed because they may help to identify the most vulnerable subjects. Because ancient Greek physicians already struggled with these issues and because of the striking accuracy of some of their observations on body hydration, the article starts with a summary of the classical concepts of changes in body hydration as a cause of aging.

HYDRATION AND AGING

The oldest European theories on aging were based on the hypothesis that all life is wet and that aging is caused by dehydration [22]. Homer compared an old woman with a dried olive-branch, and Alkmaion (540 B.C.) stated that health depends on a proper balance between the wet and dry, and the cold and warm [23]. However, within the Hippocratic works there is already a controversy about body hydration. Most Hippocratic authors attribute aging to the loss of innate heat and humidity, but in the book "The Diet" Hippocrates says: "The elderly are cold and moist, because the fire burns out in their bodies and the watery element flows in; withdrawal of dryness and occupation by the wet" [24]. Aristotle disagreed with this view on aging in his: "On Youth and Old Age, On Life and Death and On Respirations": "One should know that living beings are moist and warm and that these characteristics may be attributed to life, no matter what it looks like. However, old age is dry and cold" [23]. Later, Galen (129-200 A.D.) combined the doctrine of the four humours with the decline of innate heat and body water [25]. Galen also stressed the difficulty to diagnose dehydration in elderly subjects. Western medicine was dominated by Galen's ideas during the Middle Ages. Possibly as a result of this 'dehydration-theory' it became fashionable in that period for elderly persons to take special baths to become rehydrated and more youthful.

It was only at the end of the seventeenth century, when the modern scientific era started, that the humoral theory including the dryness of old age was abandoned [26]. Christoph Hufeland said that the aging process itself dried the body, narrowed the vessels and accumulated earthy material [25]. From that time body hydration was not regarded anymore as a cause, but rather as a consequence of aging. However, in general medicine the hypothesis was recently raised again that a decrease in intracellular water and the resulting change in cell shape might be very important triggers for proteolysis and catabolism [27]. The possibility of dehydration as one of the factors of aging and cell loss was also rediscussed recently [28]. More specifically, it has been suggested that recurrent dehydration may accelerate brain aging [29]. However, these hypotheses lack empirical data, just as the ancient assumptions on the role of dehydration in the aging process. Likewise, twentiest century geriatrics has to confess that Galen's difficulties in diagnosing dehydration have not been resolved. Therefore, studying body hydration and dehydration is still necessary in gerontology and geriatrics.

METHODS TO ASSESS HYDRATION

Chemical analysis of human cadavers is the most accurate and direct measurement of body hydration. However, these analyses have not been carried out frequently and -to our knowledge- none of the other methods applied in measuring body hydration is validated against direct human cadaver analysis. Broïek introduced the concept of an empirical "reference body" based on the chemical analysis of three male cadavers (mean age: 35 yrs) [30]. This "reference body" contains 62.43% of water per kilogram body weight and 73.7% water per kilogram fat-free mass (FFM). Reference values of body composition have also been described for children, but not for elderly subjects [31, 32]. An important limitation of cadaver analysis is the intrinsic impossibility to measure extracellular and intracellular water (ECW, ICW) separately.

Direct estimations of total body water (TBW) in living human beings are based on dilution methods using the isotopes of hydrogen deuterium (stable isotope), tritium (radioactive) or oxygen (stable) labeled water, or a nonisotopic tracer compound like antipyrine. Most validation studies of indirect bioelectrical measurements of TBW such as bioelectrical impedance analysis are based on deuterium dilution. After the equilibration of a known mass of deuterium in the body water compartment, TBW can be calculated by measuring deuterium concentration in plasma. This concentration can be determined by gas chromatography, mass spectrometry (precision: 1%) or infra red absorption (precision: 2.5%) [33]. The exact accuracy of measuring TBW by deuterium dilution in man is unknown. However, both deuterium and tritium exchange with non-aqueous hydrogen and therefore the dilution spaces measured with the oxides of these isotopes will overestimate total body water. In most cases, investigators correct for this overestimation which is assumed to be 5% of TBW [34]. The measurement of TBW with water marked with an oxygen-18 isotope is more accurate, but there is still a small overestimation of TBW (1-2%), by non-aqueous oxygen exchange [35, 36].

Indirect methods to determine TBW can be divided in property and component based techniques [37]. The most accurate property based methods predict TBW using regression formulas in which electrical conductivity or bioelectrical impedance, height, and sometimes age, sex and weight are the independent variables. Both total body electrical conductivity (TOBEC) and total body impedance are rapid, safe and non-invasive methods. TOBEC is based on the principle that the impedance of a radio frequency coil is changed when a human body is introduced. The change of impedance is related to the volume of body electrolytes. Resulting standard errors of the estimate (SEE) of TBW are smaller than 1 liter, meaning that 68% of the individual prediction errors are smaller [16, 38]. TOBEC as a measure of TBW has not been validated in the elderly. In bioelectrical impedance analysis the resistance offered by a biological conductor to a small alternating current is inversely proportional to the amount of body fluid in the conductor. Many regression formulas have already been developed to predict TBW by impedance measurements in populations with different race, sex, age and diseases [39, 40]. Recently, it has been shown that it is possible to distinguish between the extra- and intracellular water compartments using multi-frequency impedances [41]. At low frequencies, body impedance measures extracellular water only, because the current is unable to pass the cell membrane. With increasing frequency the current passes the cell membrane, so that at high frequencies body impedance is a measure of total body water. In a validation study on 117 healthy elderly subjects, SEEs for the prediction of TBW were 12.3% and 7.4% for men and women, respectively, which was larger than the prediction errors in younger populations [40]. This may be due to changes in body build with age which affect body fluid distribution. These changes are primarily caused by highly individual processes like osteoporosis and decrease in muscle mass. Therefore, the error of a population based prediction formula of TBW by means of the impedance index (length^2/impedance) will be larger for individual subjects. Absolute changes in body water, introduced by a diuretic drug, were not predicted accurately at either the group or the individual level [42]. In general, the responsiveness of bioelectrical impedance to changes in body composition has been questioned, but so far this has not been studied empirically in the elderly population [43].

TBW can also be estimated by using prediction formulas in which other components of the human body, such as the total amount of exchangeable sodium and potassium or the FFM are the independent variables. Obviously, these variables must be measured first. The underlying concept of prediction formulas for body water compartments based on these components is that there exists a stable quantitative relationships between TBW, ECW or ICW on the one side and body cell mass and fat-free mass on the other. The validity of these assumptions has been questioned seriously in elderly subjects and predictions based on these components probably have larger errors than the before mentioned bioelectrical techniques [44-46].

ECW and plasma volume can be measured directly by using several dilution techniques and estimated indirectly, based on a wide variety of techniques. There are a considerable number of possible diluents, of which isotopes of bromide are the most popular for measuring ECW. Bromide in plasma can be detected in several ways, of which the high-pressure liquid chromatography is very sensitive and has a small coefficient of variation in repeated measurements (<2.5%) [47]. Bromide-space is larger than ECW and therefore correction factors are introduced [34]. Low frequency bioelectrical impedance has been validated in the elderly as a an indirect measure of ECW with a prediction error of about 10% [40]. However, a valid prediction of the absolute changes in ECW, based on population derived prediction equations, is only possible in individual subjects when the change in body water reflects the initial ratio of ECW and ICW [41].

Unfortunately, ICW cannot be measured directly. Generally, it is calculated as the difference between TBW and ECW, but there are also prediction formulas of ICW based on the amount of exchangeable potassium. Precision and accuracy of ICW estimates depend completely on the way in which the other water compartments were measured.

Many factors should be considered in selecting a technique for clinical or field measurements of body water compartments [48]. It has to be clear what precision and accuracy is required and how long a measurement may take. Each method should be judged on its price, availability, technical difficulty, maintenance and calibration. For clinical use it has to be emphasized that only very few techniques are validated in geriatric patients. To be applicable as a bedside measurement in frail elderly subjects, the acceptability is very important: measurements should be harmless, noninvasive, quick, simple and should not be frightening. At present, most instruments are still at the stage of preclinical research.

EFFECTS OF AGING ON BODY HYDRATION

Recent cross-sectional and longitudinal studies in healthy elderly populations have unequivocally confirmed the classical dogma of a decrease in body hydration with increasing age only in the sense of a decrease in the absolute amount of TBW. Watson and Schoeller reviewed the literature on changes in body water with age and found differences in the patterns of decline in TBW between men and women [49, 50]. However, because of large between-subject variability in body build and weight in the elderly, the effect of age on TBW per kilogram body weight and per kilogram fat-free mass (TBW/FFM) is much more important. True age effects can only be studied in longitudinal studies, but -as far as we know- there is only one longitudinal study on body hydration. Steen et al. managed to study 23 subjects at ages 70, 75, 79 and 81 [51, 52]. These 23 were the only healthy subjects that could be re-examined out of an initial group of 105 subjects who were included when they were 70. In the 11 year follow-up there was a decrease in TBW, but an increase in the percentage of total body water per unit of body weight. This relative increase was probably caused by a decrease in both weight and percent body fat in this group. The decrease in TBW in Steen's study was primarily based on a decrease in ECW. Their estimations of ECW were based on measurements of body potassium. Therefore, it had to be assumed that the potassium content of the body cell mass does not change with increasing age. This assumption, however, was shown to be wrong at least in elderly women in a recently conducted study [45].

Unfortunately, only cross-sectional studies are available for the comparison of body hydration in healthy subjects aged under and over 60. Data compiled by Fanestil and Hays showed that the percentage of body hydration in 30 year old subjects was 9.1% and 4.7% larger for men and women, respectively, than the body hydration in subjects older than 60 [53]. Most cross-sectional studies found that the lower TBW in the elderly was due to a decrease in ICW, while ECW remained constant or was slightly smaller or larger than in younger subjects. As an example of such a cross-sectional comparison own data on body hydration in a young adult population (N=139) and a healthy elderly population (N=117) are presented (Table 1). Though the data were acquired in different studies [40, 54], the subjects were selected in the same period, from the same Dutch population, and exactly the same measurement techniques were applied. These data show that the smaller TBW in these elderly subjects was primarily due to a decrease in ICW for the men, or to a decrease in both ECW and ICW for the women.

Table 1

Cross-sectional comparison of subject characteristics and data on body hydration between healthy young and elderly subjects as presented in means (and standard deviations).

	Young women (n=63)	Elderly women (n= 81)	Young men (n=76)	Elderly men (n=36)
Age (y)	26 (6)	72 (5)	26 (7)	72 (6)
Body weight (kg)	66.0 (11.0)	67.5 (9.9)	75.0 (8.7)	78.4 (10.6)
Body mass index (kg/m2)	23.0 (4.4)	25.9 (3.8)**	22.2 (2.2)	25.4 (3.3)**
Body fat content (%)***	27.2 (6.9)	41.5 (6.2)**	13.1 (4.8)	32.3 (5.7)**
TBW (kg)	33.1 (3.3)	31.6 (3.5)**	45.3 (4.8)	41.9 (5.1)**
ECW (kg)	14.4 (1.4)	13.7 (1.7)**	18.2 (2.2)	17.5 (2.7)
ICW (kg)	18.8 (2.2)	17.9 (2.9)*	27.1 (3.1)	24.4 (4.3)**
ECW/TBW	0.43 (0.02)	0.43 (0.05)	0.40 (0.02)	0.42 (0.06)

Notes: TBW, total body water, measured by deuterium dilution; ECW, extracellular water, measured by bromide dilution; ICW, intracellular water (calculated as the difference between TBW and ECW); Significancy of differences within sexes: * $P < 0.05$; ** $P < 0.01$; *** from body density, which was measured by underwater weighing.

Only five studies have investigated the effect of aging on hydration of fat-free mass [44, 45, 55-57]. Such a study requires body composition to be determined in a four compartment model (fat, protein + glycogen, water and mineral) and not in a two compartment model (fat, fat-free mass), because this is the only way to assess body water and body fat independenltly [46, 58]. Four of the five cross-sectional studies did not show a difference in hydration of FFM between aged and non-aged groups [44, 45, 55, 57]. In a comparison of a small group of young and elderly women (n=20, n=18, respectively) Kadijk et al. found that elderly women had a significantly larger TBW/FFM ratio (0.737 vs. 0.723) [56]. However, in studies with a small number of subjects results are more likely to be confounded by the inclusion of some subjects who were not in euvolemic condition, the considerable between-subject variability in body hydration and the effect of outliers. Therefore, it is still valid to assume that hydration of fat-free mass does not change with increasing age, although the final conclusions on age-related changes in body hydration can only be drawn following a large longitudinal study. despite the lack of appropriate data for practical aims it is still valid to apply the percentage hydration of FFM, determined by chemical cadaver analysis in young adult subjects (73 ± 3%), as an estimate of body hydration in elderly men and women [30, 50, 59, 60]. When the TBW/FFM ratio plays a crucial part in a research project it should be measured by a multi-compartment methodology in that population. The relative constancy of the TBW/FFM ratio implies that absolute decrease in TBW with age can be seen as an indicator of loss of FFM [50]. Within this constancy there is some redistribution of body water over extracellular and intracellular compartment. Most cross-sectional studies showed a higher ECW/ICW in the elderly, but there is a very large between-study variability in this ratio (0.54-1.20), depending on the measurement techniques that were used [40, 45, 60, 61].

The ability to translate these epidemiological data obtained in elderly populations on body hydration accurately to individual elderly subjects depends largely on their within- and between-subject variability in body hydration. However, up till now, there are no data available on the short- and long-term within-subject biological variability in body hydration in elderly subjects. It has been suggested that between-subject variability in TBW, in the ratio of intra- to extracellular fluids, and in the hydration of FFM increases with age [46, 50], but there is no study that tested this hypothesis. The longitudinal data from Steen et al. do not show an increasing variance in body hydration from 70 to 81 years [52]. As a kind of meta-analysis, we tested variances of body hydration variables in young and aged subjects, as presented in studies from Fülop et al., Mazariegos et al., Visser et al. and Ellis, with variance ratio tests ('Snedecor's F-test') for significance of differences in variability [40, 45, 60, 61]. There turned out to be only a significantly larger variability in the elderly in Mazariegos's TBW/FFM-ratio and Visser's ECW/TBW-ratio, but not in the between-subjects variability in TBW, ECW and ICW in any of these studies. Therefore, although none of the studies was designed to test this hypothesis, they do not support a general age-related increase in the heterogeneity of body hydration.

It is largely unknown how the before mentioned changes in body hydration are reflected in the hydration of individual organs and tissues. As fat-free mass consists primarily of muscle it is unlikely that muscle hydration will change considerably, but there are no data supporting this hypothesis. The aged skin often seems to be much more dry in the elderly. This is only partly explained by the small decrease in water content of the stratum corneum of the skin [62, 63]. Other histopathological changes must contribute substantially to the 'dry' appearance of old age skin.

RISK FACTORS FOR DEHYDRATION

Dehydration can be defined as a clinically relevant decrease of a subject's optimal amount of TBW. Dehydration may occur with or without loss of electrolytes. The severity of dehydration depends more on the relative than on the absolute loss of TBW, ICW and ECW [64]. Therefore, the reduction in total body water as unavoidable part of aging is clearly an intrinsic risk factor for the development of dehydration in the elderly. The smaller a subject's body weight and optimal amount of TBW, the sooner a small loss of body water will cause symptoms and signs of dehydration. Reduced thirst and renal water conservation capacity are also risk factors, probably associated with aging per se [5, 7, 8, 65]. However, if elderly subjects are functioning independently they fulfill their daily needs for water easily with bouts associated with their meals and social drinks [6, 66]. The limited capacity of homeostatic mechanisms to maintain fluid balance only becomes important when fluid balance is at risk.

Environmental and disease-related risk factors for dehydration have a very high prevalence in elderly subjects. Lavizzo-Mourey identified the most important risk factors for dehydration in a large prospective study on a nursing home population [11]. Being over 85 years old and female, having more than four chronic diseases, taking more than four medications, and being bedridden were significant risk factors in developing a moderate degree of dehydration. In case of severe dehydration the odds ratios for these risk factors were much higher and also the season (winter), inability to feed oneself, poor mobility and a low level of care were significant risk factors. Suffering from Alzheimer's disease may still be a risk factor, after having controlled for the beforementioned factors, because it is asociated with a low arginine vasopressine (AVP) level [67]. Subjects in an AVP deficient state are prone to dehydration because of having a poor water concentrating capacity. Lavizzo-Mourey's risk factors are presented in table 2, together with the most important causes of hypernatremic dehydration [14, 68-72], as the most important triggers to alert physicians and nurses to the possibility of dehydration in elderly patients.

Table 2
Risk factors for dehydration in elderly patients

Non-pathological	Age > 85
	Female
	Low total body water, low body weight
	Decline in maximal renal water- and salt conservating capacity
	Lower responsiveness of thirst
Functional	Poor mobility
	Comprehension/communication problems
	Oral intake less than 1500 ml per day
	Hand dexterity/body control problems
	Self neglect
Environmental	Hospitalization
	Insufficient care givers/ Understaffed institution
	Insufficiently skilled care givers/staff
	Winter season and high temperature (heating/weather)
Disease-related	Suffering from Alzheimer's disease or from more than 4 chronic diseases
	Fluid loss by: diarrhea, fever, vomiting, bleeding, fever, tachypnoea, artificial ventilation, polyuria, decubitus, burns
	Reduced intake by: dysphagia, anorexia, acute confusion, depression, dementia
	Previous episode of dehydration, fear of incontinence, unexplained weight loss
Iatrogenic	Drug-related: laxatives, diuretics, lithium, hypnotics
	High protein intake (oral/enteral/parenteral)
	Dietary restriction of fluids, salt
	Dianostic procedures requiring fasting

METHODS TO ASSESS DEHYDRATION IN THE ELDERLY

Galen already noted that it was hard to diagnose dehydration in the elderly: "Doctors often say that old age is wet, because they are mislead by the flood of wet excretions: tearful eyes, full of catarrh, slavering mouth, lungs full of fluid, stomach filled with phlegm"[22]. Eighteen centuries later, clinicians are still frequently mislead in diagnosing dehydration in geriatric patients. This was oficially recognized in 1995 by the American Medical Association by warning their members that there exists no absolute definition of dehydration and that the signs and symptoms of dehydration may be vague, deceptive or even absent in the elderly [72]. Classical signs of dehydration such as loss of skin turgor (or more correctly the increase in skin recoil time), increased thirst and orthostatic hypotension have a low specificity and sensitivity in geriatrics [6, 73-75]. Even in pediatrics their value is doubted and not supported by empirical data [76]. A careful examination of cardiac parameters, jugular venous pressure, orthostatic changes in pulse and blood pressure, axillary moisture, and hydration of mucous membranes only had a sensitivity of 46% and a specificity of 48% in detecting hyponatremic hypovolemia in a non-aged population [77]. Probably the diagnostic value of such an examination is even less in elderly patients. In geriatric patients dehydration often causes atypical symptoms such as confusion [16], obstipation [21], or less frequently fever [17], or falls. Confusion, obstipation and falls are part of the very frequently occurring 'Geriatric giants'[78], and therefore their specificity is far to low to be useful to diagnose dehydration.

In discussing the clinical assessment of dehydration two important destinctions should be made. First, diagnostic instruments should be categorized as discriminitive or evaluative measures [79]. A discrimitive measure should be able to detect dehydrated patients in the first examination of unknown patients. An evaluative measure should be able to detect dehydration in monitoring a patient's fluid balance over time. Secondly, dehydration should be characterized as dehydration with or dehydration without concomittant loss of electrolytes. Three forms of dehydration can be distinguished on the basis of the plasma tonicity: hypertonic, isotonic and hypotonic dehydration. Tonicity or effective osmolality is the concentration of particles that cannot penetrate cell membranes and it is a measure of movement of water across a semipermeable membrane. Hypertonic dehydration results if water losses are greater than sodium losses. A lot of studies on dehydration are limited to hypertonic dehydration [14, 15, 70]. This diagnosis is easy to make by laboratory tests and unequivocal (e.g. serum sodium levels >150 mmol/L or serum osmolality > 300 mosmol/L), but neglects the frequently occurring isotonic and hypotonic dehydration. Isotonic dehydration results from a balanced loss of water and electrolytes (e.g. by vomiting and diarrhea) and hypotonic dehydration results when loss of electrolytes exceeds water loss (e.g. by overuse of diuretics). Hyponatremia, which has a higher prevalence than hypernatremia in the elderly, was shown to be primarily based on volume contraction in 29% of a population with a mean age of 60 years [80]. How often isotonic and hypotonic dehydration occur has never been studied systematically, probably because of the difficulties in diagnosing it correctly. A proper diagnostic approach to dehydration in clinical practice should be sensitive and specific for all three forms of dehydration.

The initial assessment of fluid status of a geriatric patient is often very difficult. It should result in answering not only the question wether there is dehydration, but, if a patient is dehydrated, it should also result in describing the type of dehydration, its development in time, and its severity. Many studies have been performed in a quest for a single measure that should be able to discriminate dehydrated and not-dehydrated or euvolemic patients. However, decreased intraocular pressure [81], absent axillary sweating [82], increased plasma specific gravity or increased cerebrospinal fluid protein did not fulfill this need [83-85]. Presumably plasma arginine vasopressine (AVP) levels will also not discriminate between dehydrated and non dehydrated subjects: although there is a steep rise of AVP in dehydrated elderly subjects there are no data to define a normal range [5]. AVP levels are said to increase or remain stable in normal aging [86, 87], and are influenced by dementia and all kind of drugs [67, 88]. The same problems are likely to occur in attempts to validate other endocrine measures as tools to diagnose dehydration. Such a one dimensional approach to diagnose dehydration in elderly patients is probably deemed to be a search for the holy grail, partly because of the diverse nature of dehydrated conditions and partly because of the heterogeneity of the geriatric populations. Clinical application of dilution methods to measure TBW, ECW and ICW would also be of little help in detecting mild and moderate degrees of dehydration, if a patient's optimal state of fluid balance has not been quantified. It seems more valuable to select a set of clinical signs and symptoms, and laboratory measures that have proved to be useful in the discriminative diagnosis of dehydration with and without salt depletion in the elderly (Table 3) [9, 64, 89]. Gross et al. found that the seven signs which were correlated well with dehydration severity (Kendall's tau $\geq$ 0.35, P<0.01) but were unrelated to patient age, (Kendall's tau $\leq$ 0.20, P>0.05) were the most valuable indicators of dehydration in the elderly [90]. A problem with Gross's seven signs is that there remains some subjectivity in assessing them. Therefore, one should also include a cardiovascular assessment of blood pressure and pulse rate. There is no scientific evidence for the widely used clinical guideline that loss of body water, i.e. water loss without concomitantly losing electrolytes, is more likely to give confusion in the elderly than combined loss of salt and water. As suggested by the very high prevalence of acute confusional states, geriatric patients may become easily confused by every disturbance of fluid balance, whatever its nature is.

Table 3

Important clues from medical history, physical and laboratory examinations of geriatric patients in the initial assessment of dehydration with and without concomitant loss of electrolytes.

Clue	Water deficiency	Water+Electrolyte deficiency
Medical history	Recently >3% weight loss Impaired water intake Increased perspiration (fever, tachypnoea, heat)	Recently >3% weight loss Vomiting, diarrhea, diuretic drug use, diabetes, bleeding
Physical Examination	+	+
Tongue dryness	+	+
Longitudinal tongue furrows	+	+
Dry mucous membranes mouth	+	+
Upper body muscle weakness	+	+
Confusion	+	+
Speech difficulty	+	+
Sunken eyes	+	+
Blood pressure	$=/\downarrow$	$\downarrow\downarrow$
Pulse rate	$=/\uparrow$	$\uparrow\uparrow$
Laboratory tests		
Serum creatinine	$\uparrow$	$\uparrow$
Serum urea	$\uparrow$	$\uparrow\uparrow$
Tonicity	$\uparrow\uparrow$	$=/\downarrow$
Urinary output	$\downarrow$	$\uparrow/=/\downarrow$
Urinary sodium concentration	$\downarrow$	$\uparrow=/\downarrow$

Notes: +, present; $\uparrow$, increased; $\uparrow\uparrow$, clearly increased; $\downarrow$, decreased; $\downarrow\downarrow$, clearly decreased; =, unchanged.

Traditionally, serum creatinine, blood urea nitrogen (BUN) and the BUN/creatinine ratio are advocated as useful laboratory measurements in detecting dehydration and other pre-renal pathology [91]. However, reference ranges for urea and creatinine in elderly subjects without evidence of renal impairment showed to be much wider than reference ranges found in younger populations [92]. Moreover, serum urea is more than creatinine dependent on abnormalities in protein metabolism, on increases by gastrointestinal bleeding and on other causes of pre-renal insufficiency [93]. Consequently, in the study of Bowker et al. only 50% of the elderly patients with one or more pre-renal causes of uremia had urea concentrations outside the age-adjusted reference range [92]. Data for the sensitivity and specificity of serum urea, creatinine and BUN/urea ratios in detecting dehydration are still failing. Osmolality is frequently advised in determining fluid balance [72], but effective osmolality is more appropriate in determining the need for rehydration (i.e. E_{osmol} = 2 X [serum sodium + potassium concentration, (mEq/L)] + [serum glucose concentration (mmol/L)]) [94, 95]. Especially in case of chronic renal insufficiency osmolality may be misleading in diagnosing the real nature of dehydration because urea levels do contribute to osmolality, but are in fact ineffective osmoles that can easily pass semipermeable membranes. Despite a reduction in maximal renal concentration capacity in elderly subjects, urinary output and sodium concentration may give additional information in assessing body fluid state [96]. Some investigators tried to combine the most sensitive indicators in a dehydration rating scale, but these scales have never been validated in geriatric populations [16, 89]. Therefore at present a hydration rating scale may only be useful in designing research protocols, not in clinical practice. The initial assessment of duration and severity of dehydration has to rely on information from the patient, family, care givers or referring physicians. Documented and accurately measured weight changes might be invaluable, but are mostly not available.

In evaluating fluid balance to detect dehydration in geriatric patients who are already known, for instance in long term care, repeated measurements of a few laboratory variables are probably sufficient. Unfortunately, it is not yet known which variables have the highest responsiveness to dehydration. Weinberg showed that serial measurements of serum osmolality, sodium concentration and BUN/urea ratio were characterized by high inter-individual and low intra-individual variability [97]. This is one important precondition for a good responsiveness. Another important precondition for a good responsiveness to dehydration is that the variable should change significantly whenever a patient's fluid balance changes from euvolemic to dehydrated condition [79]. Probably, regular measurements of body weight or a correctly recorded fluid balance over time, and serial serum sodium and creatinine concentrations would suffice for monitoring fluid balance. However, daily body weights may be very hard to obtain in functionally impaired elderly patients and intake and output charts are notoriously unreliable because of high prevalence of incontinence and inaccurate recording [72]. Therefore, new measurement techniques of body water compartments might be useful as an evaluative tool. Important prerequisites for application of these instruments in geriatrics are that they should be non-invasive, quick and not threatening and that they should not require much co-operation of the patients. Bioelectrical impedance analysis fulfills these criteria and has even been used without problems in centenarians in a study on body composition [98]. The limited ability to estimate fluid compartments in individual patients and the between-subjects variability in TBW and ECW restricts it application of impedance analysis to monitoring fluid balance. It has been shown that impedance measurements can be used in monitoring changes in body composition during refeeding and in changes in body water compartments in critically ill patients [99, 100]. However, these were studies in younger populations and the responsiveness of bioelectrical impedance analysis to changes in fluid balance still has to be proved in geriatric patients. The total body water deficit can be estimated by the weight loss in a short period, and the free water deficit (FWD) with a formula using serial laboratory measurements [12]: FWD (L) = Baseline weight (kg) X TBW% - {[E_{osmol}-euvolemia/E_{osmol}-dehydration] X Current weight (kg)X TBW%}; where TBW% is the relative body hydration (0.47 for women, 0.53 for men, data from Table 1), E_{osmol}-euvolemia is the baseline effective osmolality in euvolemic state and E_{osmol}-dehydration is the current effective osmolality.

CONCLUSIONS

Recent findings on the effect of age on body hydration and on diagnosing dehydration confirm ancient, prescientific notions in medicine, which stated that aging means loss of body water and that dryness of the body is very difficult to assess. In the development of gerontology water conservation has served as a very useful model to study the physiology of aging [101]. The age-related failure of homeostasis to compensate stressful disturbances has been demonstrated very clearly in disturbances of fluid balance. A major challenge for gerontologists is to design and perform longitudinal studies on the effect of aging on body hydration, using state-of-the art techniques to provide answers to the questions that cannot be answered from the available cross-sectional studies. The most important task for geriatricians is to increase their alertness for the possibility of disturbances of fluid balance and to improve their competency of early detection of dehydration. The enormous impact of dehydration in the elderly in terms of mortality, morbidity and health care expeditures warrants further research efforts on this topic. Urgently, a dehydration rating scale has to be validated, the responsiveness of bioelectrical impedance measurements and laboratory tests in monitoring fluid balance has to be determined, and preventive and therapeutic strategies need to be evaluated. More research is also needed on the clinical effects of disturbances in the homeostasis of intracellular water, before dryness can be abondened definitely as a cause of aging.

REFERENCES

1. Kuczmarski RJ. Need for body composition in elderly subjects. Am J Clin Nutr 1989; 50:1150-7.
2. Lindeman RD, Tobin J, Shock NW. Longitudinal studies on the rate of decline in renal function with age. J Am Geriatr Soc 1985; 33:278-85.
3. Malmrose LC, Gray SL, Pieper CF, et al. Measured versus estimated creatinine clearance in a high-functioning elderly sample: MacArthur Foundation study of successful aging. J Am Geriatr Soc 1993; 41:715-21.
4. Salive ME, Jones CA, Guralnik JM, Agodoa LY, Pahor M, Wallace RB. Serum creatinine levels in older adults: relationship with health status and medications. Age Ageing 1995; 24:142-50.
5. Davies I, O'Neill P, McLean KA, Catania J, Bennett D. Age-associated alterations in thirst and arginine vasopressin in response to a water or sodium load. Age Ageing 1995; 24:151-9.
6. Phillips PA, Rolls BJ, Ledingham JGG, Morton JJ. Body fluid changes, thirst and drinking in man during free access to water. Physiol Behav 1984; 33:357-63.
7. Phillips P, Rolls BJ, Ledingham JGG, et al. Reduced thirst after water deprivation in healthy elderly men. N Engl J Med 1984; 311:753-9.
8. Phillips PA, Johnston CI, Gray L. Disturbed fluid and electrolyte homeostasis following dehydration in elderly people. Age Ageing 1993; 22:26-33.
9. Leaf A. Dehydration in the elderly. N Engl J Med 1984; 311:791-2.
10. Warren JL, Edward Bacon W, Harris T, Marshall McBean A, Foley DJ, Phillips C. The burden and outcomes associated with dehydration among US elderly, 1991. Am J Public Health 1994; 84:1265-9.
11. Lavizzo-Mourey R, Johnson J, Stolley P. Risk factors for dehydration among elderly nursing home residents. J Am Geriatr Soc 1988; 36:213-8.
12. Warren JL, Harris T, Phillips C. Dehydration in older adults. JAMA 1996; 275:911-2.
13. Antonelli Incalzi R, Gemma R, Capparella O, Terranova L, Sanguinetti C, Carbonin PU. Post-operative electrolyte imbalance: its incidence and prognostic implications for elderly orthopaedic patients. Age Ageing 1993; 22:325-31.
14. Himmelstein DU, Jones AA, Woolhandler S. Hypernatremia in nursing home patients: an indicator of neglect. J Am Geriatr Soc 1983; 31:466-71.
15. Mahowald JM, Himmelstein DU. Hypernatremia in the elderly: relation to infection and mortality. J Am Geriatr Soc 1981; 29:177-80.
16. Seymour DG, Henschke PJ, Cape RDT, Campbell AJ. Acute confusional states and dementia in the elderly: the role of dehydration/volume depletion, physical illness and age. Age Ageing 1980; 9:137-46.
17. Balcar JO, Sansum WD, Woodyatt RT. Fever and the water reserve of the body. Arch Intern Med 1919; 24:116-28.
18. Embon OM, Rose GA, Rosenbaum T. Chronic dehydration stone disease. Br J Urol 1990; 66:357-62.
19. Olde Rikkert MGM, Hoefnagels WHL. Dehydration in geriatric patients; pathophysiology, diagnosis, therapy, and prevention. (In Dutch) Ned Tijdschr Geneeskd 1993; 137:750-3.
20. Olde Rikkert MGM, Peet JCMvd, Poelgeest AE, Hoefnagels WHL. Dehydration in geriatrics; Dry stuff? (In Dutch) Ned Tijdschr Geneeskd 1993; 137:745-7.
21. Wrenn K. Fecal impaction. N Engl J Med 1989; 321:658-62.
22. Horstmanshoff HFJ. The doorstep of old age; medical and social care for the elderly in the Greec-Roman era. (In Dutch) Ned Tijdschr Geneeskd 1995; 139:1651-6.
23. Godderis J. Ancient medicine. Physical impairments and psychiatric diseases in olde age. Peri geros. (In Dutch) Leuven: Peeters, 1989.
24. Joly R. Du rÈgime. Paris: Les Belles Lettres, 1967.
25. Gaylord SA, Williams ME. A brief history of the development of geriatric medicine. J Am Geriatr Soc 1994; 42:335-40.
26. Grant RL. Concepts of aging: an historical review. Perspect Biol Med 1963:443-78.
27. Finn PJ, Plank LD, Clark MA, Connolly AB, Hill, G.L. Progressive cellular dehydration and proteolysis in critically ill patients. Lancet 1996; 347:654-6.
28. Reiff TR. Body composition with special reference to water. In: Horwitz A, Macfayden DM, Munro H, Scrimshaw NS, Steen B, Williams TF, eds. Nutrition in the elderly. Oxford: Oxford University Press, 1989:115-22.
29. Lalonde R, Badescu R. Exploratory drive, frontal lobe functioning and adipsia in aging. Gerontology 1995; 41:134-44.
30. Brozek JF, Grande F, Anderson JT, Keys A. Densitometric analysis of body composition: revison of some quantitative assumptions. Ann NY Acad Sci 1963; 110:113-40.

31. Lohman TG. Research progress in validation of laboratory methods of assessing body composition. Med Sci Sports 1984; 16:596-603.

32. Snyder WS, Cook MJ, Nasset ES, Karhausen LR, Parry Howells G, Tipton IH. Report of the task group on reference man. Oxford: Pergamon Press, 1975:27-32.

33. Lukaski HC, Johnson PE. A simple, inexpensive method of determiningtotal body water using a tracer dose of D2O and infrared absorption of biological fluids. Am J Clin Nutr 1985; 41:363-70.

34. Forbes GB. Human body composition. London, Paris, Tokyo: Springer-Verlag, 1987:31.

35. Schoeller DA, Dietz W, Sauten D van, Klein PD. Validation of saliva sampling for total body water determination by H2O^{18} dilution. Am J Clin Nutr 1982; 35:591-4.

36. Whyte RK, bayley HS, Schwarz P. The measurement of whole body water by H2O^{18} dilution in newborn pigs. Am J Clin Nutr 1985; 41:801-9.

37. Wang ZM, Heshka S, Pierson RN, Heymsfield SB. Systematic organization of body-composition methodology: an overview with emphasis on component-based methods. Am J Clin Nutr 1995; 61:457-65.

38. Cochran WJ, Wong WW, Fiorotto Ml, Sheng HP, Klein PD, Klish WJ. Total body water estimated by measuring total-body electrical conductivity. Am J Clin Nutr 1988; 48:946-50.

39. Kotler DP, Burastero S, Wang J, Pierson RN. Prediction of body cell mass, fat-free mass, and total body water with bioelectrical impedance analysis: effects of race, sex, and disease. Am J Clin Nutr 1996; 64:489S—497S.

40. Visser M, Deurenberg P, Staveren WA van. Multi-frequency bioelectrical impedance for assessing total body water and extracellular water in elderly subjects. Eur J Clin Nutr 1995; 49:256-66.

41. Deurenberg P. Multi-frequency impedance as a measure of body water compartments. In: Davies PSW, Cole TJ, eds. Body composition technques in health and disease. Cambridge: Cambridge University Press, 1995: 45-57.

42. Deurenberg P, Schouten FJM. Loss of total body water and extracellular water assessed by multi-frequency impedance. Eur J Clin Nutr 1992; 46:247-55.

43. Forbes GB, Simons W, Armatruda JM. Is bio-electrical impedance a good predictor of body composition change? Am J Clin Nutr 1992; 56:4-6.

44. Lesser GT, Markofsky J. Body water compartments with human aging using fat-free mass as the reference standard. Am J Physiol 1979; 236:R215-20.

45. Mazariegos M, Wang Z-M, Gallagher D, et al. Differences between young and old females in the five levels of body composition and their relevance to the two-compartment chemical models. J Gerontol 1994; 49:M201-8.

46. Baumgartner RN, Heymsfield SB, Lichtman S, Wang J, Pierson RN. Body composition in elderly people: effect of criterion estimates on predictive equations. Am J Clin Nutr 1991; 53:1345-53.

47. Miller ME, Cappon CJ. Anion-exchange chromatographic detemination of bromide in serum. Clin Chem 1984; 1984:781-3.

48. Norgan NG. The assessment of the body composition of populations. In: Davies PSW, Cole TJ, eds. Body composition techniques in health and disease. Cambridge: Cambridge University Press, 1995:195-221.

49. Watson PE, Watson ID, Batt RD. Total body water volumes for adult males and females from simple anthropometric measurements. Am J Clin Nutr 1980; 33:27-39.

50. Schoeller DA. Changes in total body water with age. Am J Clin Nutr 1989; 50:1176-81.

51. Steen B, Isaksson B, Svanborg A. Body composition at 70 and 75 years of age: a longitudinal study. J Clin Exp Gerontol 1979; 1:185-200.

52. Steen B, Lundgren BK, Isaksson B. Body composition at age 70, 75, 79 and 81 years: a longitudinal population study. In: Chandra RK, ed. Nutrition, immunity, and illness in the elderly. New York: Pergamon Press, 1985:49-52.

53. Fanestil DD. Compartmentation of body water. In: Maxwell MH, Kleeman CR, Narins RG, eds. Clinical disorders of fluid and electrolyte metabolism. New York: McGraw-Hill, 1987:1-13.

54. Deurenberg P, Tagliabue A, Schouten FJM. Multi-frequency impedance for the prediction of extra-cellular water and total body water. Br J Nutr 1995; 73:349-58.

55. Cohn SH, Vartsky D, Yasamura S. Compartmental body composition based on total-body nitrogen, potassium, and calcium. Am J Physiol 1980; 239:E524-30.

56. Bergsma-Kadijk JA, Baumeister B, Deurenberg P. Measurement of body fat in young and elderly women: comparison between a four-compartment model and widely used reference methods. Br J Nutr 1996; 75:649-57.

57. Visser M, Gallagher D, Deurenberg P, Wang J, Pierson RN, Heymsfield SB. Density of fat-free body mass: relationship with race, age and level of body fatness. Am J Physiol 1997; In Press.

58. Heymsfield SB, Wang J, Lichtman S, Kamen Y, Kehayias J, Pierson RN. Body composition in elderly subjects: a critical appraisal of clinical methodology. Am J Clin Nutr 1989; 50:1167-75.

59. Knight GS, Beddoe AH, Streat SJ, Hill GL. Body composition of two human cadavers by neutron activation and chemical analysis. Am J Physiol 1986; 250:E179-85.
60. Ellis KJ. Reference man and woman more fully characterized. Biol Trace Elem Res 1990; 26:385-400.
61. Fülop T, Worum I, Csongor J, Foris G, Leövey A. Body composition in elderly people. I. Determination of body composition by mtiisotope method and the eliminiation kinetics of these isotopes in healthy elderly subjects. Gerontology 1985; 31:6-14.
62. Thune P, Nilson T, Handstad IK, Gustavsen T, Lovig Dahl H. The water barrier function of the skin in relation to the water content of stratum corneum pH and skin lipids. Acta Derm Venereol 1988; 68:277-83.
63. Berardesca E, Maibach HI. Transepidermal water loss and skin surface hydration in the non invasive assessment of stratum corneum function. Derm Beruf Umwelt 1990; 38:50-3.
64. Lindeman RD. Application of fluid electrolyte balance principles to the older patient. In: Reichel W, ed. Clinical aspects of aging. Baltimore: Williams & Wilkins, 1988:248-53.
65. Silver AJ, Morley JE. Role of the opioid sytem in the hypodipsia associated with aging. J Am Geriatr Soc 1002; 40:556-60.
66. Castro JM de. Age-related changes in natural spontaneous fluid ingestion and thirst in humans. J Gerontol 1992; 47:P321-330.
67. Albert SG, Nakra BRS, Grossberg GT, Caminal ED. Vasopressin response to dehydration in Alzheimer's disease. J Am Geriatr Soc 1989; 37:843-7.
68. Palevski PM, Bhagrath R, Greenberg A. Hypernatremia in hospitalized patients. Ann Int Med 1996; 124:197-203.
69. Long CA, Bayer AJ, Shetty HGM, Pathu MSJ. Hypernatraemia in an adult in-patient population. Postgrad Med 1991; 67:643-5.
70. Macdonald NJ, McConnell KN, Dunnigan MG. Hypernatraemic dehydration in patients in a large hopsital for the mentally handicapped. BMJ 1989; 299:1426-9.
71. Weinberg AD, Pals Jk, Beal LF, Cunningham TJ. Dehydration and death during febrile episodes in the nursing home. J Am Geriatr Soc 1994; 42:968-71.
72. Weinberg AD, Minaker KL, Council on Scientific Affairs American Medical Association. Dehydration, evaluation and management in older adults. JAMA 1995; 274:1552-6.
73. Dorrington KL. Skin turgor: do we understand the clinical sign? Lancet 1981; i:264-6.
74. Wandel JC. The use of postural vital signs in the assessment of fluid volume status. J Prof Nurs 1990; 6:46-54.
75. Lipsitz L. Orthostatic hypotension in the elderly. N Engl J Med 1989; 321:952-7.
76. Poole SR. Criteria for measurement of dehydration. Ann Emerg Med 1990; 19:730-1.
77. Chung H-M, Kluge R, Schrier RW, Anderson RJ. Clinical assessment of extracellular fluid volume in hyponatremia. Am J Med 1987; 83:905-8.
78. Fox RA, Puxty JAH. Medicine in the elderly, a problem-oriented approach. London: Edward Arnold, 1993.
79. Guyatt G, Walter S, Norman G. Measuring change over time: assessing the usefulness of evaluative instruments. J Chron Dis 1987; 40:171-8.
80. Gross PA, Pehrisch H, Rascher W, Schomig A, Hackenthal E, Ritz E. Pathogenesis of clinical hyponatremia: observations of vasopressin and fluid intake in 100 hyponatremic patients. Eur J Clin Invest 1987; 17:123-9.
81. Rhodes KM. Can the measurement of intraocular pressure be useful in assessing dehydration and rehydration? J Am Geriatr Soc 1995; 43:589-93.
82. Eaton D, Bannister P, Mulley GP, Connolly MJ. Axillary sweating in clinical assessment of dehydration in ill elderly patients. BMJ 1994; 308:1271.
83. Dauterman KW, Redett RJ, Gillespie JA, Greenough WB, Schoenfeld CN. Plasma specific gravity measures volume depletion: a common correctable and often overlooked problem in the elderly. Clin Res 1992; 40:394A.
84. Dauterman KW, Bennet RG, Greenough WB, et al. Plasma specific gravity for identifying hypovolemia. J Diarrhoel Dis Res 1995; 13:33-8.
85. Solommadevi SV. Elevated CSF protein in uremia and dehydration. J Tenn Med Ass 1982; 75:325.
86. Johnson AG, Crawford GA, Kelly D, Nguyen TV, Gyory AZ. Arginine vasopressin and osmolality in the elderly. J Am Geriatr Soc 1994; 42:399-404.
87. Duggan J, Kilfeather S, Lightman SL, O'Malley K. The association of age with plasma arginine vasopressin and plasma osmolality. Age Ageing 1993; 22:332-6.
88. Miller M. Hormonal aspects of fluid and sodium balance in the elderly. Endocr Metab Clin N Amer 1995; 24:233-51.
89. Gershan JA, Freeman CM, Ross MC, et al. Fluid volume deficit: validating the indicators. Heart Lung 1990; 19:152-6.

90. Gross CR, Lindquist RD, Woolley AC, Granieri R, Allard K, Webster B. Clinical indicators of dehydration severity in elderly patients. J Emerg Med 1992; 10:267-74.
91. Dossetor JB. Creatininemia versus uremia. Ann Int Med 1966; 65:1287-99.
92. Bowker LK, Briggs RSJ, Gallagher PJ, Robertson DRC. Raised blood urea in the elderly: a clinical and pathological study. Postgrad Med J 1992; 68:174-9.
93. Pryce JD, Durnford J. Laboratory tests for kidney function -urea or creatinine? N Engl J Med 1979; ii:481-2.
94. Warren JL, Harris T, Phillips C. Dehydration in older adults. JAMA 1996; 275:911-2.
95. Gennari FJ. Serum osmolality. N Engl J Med 1984; i:102-5.
96. Francesconi RP, Hubbard RW, Szylk PC, et al. Urinary and hematologic indexes of hypohydration. J Appl Physiol 1987; 62:1271-6.
97. Weinberg AD, Pals JK, McGlinchey-Berroth R, Minaker K. Indices of dehydration among frail nursing home patients: highly variable but stable over time. J Am Geriatr Soc 1994; 42:1070-3.
98. Paolisso G, Gambardella A, Balbi V, Ammendola S, D'Amore A, Varricchio M. Body composition, body fat distribution, and resting metabolic rate in healthy centenarians. Am J Clin Nutr 1995; 62:746-50.
99. Pencharz PB, Azcue M. Use of bioelectrical impedance analysis measurements in the clinical management of malnutrition. Am J Clin Nutr 1996; 64:485-8S.
100. Roos AN, Wetsendorp RGJ, Fr^hlich M, Meinders AE. Weight changes in critically ill patients evaluated by fluid balances and impedance measurements. Crit Care Med 1993; 21:821-7.
101. Davies I. A physiological approach to ageing. In: Horan MA, Brouwer A, eds. Gerontology, approached to biomedical and clinical research. London: Edward Arnold, 1990:84-101.

THIRST IN ELDERLY SUBJECTS

M. NAITOH, L. M. BURRELL

Department of Medicine, The University of Melbourne, Austin and Repatriation Medical Centre, Heidelberg, Victoria 3084, Australia

Key words: thirst, elderly, vasopressin

INTRODUCTION

Our population is ageing and part of the normal ageing process involves changes in fluid and electrolyte homeostatic mechanisms that adversely affect the individual and increase morbidity and mortality. The maintenance of fluid balance is essential for health. In healthy individuals fluid homeostasis is achieved through the sensation of thirst which leads to water ingestion, and stimulation of vasopressin secretion which limits the renal loss of water.

It is now well recognised that elderly individuals are less able to regulate their fluid balance in response to fluid deprivation or overhydration. Thirst is diminished with age and there is also decreased urinary concentrating ability, as well as reduced capacity to excrete a water load [1, 2]. Such changes in the homeostatic capacity of the elderly are modified by other diseases such as hypertension, cardiac and cerebrovascular disease.

This chapter describes the physiological control mechanisms for thirst and vasopressin release before discussing age related changes in these systems. It is only by increasing the awareness of the decline in homeostatic functions in the elderly that conditions such as hypo- and hypernatremia can be recognised early and corrected leading to a reduction in morbidity and mortality in the ageing population.

I - PHYSIOLOGY OF THIRST AND VASOPRESSIN RELEASE

1.1. Osmoreceptors and Neural Circuits

Thirst and vasopressin release are mediated by specialized cells known as "osmoreceptors", which are sensitive to changes in plasma osmolality. The influence of body fluid hypertonicity on thirst and vasopressin secretion was first described experimentally by Gilman [3] and Verney [4] and numerous lesion and electrophysiological studies have confirmed the localization of osmoreceptors. Andersson [5] first described that the anterior hypothalamus was the responsible area for peripheral osmotic stimuli and subsequently Peck and Novin [6] suggested that the osmoreceptor lay in the lateral preoptic area of the hypothalamus (LPO). Since then lesioning studies have provided evidence that the osmoreceptor is localized in the anterior ventral lesion of the third ventricle (AV3V) [7, 8]. These lesions spared the preoptic-anterior hypothalamic area previously implicated in the stimulation of drinking and also the supra optic nucleus (SON) and the paraventricular nucleus (PVN). The results provided the evidence that the magnocellular neurons require efferent input to release vasopressin in response to hypovolemia, and also that structures along the lamina terminalis contained essential circuits necessary for the control of fluid balance.

Three anatomically defined areas of the lamina terminalis are now known to be implicated in water balance control; two of these are circumventricular organs (CVO), the organum vasculosum of the lamina terminalis (OVLT) and the subfornical organ (SFO), which lies outside of the blood brain barrier and the third is the nucleus medianus (NM), which lies inside of the blood brain barrier.

The SFO is primarily concerned with angiotensin II (Ang II) mediated thirst [9] and vasopressin release [10], whilst the OVLT is involved in osmotically-stimulated vasopressin secretion [11, 12]. The role of NM is to integrate signals from the SFO, OVLT and peripheral cardiovascular pathways, and to provide stimulatory inputs to the magnocellular neurons for vasopressin release, and to neurons in the lateral hypothalamic area to stimulate drinking [13, 14].

A basic integrated hypothesis of the neural control of thirst and vasopressin secretion was suggested by Thrasher [13]. The principle inputs to the brain arise from osmoreceptors in the SFO and OVLT monitoring plasma osmolality and Ang II concentrations, and from peripheral cardiovascular receptors monitoring blood pressure and volume. Fibres from the SFO, OVLT and cardiovascular receptors via the nucleus tractus solitarius (NTS) converge on the NM and also send fibres to the SON and PVN to stimulate vasopressin release, and to the LPO-lateral hypothalamic area to stimulate thirst sensation and drinking. Although the magnocellular neurons of the SON and PVN are osmosensitive, they are not primarily responsible for osmotic stimulated secretion of vasopressin but rather rely on inputs from the OVLT. The magnocellular neurons send axons by way of the median eminence to the posterior pituitary where vasopressin is secreted into the blood stream. Through poorly defined afferent pathways to higher cortical centers, the awareness of thirst is perceived and motor responses involved in drinking are integrated.

1.2. Factors Influencing Thirst and Vasopressin Release

In the majority of physiological situations changes in thirst and vasopressin release occur in parallel. The main types of physiological factors to influence thirst and vasopressin release include plasma osmolality, hemodynamic factors, endocrine factors (including Ang II and atrial natriuretic peptide (ANP)), oropharyngeal / gastrointestinal / hepatic factors and finally behavioral influences. Since all these factors influence thirst and vasopressin secretion as final common pathways, they have complex interactions and changes in one factor will modify the effects of another.

Osmotic Factors

The most important stimulus to water intake and vasopressin release is plasma osmolality. The mechanism of action of the osmoreceptor cell remains to be defined, but it is postulated that the osmoreceptor cell perceives a reduction in cell volume caused by the efflux of water down an osmotic gradient created by a rise in the effective osmotic pressure of the extracellular fluid due to rise in osmotic solute; this form of thirst is often referred to as cellular thirst. The potency of the solute in stimulating thirst and vasopressin secretion will be inversely proportional to its rate of entry into the osmoreceptor cells; cell membranes exclude sodium, sucrose and mannitol but are relatively permeable to glucose and urea [15].

Whether the same osmoreceptor neurons serve both thirst and vasopressin release is unclear. In the majority of physiological situations changes in osmoregulated thirst and vasopressin release occur in parallel, but there is some experimental evidence in rats [16] to indicate the osmoreceptors are separate. In man, rare clinical situations exist indicate that osmoreceptors are anatomically distinct, such as absent thirst (adipsia) associated with normal osmoregulated vasopressin release [17].

To assess osmotically stimulated thirst in man, visual analogue scales (VAS) are commonly used [18-21]. Subjects are asked to place a mark on a 10 cm long uncalibrated line at the point representative of their thirst between the extremes of very severe thirst at 10 cms and no thirst at 0 cms. Early studies considered thirst to be a discontinuous sensation experienced at plasma osmolalities greater than those required to produce maximal vasopressin induced antidiuresis [15]. The use of VAS to provide a semi-quantitative estimation of thirst during osmotic stimulation has demonstrated that thirst is a continuous variable which rises when subjects are rendered increasingly hyperosmolar [22] and that thirst is experienced at plasma osmolalities in the normal physiological range [23].

The linear relationships between thirst or vasopressin secretion and plasma tonicity can be modulated by several other physiological factors such as blood volume, reproductive status, drugs (e.g. alcohol, lithium), psychiatric diseases (e.g. psychosis, anorexia nervosa), and hormones (e.g. ANP).

Reduced blood volume (hypovolemia) shifts the relationship to the left, whereas hypervolemia shifts it to the right. During the luteal phase of the menstrual cycle [24] and in pregnancy [25], the relationship are shifted to the left by approximately 5-10 mOsmol/kg so that thirst and vasopressin secretion are experienced at lower levels of plasma tonicity. At least for pregnancy these changes may be related to human chorionic gonadotropin [25] and / or relaxin [26].

Hemodynamic Factors

Thirst and vasopressin release may also be stimulated by non-osmotic factors such as hypovolemia and hypotension although in general these are less potent stimuli than raised plasma osmolality.

Two main types of baroreceptors are involved in the regulation of non-osmotic thirst and vasopressin secretion. High pressure baroreceptors located in the carotid sinus and aortic arch respond to changes in blood pressure, whilst changes in blood volume are seen by low pressure left atrial stretch receptors. Thirst and the release of vasopressin are stimulated by decreases in blood volume, blood pressure, or both. On the other hand increased blood pressure, blood volume, or both leads to increased firing of baroreceptors and inhibition of thirst and vasopressin secretion.

Afferent input from the baroreceptors is carried in the vagus and glossopharyngeal nerves to the nucleus of the solitary tract and then via the dorsal ascending noradrenergic bundle to the PVN and SON [27]. In man, it is thought that the high pressure arterial baroreceptors play a more important role than the low pressure volume receptors as only a 5% fall in pressure compared to a 15% fall in blood volume is necessary to stimulate vasopressin release [28]. In contrast to the linear thirst / vasopressin osmotic relationships, the relationship between thirst / vasopressin and blood pressure / blood volume is exponential.

It can be seen that the osmoregulatory system involving vasopressin release is more sensitive than the baroregulatory system as only a 2% increase in plasma osmolality is required to cause maximum antidiuresis compared to a 15-20% fall in arterial blood pressure.

Endocrine Factors

Angiotensin II
Hypovolemia and reduced blood pressure also stimulate the renin angiotensin system to cause an increase in plasma renin activity with consequent production of increased circulating Ang II. Intracerebroventricular administration of Ang II is a potent stimulator of both thirst and vasopressin release. The role of circulating plasma Ang II in the control of vasopressin and thirst is less clear because Ang II increases blood pressure which will inhibit thirst and vasopressin secretion. If however this pressor effect is limited, exogenously administered Ang II stimulates thirst and vasopressin secretion at plasma levels within the physiological range [29].

As there is also evidence for a independent brain renin angiotensin system, Ang II may act as a neurotransmitter or neuromodulatory to influence thirst and vasopressin release. At the present time the relative importance of central versus circulating Ang II is not clear.

Atrial Natriuretic Peptide
ANP is released in response to increases in blood pressure and blood volume and acts to cause a diuresis and natriuresis. In many respects therefore ANP can be considered as the physiological antagonist of the renin angiotensin system. If ANP were also able to inhibit fluid intake this effect would be additive to its diuretic action. Certainly studies in animals have shown that ANP administered intracerebroventricularly or

intravenously will inhibit osmotically stimulated Ang II stimulated drinking [30-33] and we have shown that intravenously infused ANP inhibits osmotically stimulated thirst in man [21].

Evidence to date from human and animal studies has produced conflicting results regarding the effect of ANP on vasopressin release. In man studies using pharmacological concentrations of ANP show inhibition of basal and osmotically stimulated vasopressin release [34, 35]. On the other hand, infusion of physiological concentrations of ANP does not affect osmotically stimulated vasopressin release [21].

Environmental Factors

Environmental factors such as temperature, humidity, water availability, food availability and type may also affect thirst and vasopressin secretion by altering fluid losses. Under hot conditions elderly individuals often have difficulty maintaining fluid balance as despite increased plasma osmolality they have less thirst and are also slower at replacing their fluid deficits compared to younger subjects [36]. The palatability of the fluid available for drinking is also important and if unpalatable may limit the amount of water intake. On the other hand if the fluid is very palatable, increased water intake may occur leading to hyponatremia, as secretary mechanisms in the elderly are impaired. The temperature of the drinking water also determines the volume drunk, as does the effort required to obtain the drinking water.

1.3. Satiety

Accurate monitoring of the amount of fluid consumed must occur as in general animals do not over compensate when correcting fluid losses. Mechanisms responsible for the termination of thirst and drinking appear to be different from those which initiate it. Drinking in man produces a rapid fall in thirst appreciation and plasma vasopressin concentrations prior to any change in plasma osmolality or blood volume [37-39]. These data suggest the termination of thirst and drinking is not solely due to abolition of the osmotic stimulus. It is now generally believed that the mechanism responsible for the termination of drinking and the rapid suppression of vasopressin and thirst appreciation involves an inhibitory oropharyngeal neuronal pathway [40], rather than hypothalamic osmoreceptors.

As ANP has antidipsogenic properties it may be involved in the termination of drinking. Physiological increases in plasma ANP inhibit thirst appreciation [21] and subsequent water intake in hyperosmolar man [41].

II - AGE ASSOCIATED CHANGES IN THE PHYSIOLOGICAL VARIABLES INVOLVED IN WATER HOMEOSTASIS

Normal ageing is associated with many changes in homeostatic mechanisms. The result of such changes is that the elderly person is at increased risk for the development of significant changes in salt and water balance and increased morbidity and mortality.

There is now considerable evidence that thirst declines as age increases [42-45], whilst vasopressin secretion tends to increase with age. The results of these changes mean that in association with reduced renal concentrating ability (despite normal or elevated vasopressin secretion), the elderly are predisposed to dehydration through reduced thirst and water loss.

2.1. Decreased Sensation of Thirst

The precise mechanism for reduced thirst perception in the elderly remains to be elucidated but may be due to reduced osmotic sensitivity [43]. In one study the elderly subjects (67-75 years) and young healthy controls (20-31 years) were deprived of water for 24 hours and then offered access to water. During the period of water deprivation, plasma osmolality increased more in the elderly subjects as did plasma vasopressin. However, the maximum urine osmolality in the elderly was significantly lower than that of the younger subjects. There was a striking difference in the water intake and thirst in between the elderly and young. During the 60 minute period in which water was available the elderly drank 257±57 ml compared to the young control group who drank 601±72 ml. The elderly group did not actually drink sufficient amounts of water to return plasma osmolality to normal.

A reduced response to a fall in blood pressure or blood volume may also occur in the elderly but as severe hypovolemia and / or hypotension are required to stimulate thirst in man [28]. It is unlikely that changes in blood volume or blood pressure influence either the secretion of vasopressin or thirst stimulation in the elderly.

On the other hand, changes in various neurotransmitters may influence thirst in the elderly. For example, central levels of dopamine are reduced with ageing [46, 47] and as dopamine facilitates drinking in animals [48], a reduction in central dopamine may be responsible for reduced thirst in drinking in the elderly patient. Changes in endogenous opiod peptides and their receptors may play a part in reduced thirst in the elderly [49]. Reduced levels of endorphins in the hypothalamus [50] and decreased density of central opiod receptors [51] have been described in the aged rat. Naloxone, the opiod antagonist in known to reduce drinking by acting centrally [52] and there is a decrease responsiveness to naloxone induced reduction in water intake in elderly mice [49], whilst exogenous opiod agonist increase water intake in young animals [53].

It is also likely that there are changes with ageing in poorly defined pathways that bring thirst to consciousness [1]. It is well known that elderly individuals with pre-existing cerebrovascular disease have reduced thirst and experience episodes of significant hypertonicity and hypernatremia despite their ability to communicate the desire for water and obtain it [54].

2.2. Increased Osmoregulated Vasopressin Secretion

To date morphometric and immunocytochemical studies indicate no change in the SON and PVN which are responsible for the production of vasopressin with ageing [5]. Data is conflicting as to whether circulating levels of vasopressin are significantly altered during the ageing process. A number of studies have shown no change [56-58], other lower vasopressin levels [59-61] and others elevated vasopressin levels [62-64] in elderly compared to younger subjects.

In studies in which elderly subjects were either water deprived [42] or had hypertonic saline infused to stimulate vasopressin and thirst [56, 65], circulating vasopressin levels in the elderly were higher than those of younger subjects. Thus for any given level of osmotic stimulus there appears to be an increased release of vasopressin in the elderly which suggests either that there is a reduction in an inhibitory input to osmoregulation with age or that there is increased osmoreceptor sensitivity with increasing age.

These findings are interesting as under normal circumstances changes in osmotically regulated thirst and vasopressin release occur in parallel. Although there may be separate osmoreceptors for thirst and vasopressin secretion (see above), it would seem unlikely that only one type of osmoreceptor neuron would be affected by ageing. It may be, therefore, that there are changes with ageing in poorly defined pathways that bring thirst to consciousness [1] as discussed above which accounts for the dichotomy between thirst and vasopressin release in the elderly.

2.3. Blunted Renal Response to Vasopressin

Increasing age is also associated with declining urinary concentrating ability in man [42, 66]. After 24 hours of water deprivation, the elderly showed lower urinary osmolality, even though their plasma sodium and osmolality after deprivation were significantly higher than young controls [42]. The mechanism responsible is likely to be the result of poor renal responsiveness to circulating vasopressin. This can also be partly accounted for by the reduction in nephron numbers in old age [45]. Miller [67] described that the age-related increase in vasopressin secretion may result in decreased responsiveness to this hormone through down regulation of renal vasopressin receptors, although the changes in basal plasma vasopressin level during normal aging are conflicting as described above.

2.4. Age-Related Changes in ANP and Renin-Angiotensin-Aldosterone System

The normal aging process affects other hormonal systems involved in regulating water balance such as Ang II, a potent stimulator for thirst and vasopressin secretion, and ANP, an endogenous inhibitor of the renin-angiotensin system.

Basal levels of ANP increase with increasing age [2, 68-70] and the ANP rises in response to stimuli such as saline infusion [69], head-out water immersion [70] and exercise [2] also increases with age. Elevated circulating ANP levels are accompanied by a reduction in the activity of renin-angiotensin-aldosterone system due to decreased renin production in the kidney [71, 72] and a decrease in aldosterone concentration secondary to elevated ANP and reduced plasma renin activity. Taken together these effects of ANP may result in age-related renal sodium and water loss. Of interest is that after 24 hour water deprivation, the elderly showed higher plasma ANP levels than control young subjects, even though they were more dehydrated as confirmed by higher plasma osmolality, plasma sodium and hematocrit [44].

Thus in aged people, increased ANP secretion and decreased Ang II may be partially responsible for a reduction in thirst sensation. We have previously shown that physiological infusions of ANP (15-20 pmol/L) along with hypertonic saline in young volunteers will blunt osmotically-stimulated thirst whilst having no effects on vasopressin release [21, 73]. Although similar studies have yet to be performed in the elderly, this data does suggest that in the elderly subjects elevated ANP may play a role in reduced thirst.

2.5. Effects of Ageing on Satiety

Changes in satiety with ageing have also been reported. Phillips et al [44] examined changes in thirst and plasma vasopressin responses to oral water load (10 ml/kg within 5 min) in old and young 24-hour water deprived subjects. In the elderly vasopressin secretion was not inhibited immediately upon drinking as seen in the younger subjects. The elderly did show appropriate inhibition of water deprivation-induced thirst after drinking although their thirst was reduced compared to the younger subjects. Thus, the elderly individual has reduced oropharyngeal inhibition of vasopressin secretion but maintains inhibition of thirst after drinking.

2.6. Risks of Ageing

The elderly are more likely to have medical disorders and / or be taking medications, both of which can influence fluid homeostasis. For example, in diabetes mellitus, increased blood glucose levels cause cellular dehydration and stimulation of thirst and vasopressin secretion. In conditions such as heart failure, glucocorticoid deficiency, hypercalcemia and hyperkalemia, excessive thirst may also occur. It is unclear if excess thirst is due to changes in plasma volume, osmoreceptor sensitivity, hormonal changes or whether they are secondary to psychological factors or changes in renal function.

The use of drugs with anticholinergic side effects (e.g. antihistamines, phenothiazines and atropine) may stimulate drinking, probably secondary to a dry mouth rather than a central neurological effect. Other drugs used by the elderly can cause hyponatremia by stimulating the release of vasopressin from the neurohypophyseal system or by potentiating its renal effects (e.g. tricyclic antidepressants, vincristine, carbamezepine etc.).

In summary, the hormonal changes associated with ageing, the occurrence of other medical condition and the use of medications increases the likelihood of conditions such as hyper- and hypo-natremia. Awareness of the homeostatic changes with age and the relations with disease and drugs will lead better management of fluid disorders in the elderly patient and hopefully a reduction in morbidity and mortality.

REFERENCES

1. Phillips PA, Burrell LM. Thirst. In: Bittar, E. & Bittar, N., eds. Principles of Medical Biology , 1997: in press.
2. Miller M. Hormonal aspects of fluid and sodium balance in the elderly. Endocrinol Metab Clin North Am. 1995;24:233-253.
3. Gilman A. The relation between blood osmotic pressure, fluid distribution and voluntary water intake. Am J Physiol 1937;120:323-328.
4. Verney EB. The antidiuretic hormone and the factors which determine its release. Proc Royal Soc London 1947;135:135.
5. Andersson B. The effect of injections of hypertonic NaCl solutions into different parts of the hypothalamus of goats. Acta Physiol Scand 1953;28:188-201.
6. Peck JW, Novin D. Evidence that osmoreceptors mediating drinking in rabbits are in the lateral optic area. J Comp Physiol Psychol 1971;74:134-137.
7. Buggy J, Johnson AK. Preoptic hypothalamic periventricular lesions: thirst deficits and hypernatraemia. Am J Physiol 1977;233:R44-R52.
8. Andersson B, Leskell LG, Lishajko F. Perturbations in fluid balance induced by medially placed forebrain lesions. Brain Res 1975;99:261-275.
9. Thrasher TN, Simpson JB, Ramsay DJ. Lesions of the subfornical organ block angiotensin II induced drinking in the dog. Neuroendocrinology 1982;35:36-72.
10. Iovino M, Steardo L. Vasopressin release to central and peripheral angiotensin II in rats with lesions of the subfornical organ. Brain Res 1984;322:365-368.
11. Thrasher TN, Keil LC, Ramsay DJ. Lesions of the organum vasculosum lamina terminalis (OVLT) attenuates osmotically induced drinking and vasopressin secretion in the dog. Endocrinology 1982;110:1837-1842.
12. Thrasher TN, Keil LC. Regulation of drinking and vasopressin secretion: role of the organum vasculosum lamina terminalis. Am J Physiol 1987;253:R108-R120.
13. Thrasher TN. Role of the circumventricular organs in body fluid balance. Acta Physiol Scand 1989;136 (suppl 583):141-150.
14. McKinley MJ, Denton DA, Leksell LC, Mouw DR, Scoggins BA, Smith MH, Weisinger RS, Wright RD. Osmoregulatory thirst in sheep is disrupted by ablation of the anterior wall of the optic recess. Brain Res 1982;236:210-215.
15. Zerbe RL, Robertson GL. Osmoregulation of thirst and vasopressin secretion in human subjects: effect of various solutes. Am J Physiol 1983;244:E607-E614.
16. Peck JW, Blass E. Localisation of thirst and antidiuretic osmoreceptors by intracranial injection in rats. Am J. Physiol 1975;228:1501-1509.
17. Hammond DN, Moll GW, Robertson GL, Chelmicka-Schorr E. Hypodipsic hypernatremia with hormonal osmoregulation of vasopressin. N Engl J Med 1986;315:433-436.
18. Rolls BJ, Wood RJ, Rolls ET, Lind H, Lind W, Ledingham JGG. Thirst following water deprivation in humans. Am J physiol 1980;239:R476-R482.
19. Thompson CJ, Bland J, Burd J, Baylis PH. The osmotic thresholds for thirst and vasopressin release are similar in healthy man. Clin Sci 1986;71:651-656.
20. Burrell LM, Lambert HJ, Baylis PH. The effect of drinking on atrial natriuretic peptide, vasopressin and thirst appreciation in hyperosmolar man. Clin Endocrinol 1991;35:229-234.
21. Burrell LM, Lambert HJ, Baylis PH. Effect of atrial natriuretic peptide on thirst and arginine vasopressin release in humans. Am J Physiol 1991;260:R475-R479.
22. Phillips PA, Rolls BJ, Ledingham JGG, Forsling ML, Morton JJ. Osmotic thirst and vasopressin release in humans: a double blid cross-over study. Am J Physiol 1985;248:R645-R650.
23. Phillips PA, Rolls BJ, Ledingham JGG, Morton JJ. Body fluid changes, thirst and drinking in man during free access to water. Physiol Behav 1984;33:357-363.
24. Vokes TJ, Weiss NM, Schreiber J, Gaskill MB, Roberston GL. Osmoregulation of thirst and vasopressin in during normal menstrual cycle. Am J Physiol 1988;254:R641-R647.
25. Davison JM, Shields EA, Phillips PR, Lindeheimer MD. Serial evaluation of vasopressin release and thirst in human pregnancy: role of human chorionic gonadotrophin in the osmoregulatory changes of gestation. J Clin Invest 1988;815:798-806.
26. Weisinger RS, Burns P, Eddie LW, Wintour EM. Relaxin alters the plasma osmolality-arginine vasopressin relationships in the rat. J Endocrinol 1993;137:505-510.
27. Sawchenko PE, Swanson LW. The organisation of noradrenergic pathways from the brainstem to the paraventricular and supraoptic nuclei in the rat. Brain Res Rev 1982;4:275-325.

28. Baylis PH. Posterior pituitary function in health and disease. Clin End Metab 1983;12:747-770.
29. Robinson MR, Evered MD. Pressor action of angiotensin II reduced drinking response in rats. Am J Physiol 1987;252:R754-R759.
30. Olsson K, Dahlborn K, Nygren K, Karlberg BE, Anden N, Eriksson L. Fluid balance and arterial blood pressure during intracarotid infusions of atrial natriuretic peptide (ANP) in water-deprived goats. Acta Physiol Scand 1989;263:249-257.
31. Antunes-Rodrigues A, McCann SM, Rogers LC, Samson WK. Atrial natriuretic factor inhibits dehydration and angiotensin-II induced water intake in conscious, unrestrained rat. Proc Natl Acad Sci 1985;82:8720-8723.
32. Thornton SN, Baldwin BA. Centrally injected atrial natriuretic factor inhibits angiotensin- and osmotically-induced drinking in pigs. Quart J Exp Physiol 1988;73:1009-1012.
33. Tarjan E, Denton DA, Weisinger RS. Atrial natriuretic peptide inhibits water and sodium intake in rabbits. Regulatory Peptides 1988;23:63-75.
34. Fuijo M, Ohashi M, Nawata h, Kato K, Ibayashi H, Kangawa K, Matsuo H. Alpha-human atrial natriuretic polypeptide reduces the plasma arginine vasopressin concentration in human subjects. Clin Endocrinol 1986;25:181-187.
35. Allen MJ, Ang VTY, Bennett ED, Jenkins JS. Atrial natriuretic peptide inhibits osmotically-induced arginine vasopressin release in man. Clin Sci 1988;75:35-39.
36. Miescher E, Fortney SM. Response to dehydration and rehydration during heat exposure in young and older men. Am J Physiol 1989;257:R1050-R1056.
37. Geelen G, Keil LC, Kravik SE, Wade CE, Thrasher TN, Barnes PR, Pyka G, Nesvig C, Greenleaf JE. Inhibition of plasma vasopressin after drinking in dehydrated humans. Am J. Physiol 1984;247:R968-R971.
38. Thrasher TN, Nistal-Herrara JF, Keil LC, Ramsay DJ. Satiety and inhibition of vasopressin secretion after drinking in dehydrated dogs. Am J Physiol 1981;240:E394-E401.
39. Thompson CJ, Burd J, Baylis PH. Acute suppression of plsama vasopressin and thirst after drinking in hypernatraemic humans. Am J Physiol 1987;252:R1138-R1142.
40. Seckl JR, Williams TDM, Lightman SL: Oral hypertonic saline causes transient fall of vasopressin in humans. Am J Physiol 1986;251:R214-R217.
41. Burrell LM, Palmer JM, Baylis PH. Atrial natriuretic peptide inhibits fluid intake in hyperosmolar subjects. Clin Sci 1992;83:35-39.
42. Phillips PA, Rolls BJ, Ledingham JG, Forsling ML, Morton JJ, Vrowe MJ, Wollner L. Reduced thirst after water deprivation in healthy elderly men. N Engl J Med 1984;311:753-759.
43. Phillips PA, Bretherton M, Johnston CI, Gray L. Reduced osmotic thirst in healthy elderly men. Am J Physiol 1991;261:R166-R171.
44. Phillips PA, Bretherton M, Risvanis J, Casley D, Johnston C, Gray L. Effects of drinking on thirst and vasopressin in dehydrated elderly men. Am J Physiol 1993;264:R877-R881.
45. Anonymous. Thirst and osmoregulation in the elderly. Lancet 1984;2 (8410):1017-1018.
46. Morgan DG, Finch CE. Dopaminergic changes in the basal ganglia. A generalized phenomenon of aging in mammals. Ann NY Acad Sci 1988;515:145-160.
47. Strong R: Regionally selective manifestations of neostriatal aging. Ann NY Acad Sci 1988;515:161-177.
48. Zabik JE, Sprague JE, Odio M. Interactive dopaminergic and noradrenergic systems in the regulation of thirst in the rat. Physiol. Behav. 1993;54:29-33.
49. Lalonde R, Badescu R: Exploratory drive, frontal lobe function and adipsia in aging. Gerontology 1995;41:134-44.
50. Missale C, Govoni S, Croce L, Bosio A, Spano PF, Trabucchi M. Changes of beta-endorphin and Met-enkephlin content in the hypothalamus-pituitary axis induced by aging. J Neurochem 1983;40:20-24.
51. Messing RB, Vasquez BJ, Samaniego B, Jensen RA, Martinez JLJ, McGaugh JL. Alterations in dihydromorphine binding in cerebral hemispheres of aged male rats. J Neurochem 1981;36:784-787.
52. Siviy SM, Bermudez-Rattoni F, Rockwood GA, Dargie CM, Reid LD. Intracerebral administration of naloxone and drinking in water-deprived rats. Pharmacol Biochem Behav 1981;15:257-262.
53. Reid LD. Endogenous opioid peptides and regulation of drinking and feeding. Am J Clin Nutr 1985;42 (Suppl 5):1099-1132.
54. Miller PD, Krebs RA, Neal BJ, McIntyre DO. Hypodipsia in geriatric patients. Am J Med 1982;73:354-356.
55. Fliers E, Swaab DF, Pool CW, Verwer RW. The vasopressin and oxytocin neurons in the human supraoptic and paraventricular nucleus: changes with aging and in senile dementia. Brain Res. 1985;342:45-53.
56. Helderman JH, Vestal RE, Rowe JW, Tobin JD, Andres R, Robertson GL. The response to arginine

vasopressin to intravenous ethanol and hypertonic saline in man: the impact of aging. J Gerontol 1978;33:39-47.

57. Chiodera P, Capretti L, Marchesi M, Gaiazza A, Bianconi L, Cavazzini U, Marchesi C, Volpi R, Coiro V. Abnormal arginine vasopresin response to cigarette smoking and metoclopramide (but not to insulin-induced hypoglycemia) in elderly subjects. J Gerontol 1991;46:M6-M10.

58. Duggan J, Kilfeather S, Lightman SL, O'Malley K. The association of age with plasma arginine vasopressin and plasma osmolality. Age Ageing 1993;22:332-336.

59. Faull CM, Holmes C, Baylis PH. Water balance in elderly people: is there a deficiency of vasopressin? Age Ageing 1993;22:114-120.

60. Asplund R, Aberg H. Diurnal variation in the levels of antidiuretic hormone in the elderly. J Intern Med 1991;299:131-134.

61. Clark BA, Elahi D, Fish L, McAloon-Dyke M, Davis K, Minaker KL, Epstein FH. Atrial natriuretic peptide suppresses osmostimulated vasopressin release in young and elderly humans. Am J Physiol 1991;261:E252-E256.

62. Rondeau E, Delima J, Caillens H, Ardaillau R, Vahanian A, Acar J. High plasma anti-diuretic hormone in patients with cardiac failure: influence of age. Mineral Electrolyte Metab 1982;8:267-274.

63. Kirland J, Lye M, Goddard C, Vargas E, Davies I. Plsama arginine vasopressin in dehydrated elderly patients. Clin Endocrinol 1984;20:451-456.

64. Johnson AG, Crawford GA, Kelly D, Nguyen TU, Gyory AZ. Arginine vasopressin and osmolality in the elderly. J Am Geriatr Soc 1994;42:399-404.

65. Davies I, O'Neill PA, McLean KA, Catania J, Bennett D. Age-associated alterations in thirst and arginine vasopressin in response to a water or sodium load. Age. Aging. 1995;24:151-159.

66. Miller JH, Shock NW. Age differences in the renal tubular response to antidiuretic hormone. J Gerontol 1953;8:446-450.

67. Miller M. Influence of aging on vasopressin secretion and water regulation. In: Schrier, R.W., eds. Vasopressin . 1985 pp.249, Raven Press, New York

68. McKnight JA, Roberts G, Sheridan B, Atkinson AB. Relationship between basal and sodium stimulated plasma atrial natriuretic factor, age, sex and blood pressure in normal man. J Human Hypertens 1989;3:157-163.

69. Ohashi M, Fujio N, Nawata H, Kato K, Ibayashi H, Kanagawa K, Matsuo H. High plasma concentration of human atrial natriuretic peptide in aged men. J Clin Endocrinol Metab 1987;64:81-85.

70. Tajima F, Sagawa S, Iwamoto J, Miki K, Claybaugh JR, Shiraki K. Renal and endocrine responses in the elderly during head-out water immersion. Am J Physiol 1988;254:R977-R983.

71. Tsunoda K, Abe K, Goto T, Yasujima M, Sato M, Omata K, Seino M, Yoshinaga K. Effect of age on renin-angiotensin-aldosterone system in normal subjects: simultaneous measurement of active and inactive renin, renin substrate, and aldosterone in plasma. J Clin Endocrinol Metab 1986;62:384-389.

72. Weidmann P, De Myttenaere-Bursztein S, Maxwell MH, De Lima J. Effect of aging on plasma renin and aldosterone in normal man. Kidney Int 1975;8:325-333.

73. Baylis PH, Burrell LM. The influence of atrial natriuretic peptides on vasopressin secretion and thirst: an overview. In: Jard, S. & Jamieson, R., eds. Vasopressin 1990, pp.287.

STRESS, AGING AND THIRST

J. E. GREENLEAF

Laboratory for Human Environmental Physiology, Life Sciences Division, NASA, Ames Research Center, Moffett Field, CA 94035-1000. Proof and reprint requests to: John E. Greenleaf, Ph.D. Gravitational Research Branch (239-11) NASA, Ames Research Center Moffett Field, CA 94035-1000 (415) 604-6604, fax: (415) 604-3954 e-mail: jgreenleaf@mail.arc.nasa.gov

Abstract : *After growth during adolesence, total body water decreases progressively with aging from 65% of body weight to about 53% of body wieght in the 70th decade: a majority of the loss occurs from the extracellular volume; from 42% to about 25%, respectively. Cellular volume also reaches equilibrium in the 70th decade at about 25% of body weight. Various stresses such as exercise, heat and altitude exposure, and prior dehydration attenuate voluntary fluid intake (involuntary dehydration). Voluntary fluid intake appears to decrease with aging (involuntary dehydration?); in this sense aging can be considered as a stress. Kidney function and muscle mass (80% water) decrease somewhat with aging, and voluntary fluid intake (thirst) is also attenuated. Thirst is stimulated by increasing osmolality (hypernatremia) of the extracellular fluid and by decreased extracellular volume (mainly plasma volume) which act to increase intracellular fluid volume osmolality to activiate drinking. The latter decreases fluid compartment osmolality which terminates drinking. However, this drinking mechanism seems to be attenuated with aging such that increasing plasma osmolality no longer stimulates fluid intake appropriately. Hypernatremia in the elderly has been associated all too frequently with greater incidence of bacterial infection and increased mortality. Involuntary dehydration can be overcome in young men by acclimation to an intermittent exercise-in-heat training program. Perhaps exercise training in the elderly would also increase voluntary fluid intake and increase muscle mass to enhance retention of water.*

INTRODUCTION

Water constitutes 55-65% of body weight [1] depending upon age, gender, muscle mass, and level of physical conditioning. The decrease in body water with aging accompanies the concomitant decline of striated muscle mass which is about 80% water [2]. This body hypohydration is attenuated during physical conditioning due, in part, to the accompanying increase in muscle mass. It is possible that both acute and chronic body dehydration, with accompaning plasma hypernatremia and hyperosmotemia, constitute bodily stress which may predispose it to infection and death; particularly in those confined in nursing homes and hospitals [3, 4, 5].

Prolonged bed rest with its increased confinement has been used as a model for deconditioning. Many anatomical and physiological responses, expecially the decrease in muscle mass and total body water throughout all body fluid compartments during bed rest deconditioning, also occur with aging. Because of these factors and the many deleterious effects of increasing levels of total body dehydration (Figure 1), an understanding of the control mechanisms for restoring (by drinking) and maintaining adequate body fluid volume could enhance the quality of health and performance accompanying the inexorable decrease in thirst and body water with aging.

Fig. 1
Adverse effects of total body dehydration.

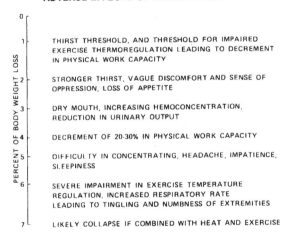

ADVERSE EFFECTS OF DEHYDRATION

PERCENT OF BODY WEIGHT LOSS	
1	THIRST THRESHOLD, AND THRESHOLD FOR IMPAIRED EXERCISE THERMOREGULATION LEADING TO DECREMENT IN PHYSICAL WORK CAPACITY
2	STRONGER THIRST, VAGUE DISCOMFORT AND SENSE OF OPPRESSION, LOSS OF APPETITE
3	DRY MOUTH, INCREASING HEMOCONCENTRATION, REDUCTION IN URINARY OUTPUT
4	DECREMENT OF 20-30% IN PHYSICAL WORK CAPACITY
5	DIFFICULTY IN CONCENTRATING, HEADACHE, IMPATIENCE, SLEEPINESS
6	SEVERE IMPAIRMENT IN EXERCISE TEMPERATURE REGULATION, INCREASED RESPIRATORY RATE LEADING TO TINGLING AND NUMBNESS OF EXTREMITIES
7	LIKELY COLLAPSE IF COMBINED WITH HEAT AND EXERCISE

This review will focus on the interaction among voluntary fluid intake; body fluid balance, and levels of physical conditioning and deconditioning (stress) in the elderly; with evaluation of possible mechanisms for the apparent resurgence of attenuated drinking with aging. For comparative purposes is a short discussion of drinking and fluid balance in infants and children. Recent reviews presenting descriptive data and discussion of mechanisms of thirst and drinking in males and females of all ages include those by Buskirk and Puhl [6], Marriott [7], and Ramsay and Booth [8].

DRINKING AND WATER BALANCE IN INFANTS (<1 YR) AND CHILDREN (1-12 YR)

Maintence of body hydration in humans is accentuated at birth when calories, other nutrients, and water are delivered to the infant in solutions of various composition. It appears that infant preferences for sweet (carbohydrates) and salty (NaCl) substances are modified innate responses that continue throughout life [9]. The sense of what should or should not be sweet, rather than an overall innate sense of sweetness, appears to be induced by dietary experience. On the other hand, the learned induction of salt preferences appears in two phases: the first is a shift from relative indifference at birth to a preference for near isotonic NaCl soutions (in relation to water) at about 4 months of age to fill the maturing muscles and cardiovascular system. Thereafter, this relative acceptance of saline leads to its aversion and rejection which occurs by 24 to 36 months of age. Thus, acceptability of fluids from birth is increased when a sweet carbohydrate is added, and a significant preference for sucrose solutions at 6 months and at 24 months of age was observed in those who had consumed sweetened water soon after birth. Also, early exposure to sweetened water before 6 months, which had subsequently been discontinued, appeared to have lasting effects on acceptance of 0.2 and 0.6 molar sucrose solutions in older children [9].

In contrast to the early and continued acceptance of carbohydrate solutions, voluntary consumption of saline solutions appears to be greater in 4 to 7 - month - old - infants than in 2 to 4 - month infants, and saline solutions were rejected in preference for water in children between 31 and 60 months of age. However, a majority of those older children chose salted (0.34 molar NaCl) soup over non-salted soup suggesting that salt intake could be increased voluntarily when consumed in a familiar medium (soup) that was perceived as food [9]. Thus, it appears that the initial change from indifference to acceptance of salt is the result of maturation, whereas dietary experience may be the explanation for the later rejection of saline solutions.

Hypernatremic dehydration. Hypernatremic (hypertonic) dehydration, a rather uncommon clinical finding in infants and children in developed countries, is usually caused by enteric disease which induces dehydration -from diarrhea, anorexia, and vomiting- resulting in depressed fluid intake [10, 11]. Many cases of enteric disease, which usually occur in the fall and winter months, are of viral origin and are accompanied by fever, hypovolemia, hyperosmotemia (hypernatremia), and often by hyperglycemia. The depressed voluntary fluid intake in the presence of significant hyperosmotemia and hypovolemia would appear to be a manifestation of stress–induced involuntary dehydration [12]. But inhibition of drinking in these sick people could be a defense mechanism to maintain hyperosmolality and increased concentrations of important plasma constituents, e.g., immune factors, for combatting the virus [13]. The degree of total body dehydration (by weight) in Australian children is often overestimated by admitting physicians. Mackenzie et al. [14] have suggested that the major clinical signs and symptoms of dehydration, such as decreased peripheral perfusion and skin turgor, deep breathing, dry mouth, and a history of increased thirst, become apparent in young children (<4 yr) at 3-4% body dehydration rather than beyond 5% thereby denying many hospital admissions and treatment with intravenous fluid. Dehydration–induced deaths constituted about 1% of all deaths in infants and children (0.5 to 73 mo) in Adelaide Children's Hospital in Australia from 1961-1993 [11].

Older children (boys and girls 9-14 yr), like adults, experience involuntary dehydration when exposed to stress such as moderate, submaximal, isotonic cycle exercise in a hot (35-39°C Tdb) environment [15, 16, 17]. With a similar percentage body weight loss from sweating, these children had a two-fold greater rise in rectal temperature (greater stress) than comparably lean adults [15]. This exercise–in–heat induced involuntary dehydration was attenuated after addition of fruit flavoring (a peripheral effect) to the drinks, and was eliminated with further addition of 2% glucose and 4% sucrose plus 18 mmol/liter NaCl [17], i.e., a central effect. Fluid consumption does not insure that it is transferred into the vascular system, as stress stimuli can inhibit gastrointestinal absorption [18].

These children could also discriminate between various levels of thirst sensations and provided reliable estimates of drink taste, and degree of sweet and sour [19, 20]. After cessation of 90 min of exercise–induced dehydration in the heat, both boys and girls drank sufficient fluid voluntarily (without eating food) to exceed their pre–exercise fluid balance levels [19], which does not generally occur in adults [21]. This "excess" drinking during recovery in heat suggests that stimuli which inhibit voluntary fluid intake were induced mainly by the exercise, and probably to a lesser extent by the environmental heat, as occurs in adult men [21].

AGING AND WATER BALANCE

Voluntary fluid intake and water balance in the elderly: ambulation-activity. Body water is lost mainly involuntarily via the skin (insensibly and by sweating), respiratory tract, and kidney; whereas normal fluid intake occurs mainly semi-voluntarily by drinking and eating. Under normal living conditions the thirst sensation, activated mainly by increased plasma osmolality and also secondarily by decreased plasma volume [12], is an adequate stimulus for sufficient fluid intake. In conjunction with eating and drinking the free and metabolic water, obtained from the diet and via reabsorption from proper kidney function, maintains body water balance within normal limits from day to day. However, under a variety of stressful conditions including increase environmental heat, physical exercise, and body dehydration, thirst is an inadequate stimulus for drinking such that the rate of voluntary fluid intake (even with normal food intake) lags considerable behind the rate of body fluid loss resulting in a prolonged period - up to 24 hr - of reduced body water [21]. This delay in rehydration from attenuated drinking is called involuntary dehydration [12, 22]. Involuntary dehydration appears to be present in the elderly (>70 yr) under essentially non-stressful conditions [23], and may be somewhat more prevalent in women who normally drink less than men [24].

It is well - documented that total body water declines with age [1, 25, 26]; after age 5 it varies between 65-55% in males and 65-45% in females (Figure 2). Because body fat contains relatively low (50%) water content [2], the lower water/weight percentages in women are probably due mainly to their relatively greater body fat content. Indeed, Lesser and Markofsky [25] found that the body water/lean body (fat free) mass remains relatively constant in both men and women accompaning the decrease in their lean body masses-mainly muscle which is about 80% water [2] - with aging. After an increase in ICV between birth and adolescense during growth, both ECV and ICV also decline with age (Figure 2). In the 70th decade ECV and ICV converge at about 25% of body weight.

Fig. 2

Total body water (TBW), and extracellular (ECV) and intracellular (ICV) fluid volumes with aging in males and females. Data from 25 yr onward represent the ± 5 yr interval. Data recalculated from ref. 1.

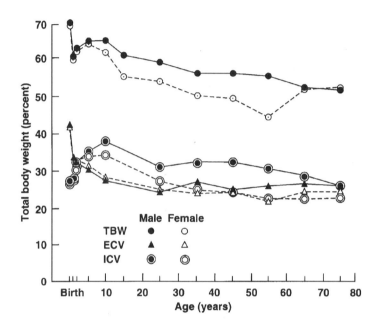

Voluntary fluid intake and water balance in the elderly: bed rest-inactivity-deconditioning. The level of physical (physiological) conditioning and deconditioning (Figure 3) can be indicated on a continous relative scale (heavy line); the eucondition (normal) range (dotted area) probably declines with aging concomitantly with the reduction in muscle mass and other functions (Figure 4). Creditor [27] has depicted many factors associated with normal aging and how they can result in confinement in a nursing home. Chief among these factors are reduced muscle strength and aerobic (work) capacity leading to deconditioning, and altered thirst and nutrition resulting in dehydration. Total body water and plasma volumes are reduced chronically in normal, healthy subjects due to a combination of diuresis and hypodipsia on the first day of bed rest; and occasionally in the presence of hyperosmotemia which should stimulate thirst and drinking [28].

Fig. 3
Body conditioning, eucondition, and deconditioning (aging?)
continuum.

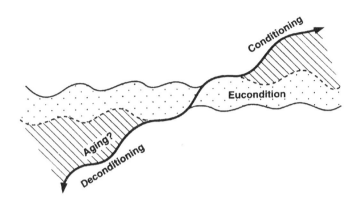

Fig. 4
Comparison of physiological functions during prolonged bed-rest,
deconditioning and aging.

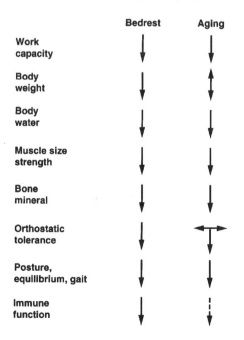

Elders appear to drink less fluid when institutionalized than when noninstitutionalized at home [29, 30]. Most fluid intake occurs between 0600 and 1800 hr in institutionalized patients who have less access to hot or cold drinks with or between meals [29]. The latter were more dependent on the nursing staff to offer fluids, which usually occurred at medication time, in a fixed and usually inadequate volume not related to the patients' desires or degree of thirst. Institutionalized patients (and the general population for that matter) do not like to drink plain tap water, which comprised only 31% of their fluid intake, when compared with 41% for the noninstitutionalized population [29]. Thus, in addition to infection and the more extensive immobility and confinement, many iatrogenic factors combine to lower fluid intake in many patients: the generalized stress of living in an unfamiliar environment, dehydration in preparation for medical test, possible mental confusion and inhibited thirst due to drugs, restricted access to beverage dispensers, no facilities to store cold drinks or to prepare warm drinks, and having drink selection and composition prepared by the institutional staff rather than by the patients.

Physiological factors influencing attenuation of drinking in the elderly. Because water is the most abundant and important compound in the body, the control of voluntary fluid intake-an interactive process involving multiple and redundant mechanisms-is particularly important for maintenance of health and well-being with aging. Thirst is a sensation all humans have experienced but a clear definition remains elusive. One definitions, "1a: a sensation of dryness in the mouth and throat associated with a desire for liquids; also: the bodily condition (as of dehydration) that induces this sensation..." [31]. It is clearly inadequate because neither a dry mouth nor body dehydration singly or together invariably result in drinking [12]. In stressful situations or conditions-such as heat exposure, exercise, or bed rest - humans lose body water via sweating or diuresis that may not be restored for 24 hr in ambulatory subjects [21], and not until reambulation in bed-rested subjects [32]. It is possible that the mechanisms causing this stress-induced involuntary dehydration (attenuated drinking) in younger humans may be similar to those causing retarded fluid intake (involuntary dehydration?) in the elderly. Morimoto et al. [33] were the first to show that loss of solutes in sweat was the cause of involuntary dehydration in subjects exposed to heat and exercise. The implication here is that aging per se is a generalized stress.

Cerebral osmoreceptors, specialized cells in the hypothalamic region, and pressure receptors in the low pressure side of the heart and systemic vascular system transduce signals to the brain that activate mechanisms to stimulate drinking [22]. Both osmol and pressure stimuli can activate arginine vasopressin (AVP) and angiotensin II (ANG II) which can act as dipsogens. Vasopressin can also be stimulated by ANG II, and the latter activated by renin from the kidney. There is some evidence for extracerebral osmoreceptors located in the oropharyngeal area, the gastric-duodenal system, and the liver-portal system [22] ; systems that meter and process fluids. This extensive redundency of osmoreceptors attests to their importance for maintaining fluid-electrolyte homeostasis. At present it is difficult to ascribe the attenuated drinking in the healthy elderly to reduced functioning of any of these osmotic or volume sensing systems. However, it is clear with increasing age that resting plasma osmolality increases progressively from 285 ± 5 mOsm • kg^{-1} at age 20 to 300 ± 5 mOsm • kg^{-1} at age 80 [34], resting plasma volume declines moderately and progressively [35], and there is also a concomitant decrease in voluntary fluid intake; that is a reduced thirst sensitivity to the hyperosmotemia and hypovolemia [36, 37]. This suggests a change in the operating "set-point" in the central osmorecptors. In addition, the sensitivity of dehydrated dogs to vasopressin, a central dipsogenic stimulant [38], appears to be inconsistent [39], but decreased kidney responsiveness to adequate secretion of AVP in old rats seems clear [40]. There is decreased activity of the renin-angiotensin-aldosterone system in old rats [41], and in healthy elderly men and women [42] which is due to reduction in active renin and not to decrease in plasma renin substrate concentration [43]. Intravenous infusion of ANG II at mildly pressor doses increased voluntary water intake in only 4 of 10 young men suggesting its unimportant role for stimulating drinking under these conditions [44]. In such an all-encompassing and basic system as water metabolism, it is not surprising that its contol mechanisms are varied and redundant. With functional deterioration in most body control systems including kidney function with aging, it will be difficult to elucidate one system or one part of the mechanism that is primarily responsible for this attenuated drinking in the normal organism because of feedback to maintain homeostasis.

Implementation of appropriate remedial treatments that increase voluntary fluid intake in non-elderly subjects may help to increase their body water and also to elucidate the mechanism of this thirst attenuation with aging. It appears that attenuated drinking in the elderly accompanies their relative reduction in total body water and associated muscle atrophy. Perhaps appropriate muscular exercise training to alleviate the muscle atrophy [45] would restore lean body mass (body water) and stimulate drinking. When exercise training is conducted in a hot environment, voluntary water intake in young men can increase from 450 ml • hr^{-1} on day 1 to about 1,000 ml • hr^{-1} after 10 hr (2 hr • day^{-1}) of classic exercise-heat acclimation, when compared with fluid intake of 129-232 ml • hr^{-1} during 2 hr of exercise alone in a cool environment [46]. It appears that the increased drinking with acclimation was more closely associated with the renin-angiotensin-aldosterone system than with activation of the sodium-osmotic-vasopressin system. Exercise training also increases plasma volume chronically in young ambulatory men with the internal thermal load contributing 40% and nonthermal factors contributing 60% to the hypervolemia [47]. Nonthermal factors appear to be exercise-induced increases in PRA and AVP that facilitated sodium and water retention, respectively, and chronic increase in plasma albumin content [48]. Exercise training during prolonged bed-rest deconditioning can increase fluid intake and also counter the hypovolemia by maintaining (influx) of plasma osmotic and protein contents [32]. Whether these or other modified remedial treatments can inouge greater fluid intake in the elderly must await further research.

REFERENCES

1. Van Loan MD, Boileau RA. Age, gender, and fluid balance. In: Body Fluid Balance: Exercise and Sport, Buskirk ER, Puhl SM (eds). Boca Raton, FL: CRC Press, 1996, p. 215-230.
2. Oser BL (ed). Hawk's Physiological Chemistry. New York: McGraw-Hill, 1965, p. 542.
3. Lavizzo-Mourey R, Johnson J, Stolley P. Risk factors for dehydration among elderly nursing home residents. J. Am. Geriatr. Soc. 36: 213-218, 1988.
4. Mahowald JM, Himmelstein DU. Hypernatremia in the elderly: Relation to infection and mortality. J. Am. Geriatr. Soc. 29: 177-180, 1981.
5. O'Neill PA, Faragher EB, Davies I, Wears R, McLean KA, Fairweather DS. Reduced survival with increasing plasma osmolality in elderly continuing-care patients. Age Ageing 19: 68-71, 1990.
6. Buskirk ER, Puhl SM (eds). Body Fluid Balance : Exercise and Sport. Boca Raton FL: CRC Press, 1996, 337 p.
7. Marriott BM (ed). Fluid Replacement and Heat Sress. Washington DC: National Academy Press, 1994, 242 p.
8. Ramsay DJ, Booth D (eds). Thirst: Physiological and Psychological Aspects. New York: Springer–Verlag, 1991, 509 p.
9. Beauchamp GK, Cowart BJ. Congenital and experiential factors in the development of human flavor preferences. Appetite 6: 357-372, 1985.
10. Finberg L. Hypernatremic (hypertonic) dehydration in infants. N. Engl. J. Med. 289: 196-198, 1973.
11. Whitehead FJ, Couper RTL, Moore L, Bourne AJ, Byard RW. Dehydration deaths in infants and young children. Am. J. Forensic Med. Pathol. 17: 73- 78, 1996.
12. Greenleaf JE. Problem: thirst, drinking behavior, and involuntary dehydration. Med. Sci. Sports Exerc. 24: 645-656, 1992.
13. Junger WG, Liu FC, Loomis WH, Hoyt DB. Hypertonic saline enhances cellular immune function. Circulatory Shock 42: 190-196, 1994.
14. Mackenzie A, Barnes G, Shann F. Clinical signs of dehydration in children. Lancet 2: 605-607, 1989.
15. Bar-Or O, Dotan R, Inbar O, Rotshtein A, Zonder H. Voluntary hypohydration in 10-to-12 year–old boys. J. Appl. Physiol. 48: 104-108, 1980.
16. Rodriguez Santana JR, Rivera-Brown AM, Frontera WR, Rivera MA, Mayol PM, Bar-Or O. Effect of drink pattern and solar radiation on thermoregulation and fluid balance during exercise in chronically heat acclimatized children. Am. J. Human Biol. 7: 643-650, 1995.
17. Wilk B, Bar-Or O. Effect of drink flavor and NaCl on voluntary drinking and hydration in boys

exercising in the heat. J. Appl. Physiol. 80: 1112-1117, 1996.

18. Gisolfi CV. Fluid balance for optimal performance. Nutr. Rev. 54: S159-S168, 1996.

19. Meyer F, Bar-Or O, Salsberg A, Passe D. Hypohydration during exercise in children: Effect on thirst, drink preferences, and rehydration. Int. J. Sport Nutr. 4: 22-35, 1994.

20. Meyer F, Bar-Or O, Wilk B. Children's perceptual responses to ingesting drinks of different compositions during and following exercise in the heat. Int. J. Sport Nutr. 5: 13-24, 1995.

21. Greenleaf JE, Sargent II F. Voluntary dehydration in man. J. Appl. Physiol. 20: 719-724, 1965.

22. Greenleaf JE, Morimoto T. Mechanisms controlling fluid ingestion: Thirst and drinking. In: Body Fluid Balance; Exercise and Sport, edited by Buskirk ER, Puhl SM. Boca Raton, FL: CRC Press Inc., 1996. p. 3-17.

23. Phillips PA, Rolls BJ, Ledingham JGG. Forsling ML, Morton JJ, Crowe MJ, Wollner L. Reduced thirst after water deprivation in healthy elderly men. N. Engl. J. Med. 311: 753-759, 1984.

24. Gaspar PM. What determines how much patients drink? Geriatr. Nurs. 9: 221-224, 1988.

25. Lesser GR, Markofsky J. Body water compartments with human aging using fat-free mass as the reference standard. Am. J. Physiol. 236: R215-R220, 1979.

26. Wolf AV. Thirst: Physiology of the Urge to Drink and Problems of Water Lack. Springfield, IL: CC Thomas, 1958, 536 p.

27. Creditor MC. Hazards of hospitalization of the elderly. Ann. Int. Med. 118: 219-223, 1993.

28. Fortney SM, Schneider VS, Greenleaf JE. The physiology of bed rest. In: Handbook of Physiology: Section 4: Environmental Physiology. III. The gravitational environment, edited by Fregely MJ, Blatteis CM. New York: Oxford University Press. Vol. 2, Chapt. 39, 1996, p. 889-939.

29. Adams F. How much do elders drink? Geriatr. Nurs. 9: 218-221, 1988.

30. Lavizzo-Mourey RJ. Dehydration in the elderly: A short review. JNMA 79: 1033-1038, 1987.

31. Gove PB. Webster's Third New International Dictionary of the English Language Unabridged. Springfield, MA: Merriam-Webster Inc., 1986. p. 2378.

32. Greenleaf JE, Vernikos J, Wade CE, Barnes PR. Effects of leg exercise training on vascular volumes during 30 days of 60 head-down bed rest. J. Appl. Physiol. 72: 1887-1894, 1992.

33. Morimoto T, Miki K, Nose H, Yamada S, Hirakawa K, Matsubara C. Changes in body fluid volume and its composition during heavy sweating and the effect of fluid and electrolyte replacement. Jpn. J. Biometeorol. 18: 31-39, 1981.

34. McLean KA, O'Neill PA, Davies I, Morris J. Influence of age on plasma osmolality: A community study. Age Ageing 21: 56-60, 1992.

35. Altman PL, Dittmer DS (eds). Biological Handbooks: Blood and Other Body Fluids. Washington DC: Federation of American Societies for Experimental Biology, 1961. p. 495.

36. Mack GW, Weseman CA, Langhans GW, Scherzer H, Gillen CM, Nadel ER. Body fluid balance in dehydrated healthy older men: thirst and renal osmoregulation. J. Appl. Physiol. 76: 1615-1623, 1994.

37. Phillips PA, Bretherton M, Johnston CI, Gray L. Reduced osmotic thirst in healthy elderly men. Am. J. Physiol. 261: R166-R174, 1991.

38. Szczepanska-Sadowska E, Sobocinska J, Sadowski B. Central dipsogenic effect of vasopressin. Am. J. Physiol. 242: R372-R379, 1982.

39. O'Neill PA, McLean KA. Water homeostasis and ageing. Med. Lab. Sci. 49: 291-298, 1992.

40. Geelen G, Corman B. Relationship between vasopressin and renal concentrating ability in aging rats. Am. J. Physiol. 262: R826-R838, 1992.

41. Jover B, Dupont M, Geelen G, Wahba W, Mimran A, Corman B. Renal and systemic adaptation to sodium restriction in aging rats. Am. J. Physiol. 264: R833- R838, 1993.

42. Weidmann P, De Myttenaere-Bursztein S, Maxwell MH, de Lima J. Effect of aging on plasma renin and aldosterone in normal man. Kidney Int. 8: 325-333, 1975.

43. Tsunoda K, Abe K, Goto T, Yasujima M, Sato M, Omata K, Seino M, Yoshinaga K. Effect of age on the renin-angiotensin-aldosterone system in normal subjects: Simultaneous measurement of active and inactive renin, renin substrate, and aldosterone in plasma. J. Clin. Endocrinol. Metab. 62: 384-389, 1986.

44. Rolls BJ, Phillips PA, Ledingham JGG, Forsling ML, Morton JJ, Crowe MJ. Human thirst: The controls of water intake in healthy men. In: The Physiology of Thirst and Sodium Appetite, edited by de Caro G, Epstein AN, Massi M. New York: Plenum Press, 1986, p. 521-526.

45. Kendrick ZV, Nelson-Steen S, Scafidi K. Exercise, aging, and nutrition. South. Med. J. 87: S50-S60, 1994.

46. Greenleaf JE, Brock PJ, Keil LC, Morse JT. Drinking and water balance during exercise and heat acclimation. J. Appl. Physiol. 54: 414-419, 1983.

47. Convertino VA, Greenleaf JE, Bernauer EM. Role of thermal and exercise factors in the mechanism of hypervolemia. J. Appl. Physiol. 48: 657-664, 1980.

48. Convertino VA, Brock PJ, Keil LC, Bernauer EM, Greenleaf JE. Exercise training-induced hypervolemia: role of plasma albumin, renin, and vasopressin. J. Appl. Physiol. 48: 665-669, 1980.

WATER METABOLISM IN THE ELDERLY IN HEALTH AND DISEASE: AGING CHANGES AFFECTING RISK FOR HYPERNATREMIA AND HYPONATREMIA

M. MILLER

From the Department of Medicine, Levindale Hebrew Geriatric Center and Hospital and the Sinai Hospital of Baltimore. Address for Correspondence: Myron Miller, M.D. Levindale Hebrew Geriatric Center and Hospital 2434 West Belvedere Avenue Baltimore, MD 21215 Phone: 410-466-8700, ext 354 FAX: 410-578-0653.

Abstract : Characteristic of the normal aging process is the development of changes in the renal, hormonal and thirst regulatory systems which are involved in the control of sodium and water balance. As a consequence, depending on the presence of accompanying disease or drug use, the elderly person is at increased risk of either sodium retention or loss and of water retention or loss. Clinically, these alterations are commonly expressed as either hyponatremia or hypernatremia. Changes in central nervous system function are often the symptomatic expression of the derangements in sodium or water balance. Thus, the impaired homeostasis of the many systems affecting fluid balance in the elderly is readily influenced by many of the disease states and medications which are often present in the elderly with resultant adverse clinical consequences. Awareness of these age-associated circumstances can allow the physician to anticipate the impact of illnesses and drugs and to implement a rational approach to therapeutic intervention and management.

Aging is associated with a number of changes in the homeostatic systems which are involved in the regulation of water and electrolyte balance [1]. These systems normally operate to maintain the composition of fluid and electrolyte compartments within a narrow range and include the hormones arginine vasopressin or antidiuretic hormone (AVP, ADH) and atrial natriuretic hormone (ANH). Other critical components are thirst perception which governs fluid intake and the kidney which is governed by hemodynamic and hormonal influences to regulate water and sodium balance. Changes which take place as part of normal aging underly the recognition by clinicians who are involved in the care of the elderly that disturbances of water and electrolyte balance are common in this age group especially when older persons are challenged by disease, drugs or extrinsic factors such as access to fluids or control of diet composition.

The confluence of normal aging changes, diseases common in the elderly and the administration of many classes of drugs can lead to water retention or loss and to hyponatremia or hypernatremia with resultant symptomatic consequences. The central nervous system is particularly sensitive to deviations in water and sodium balance and altered function may be expressed clinically by confusion, coma or seizures which may be erroneously attributed to primary disease of the central nervous system. This review will focus on the changes in the systems affecting water balance which occur with normal aging and with conditions common in the elderly.

I - RENAL CHANGES OF NORMAL AGING

1.1. Structural and Functional Changes

Normal aging is accompanied by changes in renal anatomy and in renal function (Table 1). Kidney mass undergoes progressive decline from a normal weight of approximately 250-340 grams in young adults to between 180-200 grams by age 80- 90 years. This decline is primarily due to atrophy of the renal cortex so that by the ninth decade, there is an approximately 40% loss of renal volume [2].

Histologic examination of the aged kidney reveals a decline in number of glomeruli as a function of increasing age with a corresponding increase in percent of glomeruli which are hyalinized or sclerotic [3]. This process accelerates after the age of 40 years and the decrease in cortical glomeruli may be as high as 30% in normal people by 70 years of age [4]. The residual glomeruli themselves also undergo changes with age. Thus, there is a decrease in effective filtering surface, and increase in number of mesangial cells, a decrease in number of epithelial cells and thickening of the glomerular basement membrane [5]. Along with these glomerular changes are alteration in the renal tubules as evidenced by diverticula of the distal nephron [6] and decreased proximal tubular length and volume [7]. In studies of aging animals, the amount of cholesterol in brush-border membranes on the luminal surface of proximal renal tubule cells is increased and this change is accompanied by decreased permeability of the membranes to NaCl and KCl [8].

Table 1
Aging Effects on Renal Sodium and Water Regulation

RENAL ALTERATIONS
> Decreased kidney mass
> Decline in renal blood flow
> Decline in glomerular filtration rate
> Impaired distal renal tubular diluting capacity
> Impaired renal concentrating capacity
> Impaired sodium conservation
> Impaired renal response to vasopressin

HORMONAL ALTERATIONS
> Increased vasopressin secretion (basal and stimulated)
> Increased atrial natriuretic hormone secretion
> Decreased plasma renin activity
> Decreased aldosterone production

FLUID INTAKE
> Decreased thirst perception

Renal vasculature undergoes changes as part of the normal aging process independent of vascular or renal disease. Atherosclerotic lesions are observed in larger renal arteries but do not lead to occlusion of these vessels. There is tapering of interlobar arteries, alterations in the arcuate arteries and increased tortuosity of intralobular arteries. At the level of the arteriole, hyalin deposition occurs in the vessel walls leading to atrophy of smooth muscle cells, obliteration of the arteriolar lumen and loss of the glomerular capillary tuft. These changes take place primarily in the cortical glomeruli [9,10]. In the juxtamedullary area, glomerular sclerosis may lead to anastomosis between afferent and efferent arterioles with direct shunting of blood between these vessels. Blood flow to the medulla, through the arteria rectae, is maintained in old age.

Anatomical changes in the kidney which occur with age are paralleled by alterations in renal function, although a direct relationship between anatomical and functional changes is not firmly established. Renal blood flow declines during the course of normal aging by approximately 10% per decade after young adulthood so that by the age of 90 years the renal plasma flow is approximately 300 ml/min - a reduction of 50% of the value found at 30 years of age [11]. The decrease in renal perfusion is most extensive in the outer cortex with lesser impairment of inner cortex and minimal effect on the medulla.

Glomerular filtration rate (GFR) remains relatively stable until age 40, after which it undergoes decline at an annual rate of approximately 0.8 ml/min per $1.73M^2$ [12]. There is considerable variability of this renal alteration within the elderly population so that decline in GFR is not seen in all aged individuals [13].

1.2. Renal Factors Affecting Sodium and Water Retention or Loss

Renal Sodium Retention

Several situations may lead to sodium retention and accompanying water overload in the elderly. The previously described age-related decrease in renal blood flow and glomerular filtration rate favors enhanced conservation of sodium. Disease states resulting in secondary hyperaldosteronism such as congestive heart failure, cirrhosis or nephrotic syndrome are common in the elderly. Finally, certain drugs such as nonsteroidal antiinflammatory agents, which are frequently used in the elderly may promote sodium retention.

Renal Sodium Loss

Lindeman et al have shown that elderly individuals are more likely to have exaggerated natriuresis after a water load than are younger subjects [14]. In a study of 22 patients with benign hypertension, Schalekamp et al described an excess of sodium excretion related to increased patient age [15]. Epstein and Hollenberg have shown that the aged kidney's response to salt restriction is sluggish [16]. Restriction in sodium intake to 10 mEq per day was followed by a half-time for reduction of urinary sodium excretion of 17.6 hours in young individuals and 30.9 hours in old subjects. These data suggest that the aging kidney is more prone to sodium wasting. Mechanisms underlying this tendency may be multifactorial and are related to the effects of age on atrial natriuretic hormone (ANH), the renin-angiotensin-aldosterone system, and renal tubular function.

Renal Water Retention

There are only a few studies that have assessed free water clearance (CH_2O) in the senescent kidney and these suggest that there is a modest age-related impairment in the ability to dilute the urine and excrete a water load. The ability to generate free water is dependent on several factors which include: adequate delivery of solute to the diluting region (sufficient renal perfusion and glomerular filtration rate); a functional intact distal diluting site (ascending limb of Henle's loop and the distal tubule); and suppression of ADH in order to escape water reabsorption in the collecting duct [15]. The age-related decline in GFR is the most important factor in the aged kidney's diluting capacity. The presence of an age-related diluting defect that is independent of changes in GFR remains controversial.

Lindeman et al studied the diluting capacity of the aged kidney by determining the minimum urine osmolality and maximum free water clearance after water loading in three groups of men [17]. The minimal urine osmolality in young men (mean age 31) was 52 mOsm/kg, in middle-aged men (mean age 60) was 74 mOsm/kg and in the older men (mean age 84) was 92 mOsm/kg. The free water clearance was lowest in the older group. However, when these results were expressed as free water clearance per ml of GFR, the values were not different, suggesting that the defect in diluting capacity was due to an age-related reduction in GFR. Crowe al carried out a similar study in which groups of six healthy elderly subjects aged 63-80 years (mean 72) and six healthy young subjects aged 21- 26 years (mean 22) were administered a water load [18]. The peak free water clearance was 5.7 ml/min in the older group and 8.4 ml/min in the younger group. However, when adjustments were made for changes in creatinine clearance, the difference in these indices was not statistically significant.

A differing view was presented by Dontas et al who reported a significantly lower CH_2O/creatinine ratio in 26 elderly subjects from an institutional setting as compared with 11 healthy younger subjects [19]. The maximal urinary dilution (urinary/plasma osmolality) declined from 0.247 in younger subjects to 0.418 in the elderly. The authors concluded that the CH_2O defects persist following correction for a lower GFR. A smaller study in healthy elderly subjects came to a similar conclusion [20].

In addition to impaired diluting capacity, the decrease in renal plasma flow and glomerular filtration rate that occurs with aging can lead to passive reabsorption of fluid, thereby increasing the risk of water overload and hyponatremia. This effect is clinically evident in elderly patients who have congestive heart failure, extracellular volume depletion and hypoalbuminemia.

The role of diuretics, especially, thiazides, in decreasing renal diluting capacity is well known [21]. In the elderly, this effect becomes important as it is superimposed on the already diminished diluting capacity of the aged kidney. Thus the many changes in the kidney that occur with aging can increase the risk of the elderly developing water intoxication by impairing their ability to excrete excess water promptly.

Renal Water Loss

As early as 1938, Lewis and Alving observed age-related changes in renal concentrating capacity [22]. In their study of healthy men aged 40 to 101 years who underwent 24 hours of water deprivation, maximum attainable urine specific gravity declined from 1.030 at 40 years to 1.023 at 89 years. This age-related decrease in urine concentrating ability has been confirmed by others. Lindeman et al studied the response of hospitalized men aged 23 to 72 years to 24 hours of dehydration and demonstrated a progressive decline in maximum urine osmolality with increasing age [23]. Rowe et al examined urine concentrating ability in 98 healthy, active community dwelling volunteers who were participating in the Baltimore Longitudinal Study of Aging (24). After 12 hours of water deprivation, young subjects responded with a marked decrease in urine flow (1.02 ± 0.10 to 0.49 ± 0.03 ml/min) and a moderate increase in urine osmolality (969 ± 41 to 1109 ± 22 mOsm/kg), whereas elderly subjects were unable to significantly alter urine flow (1.05 ± 0.15 to 1.03 ± 0.13 ml/min) or osmolality (852 ± 64 to 882 ± 49 mOsm/kg). This effect of age persisted after correction for the age-related decrease in glomerular filtration rate.

The effect of age on renal responsiveness to vasopressin was first explored in 1958 by Miller and Shock [25]. Renal tubular response to vasopressin was measured by determining the urine-to-plasma inulin concentration ratio in 29 men who ranged in age from 26 to 86 years and who were free of clinically demonstrable cardiovascular and renal disease. The ratio fell from 118 in young men (mean age 35 years) to 77 in the middle-aged group (mean age 55 years) and to 45 in the older men (mean age 73 years).

The decreased renal sensitivity to vasopressin with age may be a result of the age-related increase in vasopressin secretion. Miller studied rats aged 8 to 9 months that were injected daily for 28 days with vasopressin to produce a two-fold increase in plasma AVP concentration [26]. Response to water deprivation or intraperitoneal desmopressin acetate (DDAVP) in these animals was decreased when compared with controls. Cyclic AMP content of renal medullary slices from control animals doubled in response to exposure to DDAVP, whereas no change was observed in the group that had received chronic vasopressin injections. These data suggest that chronic exposure of the kidney to increased vasopressin results in diminished renal responsiveness to the hormone.

Rats heterozygous for hypothalamic diabetes insipidus have half the vasopressin secretory capacity of normal rats and a reduced plasma AVP concentration. The decreased AVP secretion in these animals was found to be associated with maintenance of maximal urine concentrating capacity with age in contrast to the decline noted in aging of normal rats [26]. Thus, it appears that the aged-related increase in vasopressin secretion may result in decreased responsiveness to this hormone, perhaps through down regulation of renal AVP receptors, and may serve as the basis for decreased renal concentrating capacity in the elderly. Testosterone treatment has been reported to restore reduced AVP binding sites in the kidney of the aging rat [27].

II - VASOPRESSIN SYSTEM IN NORMAL AGING

2.1. Neurohypophyseal System

The magnocellular neurons of the hypothalamus, the supraoptic (SON) and paraventricular (PVN) nuclei, produce the peptide hormone arginine vasopressin. To date, studies have failed to observe age-related degenerative changes in these nuclei [28]. There is no evidence of the cell destruction, neuronal dropout, or loss of dendritic arborization found in other segments of the aged brain. Moreover, neurosecretory material in SON and PVN does not appear to differ in amount from that in younger subjects (Table 2) [29,30].

Morphologic data provide evidence that these nuclei, in fact, become more active with age. Fliers et al investigated age related changes in the human hypothalamic neurohypophyseal system in subjects ranging from 10 to 93 years of age [31]. The SON and PVN were identified immunocytochemically and analyzed morphometrically; cell size was used as a parameter for peptide production. A gradual increase in the size of the SON and PVN was observed after 60 years of age, suggesting that AVP production increases in senescence. In a subsequent study, Hoogendijk et al observed similar changes in the nuclear size of AVP neurons [32]. More recently, Fliers and Swaab estimated the functional properties of the magnocellular nuclei by staining for the enzyme thiamine pyrophosphate. The distribution of this marker enzyme in the Golgi apparatus in old as compared with young rats was found to be similar in the SON but increased in the PVN [33]. Possibly contributing to the maintenance of normal or increased amounts of AVP in the magnocellular neurons is the observation of a 25% reduction in the rate of axonal transport of AVP and its associated neurophysin with advancing age [34]. Thus, it appears that neurosecretory activity of hypothalamic AVP neurons does not decrease but, in fact, remains constant or is elevated with age.

Table 2
Aging Effects on the Vasopressin System

MORPHOLOGY OF THE NEUROHYPOPHYSIAL SYSTEM
Normal or increased supraoptic nucleus cell number/AVP content
Normal or increased paraventricular nucleus cell number/AVP content
Decreased suprachiasmatic nucleus cell number/AVP content
Normal extrahypothalamic nuclei cell number/AVP content
HYPOTHALAMIC VASOPRESSIN CONTENT
Normal or increased
CEREBROSPINAL FLUID VASOPRESSIN CONCENTRATION
Normal
BLOOD VASOPRESSIN CONCENTRATION
Normal or increased basal
Increased after stimulation
RENAL RESPONSE TO VASOPRESSIN
Decreased

Changes are in comparison to values observed in the young

2.2. Suprachiasmatic Nucleus

The suprachiasmatic nucleus is the major circadian pacemaker in the mammalian brain and a site of production of vasopressin [35]. A marked decrease in the volume of the suprachiasmatic nucleus, the number of cells containing vasopressin, and total cell number has been found in persons aged 80 to 100 years as compared with younger age groups [36]. In one study, a decrease of as much as 75% was observed [37]. In addition, the seasonal oscillation in numbers of vasopressin-containing neurons seen in young persons is blunted in the elderly [38]. In the rat, the age-related decrease in suprachiasmatic nucleus AVP was prevented by exposure of the animals to high intensity light [39].

2.3. Arginine Vasopressin in the Cerebrospinal Fluid in Normal Aging

Peripheral AVP seems to be effectively excluded from the CNS by the blood-brain barrier, which limits the passage of AVP under physiological circumstances [40,41]. Thus, AVP in the cerebrospinal fluid (CSF) reflects production and release from sites within the CNS.

Normal levels of AVP in the CSF range from 0.5 to 2.0 pg/mL. Several studies have documented that levels of AVP in the CSF do not change as a consequence of aging [42,43]. There is a distinct circadian rhythm of AVP concentration in the CSF under normal conditions which varies without relationship to plasma AVP levels [44]. These changes in AVP concentrations in the CSF are more pronounced in animals than in humans [41]. AVP in CSF presumably originates from vasopressinergic nerve endings or is released within the CNS and reaches the ventricles from the brain interstitial fluid through transependymal routes [41]. Little is known about the physiological stimuli that alter the concentration of vasopressin in CSF, but it is not influenced by a number of stimuli that cause release of vasopressin into the blood, that is, changes in plasma osmolality, postural changes, and nausea.

2.4. Basal Plasma Vasopressin Levels

Secretion of AVP by the neurohypophyseal system is the principal hormonal regulator of body water and is regulated by the interaction of changes in plasma osmolality, effective blood volume, and blood pressure. Conflicting data have been gathered regarding basal concentration of AVP in the blood during normal aging.

In young normal individuals, there is a diurnal rhythm of vasopressin secretion, with increased AVP secretion occurring at night [45]. This rhythm appears to be linked to the wake-sleep cycle rather than to time of day [46]. The sleep-associated peak is absent in the majority of healthy elderly persons [47,48]. Low AVP levels and the lack of definite diurnal rhythm may, to some extent, explain increased diuresis during the night in some elderly individuals [47,48]. In a study by Faull et al, healthy elderly subjects were found to have basal plasma AVP levels that were significantly lower than in young subjects [49]. In association with the reduced AVP concentration, plasma osmolality was elevated, suggesting that the elderly subjects had a water-losing state similar to partial diabetes insipidus. Clark et al also found lower plasma AVP levels in healthy elderly males [50].

Helderman et al studied eight older individuals with a mean age 59 years (range, 52 to 66) and eight younger individuals with a mean age of 37 years and demonstrated that, under basal conditions, plasma vasopressin levels did not change with advancing age [51]. Likewise, Chioderda et al found similar basal AVP levels in 30 normal men aged 22 to 81 years who were divided into three age groups: group 1, mean age 30.6 years; group 2, mean age 52.1 years; and group 3, mean age 72.5 years [52]. More recently, Duggan et al found that basal plasma levels of AVP did not differ among young, middle-aged, and elderly healthy individuals who were studied under both supine and ambulatory conditions. Furthermore, there were no differences in plasma osmolality between the groups [53].

Other studies, however, have reported elevated basal vasopressin levels in healthy elderly persons as compared with younger individuals. Frolkis et al studied healthy human subjects aged 20 to 80 years and observed a progressive rise in plasma AVP concentration with age, which become most evident in subjects older than 60 years [30]. Similar findings were also reported by Crawford et al [54]. In a study by Rondeau et al, plasma AVP levels, both in normals and in patients with heart failure, rose steadily with increasing age, and the patients with cardiac insufficiency as a group always had higher values [55]. Kirkland et al demonstrated that healthy older persons (aged 61 to 82 years) have higher basal levels of AVP than do younger subjects under identical conditions [56]. Johnson et al also demonstrated a higher basal plasma AVP concentration in health elderly subjects (age, 78.6 ± 3.1 years) as compared with younger adults (age, 35.1 ± 9.4 years). Baseline plasma AVP was strongly correlated with serum osmolality in the younger adults but not in the elderly subjects [57].

Debate exists regarding a sex-related difference in plasma AVP levels in the elderly. Aspund and Aberg reported a two-fold higher plasma AVP concentration in elderly men as compared to women [47]. Other studies, however, have failed to identify an effect of gender on basal plasma AVP [57,58].

A rise in basal plasma AVP with age cannot be attributed to age-related changes in vasopressin pharmacokinetics. Engel et al showed that no differences existed between young and old subjects in vasopressin half-life, volume of distribution, or clearance [59]. Thus, evidence of increased basal plasma vasopressin most likely reflects age-related changes in central control systems for vasopressin release.

2.5. Vasopressin Stimulation

Secretion of AVP normally varies in response to changes in blood tonicity, blood volume, and blood pressure. Hormone release is also affected by other variables such as nausea, pain, emotional stress, a variety of drugs, cigarette smoking, and glucopenia [60,61]. In recent years, a growing body of information suggests that normal aging affects the way these stimuli act and interact to influence AVP release.

The major physiologic stimulus for vasopressin secretion in humans, plasma osmolality, is regulated by hypothalamic osmoreceptors [62]. Studies performed by Helderman et al tested osmoreceptor sensitivity in the elderly. The AVP response to hypertonic saline infusion in healthy elderly persons (aged 34 to 92 years) was compared with the response in younger individuals aged 21 to 49 years. Hypertonic saline raised plasma osmolality with a consequent increase in plasma AVP in both groups, but the hormone concentrations in the older subjects were almost double those in the younger subjects. Thus, for any given level of osmotic stimulus, there was a greater release of AVP in the elderly,suggesting that aging resulted in osmoreceptor hypersensitivity [51].

Studies using water deprivation as a stimulus for vasopressin secretion have supported the concept of an age-related enhancement in vasopressin secretion. In a study by Phillips et al, a group of seven young healthy individuals (20-31 years) and a group of seven healthy elderly men (67-75 years) were deprived of water for a period of 24 hours. The older persons responded to water deprivation and hyperosmolality with higher serum concentrations of AVP than in the younger individuals [63]. Only one study has produced results which conflict with these findings. In this study, by Li et al, water deprivation for 14 hours in 30 healthy subjects aged 63 to 87 years was reported to result in mean AVP concentrations significantly lower than those in the young control group [64].

Changes in blood volume and blood pressure influence the secretion of vasopressin through effects on pressure-sensitive receptors in the neck, heart, and large arteries of the chest. Volume is perceived by low-pressure left atrial stretch receptors, whereas change in blood pressure is perceived by high-pressure baroreceptors in the carotid arteries and aorta. Decreases in blood volume, blood pressure, or both provoke the release of AVP. Conversely, a rise in volume, pressure, or both inhibits vasopressin release.

The sensitivity of the hypothalamic-neurohypophyseal axis to these volume/pressure stimuli was studied by Rowe et al [65]. Acute upright posture was assumed by 12 younger (aged 19 to 31 years) and 15 older (aged 62 to 80 years) subjects after overnight dehydration. In the older subjects, the expected change in pulse and blood pressure did not uniformly lead to increased vasopressin secretion, with only 8 to 15 older individuals experiencing increased plasma vasopressin. A subsequent study by Bevilacqua et al produced similar findings, suggesting the presence of an aged-related failure of volume/pressure-mediated vasopressin release [66].

Ethanol induces a water diuresis by inhibiting the secretion of vasopressin at a central locus. Helderman et al studied aged-related AVP response to intravenous ethanol infusion in nine young (aged 21 to 49 years) and 13 old (aged 54 to 92 years) subjects. The younger subjects demonstrated a sustained inhibition of AVP secretion during the infusion of ethanol, whereas the response in the older group was paradoxical, with initial AVP inhibition followed by break-through secretion and rebound to twice basal levels. Not only was ethanol less effective in inhibiting AVP release in the elderly but it eventually lost its suppressive effect entirely due to the introduction of a hyperosmotic stimulus resulting from the ethanol-induced constriction in plasma volume [51].

Metoclopramide, a potent CNS cholinergic agent, was found by Norbiato et al to stimulate vasopressin secretion in man [67]. This effect on vasopressin release could not be attributed to changes in known mechanisms regulating vasopressin secretion, as no alterations in plasma osmolality, heart rate, or blood pressure occurred after metoclopramide administration, In addition, the mechanism could not be linked to antidopaminergic properties of metoclopramide, as other powerful dopamine antagonists did not produce any increase in vasopressin secretion. Studies by Steardo et al carried out in the rat provided evidence that cholinergic mechanisms may be involved in metoclopramide-induced vasopressin release [68].

Norbiato et al examined the vasopressin reponse to intravenous metoclopramide injection in seven normal elderly subjects aged 65 to 80 years and in a group of normal young subjects aged 16 to 35 years [67]. Significantly higher plasma AVP concentrations were found in the older group with no significant changes in plasma osmolality, blood pressure, or heart rate. Thus, elderly subjects were found to have increased sensitivity to metoclopramide, with the mechanism presumed to be through activation of cholinergic neurons regulating hypothalamic AVP release.

Responses of AVP to cigarette smoking and insulin-induced hypoglycemia, in addition to metoclopramide, were evaluated by

Chiodera et al in 30 male subjects aged 22 to 81 years [52]. Corroborating the prior findings of Norbiato et al, the AVP response to metoclopramide was significantly higher in the older group as compared to two younger groups. The AVP response to cigarette smoking was similar; plasma AVP concentration increased 3.25 times after smoking in the older group as compared with 2.5 times in the two younger groups. In contrast, the AVP response during the insulin hypoglycemia test was identical in pattern and magnitude in all age groups.

The results of stimulation studies indicate that, in aging, AVP response to osmotic stimuli is increased due to a hyperresponsive osmoreceptor, whereas the AVP response to upright posture is reduced due to impaired baroreceptor function. Likewise, aging accentuates the AVP stimulatory response to metoclopramide and to cigarette smoking and reduces the suppressibility of AVP to ethanol. The AVP response to hypoglycemia, however, is not affected by aging.

Several possible underlying mechanisms may explain the contrasting responses to osmotic and volume/pressure stimuli. Heightened osmoreceptor sensitivity with aging may be due to impaired baroreceptor function [62] since baroreflex sensitivity declines with age, and this change affects the release of vasopressin [69]. Input from the baroreceptor to the osmoreceptor is usually inhibitory, and a defect in this reflex arc would result in a lesser dampening of osmotically stimulated ADH release.

The hypothalamic magnocellular neurons responsible for AVP secretion are responsive to cholinergic and nicotinic neurotransmitters which serve as the primary mediators for the afferent parasympathetic impulses. The heightened AVP response to both metoclopramide and smoking might represent an overall enhancement of cholinergic activity in the control of AVP secretion, which may occur as a consequence of age-related defects in baroreceptor input [69]. The finding that AVP response to insulin-induced hypoglycemia is not affected by aging may be taken as evidence that this stimulus for AVP secretion is independent of osmotic or hemodynamic changes [52].

Anatomical studies showing an increased size of the SON and PVN nuclei support the clinical data of increased basal secretion of vasopressin as well as enhanced release of AVP in response to osmotic stimuli. When coupled with the many alterations in renal function that occur with aging, these changes can increase the risk of elderly persons for hyponatremia by impairing their ability to excrete excess water promptly.

III - AGE-RELATED CHANGES IN ATRIAL NATRIURETIC HORMONE SECRETION, REGULATION AND ACTION

Atrial natriuretic hormone is synthesized, stored, and released in the atria of the heart in humans and animals. Through its action on the kidney, ANH produces a pronounced natriuresis and diuresis; through its action on blood vessels, it produces vasodilation and has been shown to decrease blood pressure in both normal and hypertensive individuals [70]. As an important regulator of sodium excretion, ANH may be a significant factor in mediating the altered renal sodium handling of age.

Ohashi et al compared 19 young normal men and 31 elderly male nursing home residents and noted a five-fold increase in mean basal ANH levels and an exaggerated ANH response to the stimulus of saline infusion in the elderly group [71]. McKnight et al also reported an age-related increase in basal ANH levels but no changes with age in the response to saline infusion [72]. Tajima et al compared ANH levels in eight young (aged 21 to 28 years) and seven healthy old individuals (aged 62 to 73 years). Baseline ANH levels were twice as high in the old subjects than in the young, and ANH response to the stimulus of head-out water immersion was greater in the elderly [73]. We have studied 40 healthy male and female subjects aged 22 to 64 years to determine the influence of age on circulating levels of ANH both under basal conditions and after physiologic stimulation of ANH release by controlled exercise. Supine exercise using a bicycle ergometer to 80% of maximum predicted heart rate resulted in marked increases in ANH. Subjects aged more than 50 years had higher baseline levels and a greater response to exercise when compared with subjects younger than 50 years. Thus, increasing age results in increased ANH basal levels and an increased ANH response to both physiologic and pharmacologic stimuli.

Heim et al suggest that the renal effects of ANH may be exaggerated in elderly versus young individuals [74]. In their study, natriuretic response to a bolus injection of ANH was higher in 12 older individuals (mean age 52.3 years) compared with 16 younger subjects (mean age 26 years). These findings require confirmation because rapid intravenous infusion of ANH results in higher ANH levels in the elderly as a result of diminished ANH clearance [75]. Jansen et al did not measure the renal action of ANH but noted no change with age in the blood pressure response to ANH intravenous infusion after correction for higher ANH levels in the elderly [76].

Atrial natriuretic hormone is known to interact with the renin-angiotensin-aldosterone system. Increases of ANH result in suppression of renal renin secretion, plasma renin activity, plasma angiotensin II, and aldosterone levels, suggesting indirect inhibition of aldosterone secretion by ANH [77]. Cuneo et al found that minimal increases in ANH within physiological levels, produced by slow-rate ANH infusion, can inhibit angiotensin II-induced aldosterone secretion in normal men, thus, suggesting a direct inhibitory effect of ANH on aldosterone release [78]. Clinkingbeard et al have confirmed that ANH can suppress aldosterone in man through both direct and indirect actions [79]. Thus, ANH may further promote renal sodium loss through inhibition of aldosterone release.

Atrial natriuretic hormone may be an important mediator of age-related renal sodium loss. This effect may be the consequence of increased basal ANH levels, increased ANH response to stimuli, increased renal sensitivity to ANH, and ANH-induced suppression of adrenal sodium-retaining hormones.

IV - AGING AND FLUID INTAKE

The ingestion of appropriate quantities of fluid to maintain a normal state of fluid balance requires that thirst perception be present, that a suitable source of fluid be available and that the individual be physically capable of obtaining and consuming the fluid. Evidence has been generated which indicates that a decline in thirst perception is an accompaniment of normal aging. In normal individuals, thirst becomes evident when plasma osmolality rises to values greater than 292 mOsm/kg (80). Study of healthy older persons (aged 67 to 75 years) has demonstrated that prolonged water deprivation capable of raising plasma osmolality to greater than 296 mOsm/kg is accompanied by diminished subjective awareness of thirst. Thus, when these individuals are subsequently presented with water, they consume significantly less than young subjects whose plasma osmolality rose to a lesser level (mean 290 mOsm/kg) following the same period of water deprivation [63]. Other studies of elderly patients with cerebrovascular accidents have similarly documented impaired thirst perception in the face of volume depletion and hyperosmolality, both normally being potent stimuli for thirst [81]. The common occurrence of cognitive impairment in the elderly can lead to failure of water seeking behavior in the presence of major physiologic stimuli for thirst. Further confounding the ability of the elderly to ingest adequate amounts of fluid is the frequent presence of physical disability (e.g., blindness, arthritis, stroke) and impaired mobility, thus limiting the capacity of the patient to gain access to fluids.

V - DRUGS AND VASOPRESSIN RELEASE

Numerous drugs taken by elderly persons can cause hyponatremia by enhancing the release of AVP from the neurohypophyseal system or potentiating the renal effects of endogenous AVP (Table 3) [82,83]. In particular, the frequent use of these drugs increases the risk for the syndrome of inappropriate ADH secretion (SIADH). For example, chlorpropamide-induced hyponatremia is most commonly observed in elderly patients. Weissman et al described five patients with symptomatic hyponatremia due to chlorpropamide, all of whom were aged 59 years or older [84].

Table 3

Drug-induced Changes in Sodium and Water Regulation

SODIUM RETENTION
      Non-steroidal anti-inflamatory agents
SODIUM LOSS
      Thiazide and loop diuretics
IMPAIRED DILUTING CAPACITY
      Thiazide diuretics
IMPAIRED CONCENTRATING CAPACITY
      Lithium
      Demeclocycline
      Potassium-losing diuretics
SYNDROME OF INAPPROPRIATE ANTIDIURETIC HORMONE SECRETION
      Psychotropic drugs
            Tricyclic antidepressants
            Selective serotonin reuptake inhibitor antidepressants
            Phenothiazines
      Antineoplastic drugs
            Vincristine
            Vinblastine
            Cyclophosphamide
      Chlorpropamide
      Carbamazepine
      Clofibrate
      Narcotics

Estimates suggest that psychotropic medications are given to approximately 50% of institutionalized elderly patients [85]. Hyponatremia with the characteristics of SIADH is recognized as a side effect of several older psychotropic agents i.e. amitriptyline, fluphenazine, thiothixene, and phenothiazine. More recently, there is evidence that the newer selective serotonin reuptake inhibitor antidepressants (SSRIs) can also induce SIADH [86,87]. Although fluoxetine is the SSRI most commonly reported to produce hyponatremia, other SSRIs including paroxetine , sertraline and fluvoxamine have also been involved [88-90]. Individuals at highest risk for SSRI-induced hyponatremia are those over the age of 65 years in whom the onset of hyponatremia typically occurs within two weeks after initiation of drug therapy.

Other drugs that have been associated with development of hyponatremia in the elderly include the antineoplastic agents vincristine, vinblastine, and cyclophosphamide. Analgesics agents, particularly the narcotics, may be responsible for the occurrence of hyponatremia in the elderly postoperative patient.

VI - HYPERNATREMIA

The renal and hormonal alterations of aging described thus far are among the factors associated with an increased risk for hypernatremia. In a study of 15,187 hospitalized patients aged more than 60 years, a 1% incidence of hypernatremia was reported, with a mean serum sodium concentration of 154 mEq/L [91]. Similarly, a study of elderly residents in a long-term care institution revealed a 1% incidence of hypernatremia, which increased to 18% when the patients were monitored over a 12-month period [92]. Of 264 nursing home patients in whom acute illness developed requiring hospitalization, 34% became markedly hypernatremic with serum sodium concentration greater than 150 mEq/L [93].

The most significant clinical manifestations of hypernatremia involve the CNS and lead to depression of sensorium, confusion and coma. There is a high morbidity and mortality in elderly patients who develop serum sodium concentrations above 148 mEq/L and such elevations of serum sodium are often a consquence of a severe underlying disease process [91,94]. Most commonly, hypernatremia is the result of loss of body water in excess of sodium losses in association with inadequate fluid intake. Frequent causes are febrile illness with increased insensible fluid loss, tachypnea with increased water loss from the lungs, diarrhea and osmotic-induced polyuria from poorly controlled diabetes mellitus or use of loop diuretics [91,94].

VII - HYPONATREMIA

Hyponatremia is a common finding in elderly persons and can lead to significant morbidity and mortality. Analysis of plasma sodium values in healthy individuals indicates an age-related decrease of approximately 1 mEq/L per decade from a mean value of 141 ± 4 mEq/L in young subjects [95]. In a population of individuals aged more than 65 years who were living at home and who were without acute illness, a 7% incidence of serum sodium concentration of 137 mEq/L or less was observed [96]. Similarly, an 11% incidence of hyponatremia was found in the population of a geriatric medicine outpatient practice [97]. In hospitalized patients, hyponatremia is even more common. An analysis of 5000 consecutive sets of plasma electrolytes from a hospital population with a mean age 54 years revealed a mean serum sodium of 134 ± 6 mEq/L, with the values skewed toward the hyponatremic end of the distribution curve [95]. A high prevalence of hyponatremia has been found in patients hospitalized for a variety of acute illnesses, with the risk being greater with increasing age of the patient [98,99].

Elderly residents of long-term care institutions appear to be especially prone to hyponatremia. In a study of 160 patients with a mean age of 72 years who resided in a chronic disease hospital, 22.5% had repeated serum sodium determinations of less than 135 mEq/L [100]. Of patients admitted to an acute geriatric unit, 11.3% were found to have serum sodium concentrations of 130 mEq/L or less [101]. A survey of nursing home residents aged more than 60 years revealed a cross-sectional incidence of 18% with serum sodium less than 136 mEq/L. When this population was observed on a longitudinal basis over a 12-month period, 53% were observed to experience one or more episodes of hyponatremia [102]. Persons with CNS and spinal cord disease were at highest risk and water load testing indicated that most patients had features consistent with SIADH. The greatest risk for the development or worsening of hyponatremia was the administration of hypotonic fluid either as an increase in oral water intake or as intravenous 0.45% saline solution or 5% glucose in water. Tube feeding is another risk factor so that the majority of patients whose nutritional support is totally from enteral feeding will develop either intermittent or persistent hyponatremia. The underlying cause appears to be sodium depletion due to the low sodium content of most tube-feeding diets [102,103]. The hyponatremia will usually resolve in response to increasing the dietary sodium intake to 2 grams per day.

There is some evidence that patients with Alzheimer's disease may be at lower risk for hyponatremia than patients with other forms of CNS disease. Vasopressin secretion may be diminished in patients with Alzheimer's disease, both under basal conditions and following stimulation by pharmacologic agents or by dehydration [104]. As a consequence, these patients are at increased risk for dehydration and it is possible that a high urine flow rate, especially at night, may be a factor in the urinary incontinence which is so common.

Idiopathic SIADH has been described in which no identifiable cause for hyponatremia could be found, suggesting that idiopathic SIADH may represent the clinical expression of physiologic changes that take place in the regulation of water balance during aging [97, 105-107]. All of the cases have been in the elderly, and there is evidence that this clinical entity is most likely to occur in the oldest age group. Race may play a role since blacks appear to be at lower risk than whites or Hispanics [97].

As with hypernatremia, hyponatremia most commonly affects CNS function and can lead to lethargy, confusion, seizures and coma. In patients who have pre-existing cognitive impairment, the development of hyponatremia has the potential to lead to further decline in cognition. Hyponatremia often is a marker for severe underlying disease with poor prognosis and high mortality [108,109].

CONCLUSION

Normal aging is accompanied by many changes in the various regulatory systems involved in the control of sodium and water balance. As a consequence of these alterations, the elderly person has a diminished capacity to withstand the challenges of illness, drugs, and physiologic stresses and, thus, has an increased risk for the development of clinically significant alterations in sodium and water balance. Awareness of these limitations of homeostasis ability allows the physician to anticipate the impact of illnesses and drugs on volume and electrolyte status of the elderly patient and will lead to a more rational approach to therapeutic intervention and management.

REFERENCES

1. Miller M, Gold GC, Friedlander DA. Physiological changes of aging affecting salt and water balance. Rev Clin Gerontology 1991; 1:215-230.
2. McLachlan M, Wasserman P. Changes in size and distensibility of the aging kidney. Br J Radiol 1981; 54:488-491.
3. Kaplan C, Pasternack B, Shah H, Gallo G. Age-related incidence of sclerotic glomeruli in human kidneys. Am J Pathol 1975; 80:227-234.
4. Kappel B, Olsen S. Cortical interstitial tissue and sclerosed glomeruli in the normal human kidney, related to age and sex. Virchows Arch (A) 1980; 387:271-227.
5. Taylor SA, Price RG. Age-related changes in rat glomerular basement membrane. Int J Biochem 1982; 14:201-206.
6. Darmady EM, Offer J, Woodhouse MS. The parameters of the aging kidney. J Pathol 1973; 109:195-207.
7. Goyal VK. Changes with age in the human kidney. Exp Gerontol 1982; 17:321-331.
8. Pratz J, Ripoche P, Corman B. Cholesterol content and water and solute permeabilities of kidney membranes from aging rats. Am J Physiol 1987; 253:R8-R14.
9. Takazakura E, Wasabu N, Handa A, Takada A, Shinoda A, Takeuchi J. Intrarenal vascular changes

with age and diseases. Kidney Int 1972; 2:224-230.

10. Ljungvist A, Lagergren C. Normal intrarenal arterial pattern in adult and aging human kidney. J Anat 1962; 96:285-298.

11. Davies DF, Shock NW. Age changes in glomerular filtration, effective renal plasma flow and tubular excretory capacity in adult males. J Clin Invest 1950; 29:496-506.

12. Rowe JW, Andres RA, Tobin JD, Norris AH, Shock NW. The effect of age on creatinine clearance in man: a cross-sectional and longitudinal study. J Gerontol 1976; 31:155-163.

13. Lindeman RD, Tobin JD, Shock NW. Longitudinal studies on the rate of decline in renal function with age. J Am Geriatr Soc 1985; 33:278-285.

14. Lindeman RD, Adler, S, Yiengst MJ, Beard ES. Natriuresis and carbohydrate-induced antinatriuresis after overnight fast and hydration. Nephron 1970; 7:289-300.

15. Schalekamp MA, Krauss XH, Schalekamp-Kuyken MP, Kolsters G, Birkenhager WH. Studies on the mechanisms of hypernatriuresis in essential hypertension in relation to measurements of plasma renin concentration, body fluid compartments and renal function. Clin Sci 1971; 41:219-231.

16. Epstein M, Hollenberg NK. Age as a determinant of renal sodium conservation in normal man. J Lab Clin Med 1976;87:411-417.

17. Lindeman RD, Lee DT, Yiengst MJ, Shock NW. Influence of age, renal disease, hypertension, diuretics and calcium on the antidiuretic responses to suboptimal infusions of vasopressin. J Lab Clin Med 1966; 68:202-223.

18. Crowe MJ, Forsling ML, Rolls BJ, Phillips PA, Ledingham JGG, Smith RF. Altered water excretion in healthy elderly men. Age Ageing 1987; 16:285-293.

19. Dontas AS, Karkenos S, Papanayioutou P. Mechanisms of renal tubular defects in old age. Postgrad Med J 1972; 48:295-303.

20. Lye M. Electrolyte disorders in the elderly. In: Morgan DB (ed), Clinics in Endocrinology and Metabolism, Philadelphia, WB Saunders, 1984, 377-398.

21. Zanuszewicz W, Heinemann H, Demartini F, et al. A clinical study of effects of hydrochlorothiazide on renal excretion of electrolyte and free water. N Eng J Med 1959; 261:264-269.

22. Lewis WH, Alving AS. Changes with age in the renal function in adult men. Am J Physiol 1938; 123:500-515.

23. Lindeman RD, Van Buren C, Raisz LG. Osmolar renal concentrating ability in healthy young men and hospitalized patients without renal disease. N Eng J Med 1960; 262:1306-1309.

24. Rowe JW, Shock NW, DeFronzo RA. The influence of age on the renal response to water deprivation in man. Nephron 1976; 17:270-278.

25. Miller JH, Shock NW. Age differences in the renal tubular response to antidiuretic hormone. J Gerontol 1953; 8:446-450.

26. Miller M. Influence of aging on vasopressin secretion and water regulation. In: Schrier RW (ed), Vasopressin, New York, Raven Press, 1985, 249-258.

27. Herzberg NH, Goudsmit E, Kruisbrink J, et al. Testosterone treatment restores reduced vasopressin-binding sites in the kidney of the aging rat. J Neuroendocrinol 1989;123:59-63.

28. Hsou HK, Peng MT. Hypothalamic neuron number of old female rats. Gerontology 1978; 24:434-440.

29. Currie AR, Adamson H, VanDyke HB. Vasopressin and oxytocin in the posterior lobe of the pituitary in man. J Clin Endocrinol Metab 1960;20:947-951.

30. Frolkis VV, Golovchenko SF, Medved VI, Frolkis RA. Vasopressin and cardiovascular system in aging. Gerontology 1982; 28:290-302.

31. Fliers E, Swaab DF, Pool Ch W, et al. The vasopressin and oxytocin neurons in the human supraoptic and paraventricular nucleus: change with aging and in senile dementia. Brain Res 1985; 342:45-53.

32. Hoogendijk JE, Fliers E, Swaab DF, et al. Activation of vasopressin neurons in the human supraoptic and paraventricular nucleus in senescence and senile dementia. J Neurol Sci 1985; 69:291-299.

33. Fliers E, Swaab DF. Activation of vasopressinergic and oxytocinergic neurons during aging in the Wistar rat. Peptides 1983; 4:165-170.

34. Fotheringham AP, Davidson YS, Davies I, et al. Age-associated changes in neuroaxonal transport in the hypothalamo-neurohypophyseal system of the mouse. Mech Aging Dev 1991;60:113-121.

35. Swaab DF, Hofman MA, Honnebier MBOM. Development of vasopressin neurons in the human suprachiasmatic nucleus in relation to birth. Dev Brain Res 1990; 52:289-293.

36. Swaab DF, Fliers E, Hoogendijk JE. Vasopressin in relationship to human aging and dementia. In: Gash GM, Boer GJ (eds), Vasopressin: Principles and Properties, New York, Plenum Press, 1987, 611-625.

37. Goudsmit E, Neijmeijer-Leloux A, Swaab DF. The human hypothalamo-ddneurohypophysial system in relation to development, aging and Alzheimer's disease. In: Swaab DF, Hofman MA,

Mirmiran M, et al (eds), Progress in Brain Research, Amsterdam, Elsevier Science Publishers, 1992, 237-248.

38. Hofman MA, Swaab DF. Influence of aging on the seasonal rhythm of the vasopressin-expressing neurons in the human suprachiasmatic nucleus. Neurobiol Aging 1995; 16:965-971.

39. Lucassen PJ, Hofman MA, Swaab DF. Increased light intensity prevents the age related loss of vasopressin-expressing neurons in the rat suprachiasmatic nucleus. Brain Res 1995; 693: 261-266.

40. Gash DM, Herman JP, Thomas GJ. Vasopressin and animal behavior. In: Gash DM, Boer GJ (eds), Vasopressin: Principles and Properties, New York, Plenum Press, 1987, 517-547.

41. Sorensen PS. Studies of vasopressin in the human cerebrospinal fluid. Acta Neurol Scand 1986; 74:81-102.

42. Mazurek MF, Growdon JH, Beal MF, et al. CSF vasopressin concentration is reduced in Alzheimer's disease. Neurology 1986; 36: 1133-1137.

43. Raskind MA, Peskind ER, Lampe TH, et al. Cerebrospinal fluid vasopressin, oxytocin, somatostatin and βendorphin in Alzheimer's disease. Arch Gen Psychiatry 1986; 43:382-388.

44. Coleman RJ, Reppert SM. CSF vasopressin rhythm is effectively insulated from osmotic regulation of plasma vasopressin. Am J Physiol 1985; 248: E346-dE352.

45. George CPL, Messerli FH, Genest J, et al. Diurnal variation of plasma vasopressin in man. J Clin Endocrinol Metab 1975; 41:332-338.

46. Nadal M. Secretory rhythm of vasopressin in healthy subjects with inversed sleep-wake cycle: evidence for the existence of an intrinsic regulation. Eur J Endocrinol 1996; 134:174-176.

47. Aspland R, Aberg H. Diurnal variation in the levels of antidiuretic hormone in the elderly. J Intern Med 1991; 299:131-134.

48. Kikuchi Y. Participation of atrial natriuretic peptide (hANP) levels and arginine vasopressin (AVP) in aged persons with nocturia. Jap J Urol 1995; 86:1651-1659.

49. Faull CM, Holmes C, Baylis PH. Water balance in elderly people: is there a deficiency of vasopressin? Age Ageing 1993; 22:114-120.

50. Clark BA, Elahi D, Fish L, et al. Atrial natriuretic peptide suppresses osmostimulated vasopressin release in young and elderly humans. Am J Physiol 1991; 261:E252-E256.

51. Helderman JH, Vestal RE, Rowe JW, Tobin JD, Andres R, Robertson GL. The response of arginine vasopressin to intravenous ethanol and hypertonic saline in man. The impact of aging. J Gerontol 1978; 33:39-47.

52. Chiodera P, Capretti L, Marches M. Abnormal arginine vasopressin response to cigarette smoking and metoclopramide (but not to insulin-induced hypoglycemia) in elderly subjects. J Gerontol 1991; 46:M6-M10.

53. Duggan J, Kilfeather S, Lightman SL, et al. The association of age with plasma arginine vasopressin and plasma osmolality. Age Aging 1993; 22:332-336.

54. Crawford GA, Johnson AG, Gyory AZ, et al. Change in arginine vasopressin concentration with age. Clin Chem 1993; 39:2023.

55. Rondeau E, Delima J, Caillens H, Ardaillou R, Vahanian A, Acar J. High plasma anti-diuretic hormone in patients with cardiac failure. Influence of age. Mineral Electrolyte Metab 1982; 8:267-274.

56. Kirkland J, Lye M, Goddard C, Vargas E, Davies I. Plasma arginine vasopressin in dehydrated elderly patients. Clin Endocrinol 1984; 20:451-456.

57. Johnson AG, Crawford GA, Kelly D, et al. Arginine vasopressin and osmolality in the elderly. J Am Geriatr Soc 1994; 42:399-404.

58. Bursztyn M, Bresnahan M, Gavras I, Gavras H. Pressor hormones in elderly hypertensive persons: racial differences. Hypertension 1990; 15(2 Suppl): I88-I92.

59. Engel PA, Rowe JW, Minaker KL, Robertson GL. Stimulation of vasopressin release by exogenous vasopressin: effect of sodium intake and age. Am J Physiol 1984; 246:E202-E207.

60. Baylis PH, Zerbe RL, Robertson GL. Arginine-vasopressin response to insulin induced hypoglycemia in man. J Clin Endocrinol Metab 1981; 53:935-940.

61. Robertson GL, Rowe JW. The effect of aging on neurohypophysial function. Peptides 1980; 1(Suppl 1): 159-162.

62. Robertson GL, Shelton RL, Athar J. The osmoregulation of vasopressin Kidney Int 1976; 10:25-37.

63. Phillips PA, Rolls BJ, Ledingham JGG, et al. Reduced thirst after water deprivation in healthy elderly men. N Engl J Med 1984; 311:753-759.

64. Li CH, Hsieh SM, Nagai I. The response of plasma arginine vasopressin to 14 h. water deprivation in the elderly. Acta Endocrinol 1984; 150:314-317.

65. Rowe JW, Minaker KL, Robertson GL. Age-related failure of volume pressure mediated vasopressin release in man. J Clin Endocrinol Metab 1982; 54:661-664.

66. Bevilacqua M, Norbiato G, Chebat E, et al. Osmotic and nonosmotic control of vasopressin release

in the elderly: effect of metoclopramide. J Clin Endocrinol Metab 1987; 54:1243-1247.

67. Norbiato G, Bevilacqua M, Chebat E, et al. Metoclopramide increases vasopressin secretion. J Clin Endocrinol Metab 1986; 63:747-750.

68. Steardo L, Iovino M, Monteleone P, et al. Evidence that cholinergic receptors of muscarinic type may modulate vasopressin release induced by metoclopramide. J Neurol Transm 1990; 82:213-217.

69. Gribbin B, Pickering TG, Sleight P, et al. Effect of age and high blood pressure on baroreflex sensitivity in man. Circ Res 1971; 29:424-431.

70. Espiner EA, Richards AM, Yandle TG, Nicholls MG. Natriuretic hormones. Endocrinology Metab Clin N Am 1995; 24: 481-509.

71. Ohashi M, Fujio N, Nawata H, et al. High plasma concentrations of human atrial natriuretic polypeptide in aged men. J Clin Endocrinol Metab 1987; 64:81-85.

72. McKnight JA, Roberts G, Sheridan B, Brew Atkinson A. Relationship between basal and sodium stimulated plasma atrial natriuretic factor, age, sex and blood pressure in normal man. Human Hypertens 1989; 3:157-163.

73. Tajima F, Sagawa S, Iwamoto J, Miki K, Claybaugh JR, Shiraki K. Renal and endocrine responses in the elderly during headout water immersion. Am J Physiol 1988;254:R977-R983.

74. Heim JM, Gottmann JW, Strom TM, Gerzer R. Effects of a bolus dose of atrial natriuretic factor in young and elderly volunteers. Eur J Clin Invest 1989; 19:265-271.

75. Ohashi M, Fujio N, Nawata H, Kato K, Matsuo H, Ibayashi H. Pharmacokinetics of synthetic alpha-human atrial natriuretic polypeptide in normal men: effect of aging. Regul Pept 1987; 19:265-271.

76. Jansen TL, Tan AC, Smits P, de Boo T, Benraad TJ, Thien T. Hemodynamic effects of atrial natriuretic factor in young and elderly subjects. Clin Pharmacol Ther 1990; 48:179-188.

77. Genest J, Larochelle P, Cusson JR, Gutkowska J, Cantin M. The atrial natriuretic factor in hypertension: state of the art lecture. Hypertension 1988; 11(Suppl 1): 13-17.

78. Cuneo RC, Espiner EA, Nicholls MG, Yandle TG, Livessey JH. Effect of physiological levels of atrial natriuretic peptide on hormone secretion: inhibition of angiotensin-induced aldosterone secretion and renin release in normal man. J Clin Endocrinol Metab 1987; 65:765-772.

79. Clinkingbeard C, Sessions C, Shenker Y. The physiological role of atrial natriuretic hormone in the regulation of aldosterone and salt and water metabolism. J Clin Endocrinol Metab 1990; 70:582-589.

80. Robertson GL. Thirst and vasopressin function in normal and disordered states of water balance. J Lab Clin Med 1983;101:351-371.

81. Miller PD, Krebs RA, Neal BJ, McIntyre DO. Hypodipsia in geriatric patients. Am J Med 1982; 73:354-356.

82. Miller M, Moses AM. Drug-induced states of impaired water excretion. Kidney Int 1976; 10:96-103.

83. Moses A M, Miller M, Streeten DHP. Pathophysiologic and pharmacologic alterations in the release and action of ADH. Metabolism 1976; 25:697-721.

84. Weissman P, Shenkman L, Gregerman RI. Chlorpropamide hyponatremia: drug-ddinduced inappropriate antidiuretic-hormone activity. N Engl J Med 1972; 284:65-71.

85. Stewart RB, May FE, Hale WE, et al. Psychotropic drug use in an ambulatory elderly population. Gerontology 1982; 28:328-335.

86. Sharma H, Pompei P. Antidepressant-induced hyponatremia in the aged. Avoidance and management strategies. Drugs Aging 1996; 8:430-435.

87. Liu BA, Mittmann N, Knowles SR, Shear NH. Hyponotremia and the syndrome of inappropriate secretion of antidiuretic hormone associated with the use of selective serotonin reuptake inhibitors: a review of spontaneous reports. Canadian Med Assoc J 1996; 155:519-527.

88. Cohen BJ, Mahelsky M, Adler L. More cases of SIADH with fluoxetine. Am J Psychiatry 1990; 147:948-949.

89. Gommans JG, Edwards RA. Fluoxetine and hyponatremia. N Z Med J 1990; 103:106.

90. Hwang AS, Magraw RM. Syndrome of inappropriate secretion of antidiuretic hormone due to fluoxetine. Am J Psychiatry 1989;146:399.

91. Snyder NA, Feigel DW, Arieff AI. Hypernatremia in elderly patients. A heterogenous, morbid, and iatrogenic entity. Ann Intern Med 1987; 107:309-319.

92. Miller M, Morley JE, Rubenstein LA, Ouslander J, Strome S. Hyponatremia in a nursing home population. The Gerontologist 1985; 25:11.

93. Lavizo-Mourey R, Johnson J, Stolley P. Risk factors for dehydration among elderly nursing home residents. J Am Geriatr Soc 1988; 36:213-218.

94. Palevsky PM, Bhagrath R, Greenberg A. Hypernatremia in hospitalized patients. Ann Intern Med 1996; 124:197-203.

95. Owen JA, Campbell DG. A comparison of plasma electrolyte and urea values in healthy persons and in hospital patients. Clin Chem Acta 1968; 22:611-618.

96. Caird FI, Andrews GR, Kennedy RD. Effect of posture on blood pressure in the elderly. Br Heart J 1973; 35:527-530.
97. Miller M, Hecker MS, Friedlander DA, Carter JM. Apparent idiopathic hyponatremia in an ambulatory geriatric population. J Am Geriatr Soc 1996;44:404-408.
98. Anderson RJ, Chung H, Kluge R, Schrier RW. Hyponatremia: a prospective analysis of its epidemiology and the pathogenetic role of vasopressin. Ann Intern Med 1985; 102:164-168.
99. Hochman I, Cabili S, Peer G. Hyponatremia in internal medicine ward patients: causes, treatment and prognosis. Isr J Med Sci 1989; 25:73-76.
100. Kleinfeld M, Casimir M, Borra S. Hyponatremia as observed in a chronic disease facility. J Am Geriatr Soc 1979; 27:156-161.
101. Sunderam SG, Mankikar GD. Hyponatremia in the elderly. Age Ageing 1983; 12:77-80.
102. Miller M, Morley JE, Rubenstein LZ. Hyponatremia in a nursing home population. J Am Geriatr Soc 1995; 43:1410-1413.
103. Rudman D, Racette D, Rudman IW, et al. Hyponatremia in tube-fed elderly men. J Chronic Dis 1986; 39:73-80.
104. Miller M. Hormonal aspects of fluid and sodium balance in the elderly. Endocrinology Metab Clin N Am 1995; 24:233-253.
105. Crowe M. Hyponatremia due to syndrome of inappropriate antidiuretic hormone secretion in the elderly. Irish Med J 1980; 73:482-483.
106. Ditzel J. Hyponatremia in an elderly woman and inappropriate secretion of antidiuretic hormone. Acta Med Scand 1966; 179:407-416.
107. Goldstein CS, Braunstein S, Goldfarb S. Idiopathic syndrome of inappropriate antidiuretic hormone secretion possibly related to advanced age. Ann Intern Med 1983; 99:185-188.
108. Kennedy PGE, Mitchell DM, Hoffbrand BI. Severe hyponatremia in hospital inpatients. Br Med J 1978; 2:1251-1253.
109. Tierney WM, Martin DK, Greenlee MC, Zerbe RL, McDonald CJ. The prognosis of hyponatremia at hospital admission. J Genl Int Med 1986;1:380-385.

DEHYDRATION AS A PRECIPITATING FACTOR IN THE DEVELOPMENT OF ACUTE CONFUSION IN THE FRAIL ELDERLY

J. MENTES, K. CULP, B. WAKEFIELD, P. GASPAR, C. G. RAPP, P. MOBILY, T. TRIPP-REIMER

Iowa Veteran's Affairs Research Consortium College of Nursing University of Iowa Correspondence to: Janet Mentes College of Nursing University of Iowa Iowa City, Iowa 52242 (319) 335 7057 (phone) (319) 353 5535 (fax) jmentes@blue.weeg.uiowa.edu (e-mail).

Abstract : *Frail elders are at increased risk for underhydration/dehydration, which often goes undetected until more dramatic symptoms, such as acute confusion, highlight the problem. Decline in functional and/or cognitive status, as well as death are known outcomes of both dehydration and acute confusion. It is, therefore, crucial to prevent or intervene in a timely manner to improve outcomes for frail elders. This paper reviews the relationship between acute confusion and dehydration, introduces an intervention model to help practitioners prevent acute confusion by eliminating precipitating factors, such as dehydration and discusses the challenge of developing a clinical guideline for hydration management in long term care (LTC) residents.*

Keywords : *acute confusion, delirium, dehydration, clinical practice guidelines, long term care.*

INTRODUCTION

Frail elders, particularly long term care (LTC) residents, are at high risk for underhydration/dehydration due to age related changes that place them in a delicate state of physiologic homeostasis that can easily be disrupted with the addition of even minimal physiologic stress. Dehydration is a prevalent yet easily prevented/treated problem of the elderly [1, 2] ; however, the importance of maintaining adequate hydration in elderly patients is often overlooked until more dramatic symptoms, such as acute confusion, highlight the problem. With the onset of acute confusion and the brain dysfunction it heralds, the elder's prognosis becomes significantly more dire. It is important to monitor the hydration status of geriatric patients carefully to prevent further decline in functional health which is a known consequence of acute confusion [3-5].

This paper reviews the relationship between acute confusion and dehydration, introduces an intervention model to help practitioners prevent acute confusion by eliminating precipitating factors and discusses the challenge of developing a clinical practice guideline for hydration management in long term care (LTC) residents.

ACUTE CONFUSION

Acute confusion (AC) can be characterized as a state of brain dysfunction that has an acute onset, brief duration, and fluctuating course. This transient state of dysfunction is signalled by impaired orientation and memory, disorganized thinking and perception, increased distractibility, disrupted sleep wake cycle, and hyper and/ or hypoactive behavior [6, 7]. Neelon & Champagne [8] indicate that three areas of the brain are most likely affected by AC: the cortical and midbrain structures responsible for thinking, perception and memory; the reticular activating system responsible for attention and wakefulness; and the autonomic system responsible for psychomotor and regulatory functions. Despite the global dysfunction caused by AC, it is clearly a transient dysfunction caused by physiologic, psychologic or environmental factors. Acute confusion has the potential for resolution and can be prevented in many cases if the appropriate precipitants (ie. fluid imbalance) are vigilantly monitored in susceptible elders.

In recent years the problem of AC has primarily been explored with hospitalized elders in general medical or surgical units; data from LTC settings are virtually nonexistent. Therefore the literature on AC in acute care settings will be reviewed with the assumption that the epidemiologic parameters are at least as prevalent in LTC settings, given that residents are older, frailer and more cognitively impaired than most hospitalized patients. This assumption is supported by a pilot study conducted through the Iowa Veteran's Affairs (VA) Research

Consortium. Culp et al. [9] followed 37 subjects in two VA long term care facilities to ascertain the incidence and antecedent conditions of AC in this population. Findings indicate that the incidence was indeed high, with 15 subjects (40.5%) exhibiting AC over a two week observation period.

Incidence rates for AC in hospitalized elders have been documented from as low as 12% to as high as 80% [10] with 20-40% being the most frequently reported range [6, 11 16]. The wide variance in rates of AC is likely related to different modes of measurement, methodological issues, and type of treatment setting.

Duration of AC episodes vary and have been reported to last from 1 day [15] to 60 days [13]. Sirois [17] documented consultation cases of delirium in hospitalized elders and reported varying degrees of duration: less than 24 hours 20%; 1-3 days 30%; 3-5 days 17%; 5-10 days 20%; up to 30 days 13%. This variability in duration rates is compounded by the fact that in about 10% of patients AC recurs [15]. Levkoff and associates [18] suggest that there is only a partial resolution of all AC symptoms on discharge; in fact, their study reported that only 4% of patients with AC experienced complete resolution of all new AC symptoms by discharge; and that by six month followup a remarkably small percentage (17.7%) of patients had experienced resolution of symptoms.

Additionally, it has been documented that patients who suffer an AC episode while hospitalized experience poorer outcomes than patients who do not (See Table 1). Negative sequelae include: a longer length of stay, increased mortality during and post hospitalization, discharge to a higher level of care, and future institutionalization.

Table 1
Outcomes for Hospitalized Elders Experiencing an Acute Confusion Episode

Outcome Variable	Likelihood with AC
Hospital stay	1.5-1.75 times increased [4, 12]
In hospital mortality	2.6-8 times increased [4, 12]
Six month mortality	2.0 times increased [18]
Two year mortality	1.8 times increased [3]
Discharge to higher level of care	5.3-7.0 times increased [12, 18]
Institutionalized two years post AC episode	2.6 times increased [5, 12, 18]
Cost of hospitalization	1.5 times increased [4]

The equally dismal outcomes for dehydrated elderly patients in terms of morbidity and mortality further complicate the clinical picture [19]. Thus, an important etiologic question is posed, what comes first, AC or dehydration? The model proposes that dehydration is a primary precipitating factor in the development of AC in frail elders, and forms the basis for future intervention research.

INTERVENTION MODEL

The epidemiological prevention model described in this paper is based on the premise that two conditions are necessary for AC to develop: a vulnerable patient and precipitating factors [20] which are further categorized according to Neelon & Champagne's [8] patterns of onset of AC. The model allows practitioners to anticipate which elderly residents are vulnerable to AC given specific individual risk and precipitating factors, and at what point during their treatment the AC may occur. Synthesis of this information can help the geriatric practitioner to prevent episodes of AC in long term care residents. Prevention of AC is essential to avoid poor outcomes, such as, increased mortality; and decreased cognitive and functional status that occur as a result of AC [3 5].

Four major, interlocking concepts of the Pathogenesis and Intervention Model for Acute Confusion are explicated next (see Figure 1). These four concepts include: precipitating factors, individual acute confusion trajectory, intervention trajectory, and outcomes.

Table 2
Common Precipitating Factors of Acute Confusion

Condition	Description
Infection [4, 16]	Urinary tract
	Respiratory
Medications [6,11,13,16]	CNS agents
	Anticholinergics
Hypoxia [21]	Pulse oximetry < 90
	Receiving oxygen
Fluid/Electrolyte Imbalance	**Abnormalities**
Electrolytes [6, 11]	Na, K, glucose
Kidney failure [4, 6, 11]	Azotemia, proteinuria
Dehydration [9, 12,34]	BUN/Creat ratio
	< 1 liter fluid intake/day
Setting [13]	Unfamiliar hospital environment

Figure 1
Pathogenesis and Intervention Model of Acute Confusion

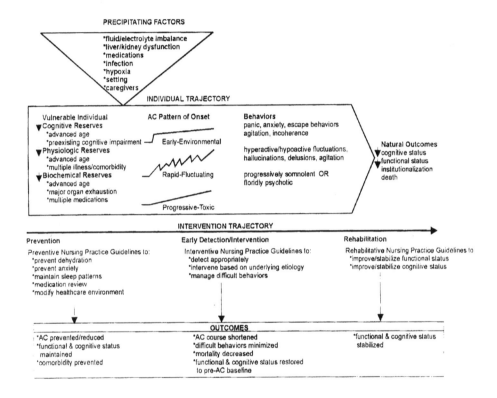

Precipitating Factors

Precipitating factors are health related or health setting related factors that interact with the vulnerabilities of the elderly individual to increase the risk of the development of AC (See Table 2). Precipitating factors that have been most frequently identified in the literature include: infection [3, 16], multiple medication usage [6, 11,16], hypoxia [21], fluid/electrolyte imbalances [6, 9, 11, 22] and liver and kidney dysfunction[4,6,11,12]. Less frequently identified conditions include: temperature imbalance [11], fracture on admission [11] and environmental issues [13]. Precipitating factors identified by Culp et al. [9] in a pilot of long term care veterans included: urinary tract infections, serum electrolyte/fluid imbalance, hypotension, hypoxia and medication induced AC. Other less well studied precipitating factors are proposed in this model, and include the type of healthcare setting, in this case the long term care setting, with concommitant norms and expectations of the setting, as well as the type and number of healthcare provider in the setting.

Individual AC Trajectory

The individual AC trajectory includes the vulnerable individual who develops a specific onset pattern of AC based on individual health characteristics. AC symptoms are exhibited in distinctive behavioral manifestations which reflect the AC onset pattern. Characteristics that indicate vulnerability in elderly individuals are: advanced age [23], >80 years [16]; preexisting cognitive impairment [6,11,12,14,16,21]; and multiple illnesses [11,12,14]. Less frequently cited characteristics are: male gender [16], vision impairments [12], and history of alcoholism [14].

The identified onset patterns for AC are: early onset, rapid onset fluctuating course, and progressive onset toxic course [8]. As postulated by Neelon & Champagne [8], patients in the early onset pattern who are most susceptible to AC, are those with a preexisting cognitive impairment which would put them at increased risk for an environmentally induced AC episode, perhaps triggered by changes in the treatment environment. If other risk factors are also present, a high degree of risk can be assumed; for example, if a patient with preexisting dementia, over 70 years of age was newly admitted to the nursing home and had been taking psychoactive drugs to manage the behavioral consequences of his/her dementia, he/she would be at very high risk for developing AC early on after nursing home admission. Residents with decreased cognitive reserve typically manifest AC with the following behaviors: panic, anxiety, escape behaviors, sundowning, agitation and/or incoherence.

The rapid onset fluctuating pattern is manifested in the elderly individual with multiple diseases affecting several body systems or with a terminal disease. Implicit with this scenario is the likelihood that this elder will be taking multiple drugs for various diseases. If the elder develops an infection or physiologic imbalance, particularly hypoxemia or dehydration, then he/she is at high risk for developing AC. Temporally, the elder at risk could develop AC at any time during his/her stay in long term care, but the risk is higher during the winter months when flu and upper respiratory diseases are more prevalent. Residents with decreased physiologic reserves typically manifest AC with the following behaviors: hyperactive/hypoactive fluctuations, hallucinations, delusions and/or agitation.

The progressive onset pattern develops more insidiously as the vulnerable elder, who is older, physically frail, and receiving multiple medications, either develops a drug toxicity or exhibits major organ system exhaustion, which presents as AC. Events of this nature are particularly likely for LTC residents who have been taking multiple medications for decades with no ill effect; but now, because of increased age and/or major organ exhaustion can no longer tolerate the dosages. The onset of this pattern may look like chronic confusion, in that a suboptimal, preconfusional state may occur, giving the impression that the patient is not suffering from an acute episode of confusion. Residents with decreased biochemical reserves typically manifest AC with the following behaviors: floridly psychotic and agitated (as with delirium tremens) or progressive somnolence.

Intervention Trajectory

The intervention trajectory as depicted in the intervention model in Figure 1, includes those actions designed to prevent, provide early detection and intervention, or to provide rehabilitation for an episode(s) of AC based on the elderly individual's vulnerabilities and the presence of precipitating factors. Preventive interventions, such as hydration management or preventing hypoxia, are those actions that prevent the occurrence of AC, whereas, early detection and intervention are actions that systematically screen elders at risk for AC and therefore reduce the impact of AC. Early detection and intervention actions would include development of a risk profile for AC or inservice educational programs designed to help staff recognize AC and to manage concomitant agitation. Rehabilitation includes all actions that restore cognitive and functional status following an AC episode.

As a first step in developing a guideline to prevent AC through hydration management, a review of AC intervention literature identified interventions already tested and any flaws in the research designs used to test these interventions. A synopsis of these studies follows.

Intervention Studies

The earliest intervention studies were conducted with patients suffering from postoperative delirium/ AC and sought to prevent development or promote early intervention for the confusion. Intervening with this patient population is logical since the change in patient status is rapid, obviously deviant from "normal" preoperative behavior and preceded by a documented stressor, the surgical intervention. This clinical picture is congruent with Neelon & Champagne's [8] rapid onset pattern in the patient with low physical reserve. However, rather than identifying physiologic interventions, researchers in the surgical setting primarily tested psychosocial-environmental interventions such as providing orientation, clarification and environmental modifications [24,25]; using family members to orient and support the confused patient [26,27]; providing consistent contact with the same caregiver [25]; and providing preoperative education about AC [28]. Despite this discrepancy between etiology and interventions, several studies showed statistically significant reductions in AC [25] or comfort with the experience of AC [28]. However, as much as 40% of the surgical patients receiving the intervention still developed AC, causing researchers to question whether the interventions were clinically significant.

When physiologic interventions were implemented, they were tested in a general medical hospital population and were a part of a broad based protocol of clinical interventions, including the psychosocial measures cited above. Nagley's [29] treatment variable included the consistent application of sixteen basic care measures; for example, regulation of room temperature, routine ambulation of patients, and having personal possessions within reach. Although Nagley sought to prevent AC episodes, her quasi-experimental study had several flaws. First, instrumentation was problematic because no instruments specific to AC had been developed at the time of the study and second, contamination between treatment and control groups was likely given that the study units were in the same hospital.

Of the more recent intervention studies, only one has examined prevention of AC. Gustafson et al. [30] demonstrated a lower incidence, shorter duration and less severity in postoperative AC by using a geriatric anesthesiological intervention that included comprehensive assessment and prevention of intraoperative hypoxemia. Other studies have focused on early detection and intervention in episodes of AC in hospitalized elders. Specifically, these studies have tested the effectiveness of nursing care protocols developed by Geriatric Clinical Nurse Specialists (CNS) [31] or Geriatrician Liaison nurse teams [32] in the care of acutely confused elders, or evaluated medical staff educational programs for the early detection of AC in hospitalized elders [33]. Both Cole et al. [32] and Wanich et al. [31] found no significant decrease in the incidence of AC with the use of care protocols or physician nurse teams; however, Wanich et al. [31] did find significant improvement in functional status among elders receiving care based on protocols designed by a Geriatric CNS. Rockwood et al. [33] found that a medical educational program was effective in increasing the recognition of AC in a hospitalized population of elders.

Rationale for Hydration Management Guideline

As this review highlights, the proposed clinical practice guideline must be sufficiently precise in order to examine the true effect of an intervention on the prevention of AC. Therefore, of the five interventions identified in Figure 1 (prevent dehydration, prevent anxiety, maintain sleep patterns, review medications, and modify healthcare environment), hydration management was selected for development and testing. The decision to develop a hydration management guideline (HMG) was based on the fact that multiple studies have identified dehydration [6,9,22,34] or laboratory data indicative of dehydration [11,12] as a significant precipitating factor of AC. Further, dehydration may serve as an antecedent condition for other documented precipitants of AC, such as infections and medication toxicity, as well as being a precipitant itself. In addition, dehydration is more likely to be prevented through direct clinical actions than either infections or medication toxicity. Recent attention has further highlighted the prevalence of dehydration in elderly, retired Medicare patients, with 6.7% of Medicare hospitalizations in 1991 having dehydration as 1 of 5 reported diagnoses [19]. Significant numbers of these same Medicare patients also had acute infections, like pneumonia or urinary tract infections, as a concomitant diagnosis [19].

The term dehydration is used to signify different fluid/electrolyte problems, usually based on the concentration of sodium [35,36]. Although many different types of dehydration are encountered in the nursing home, the most prevalent type is a subclinical state of dehydration or chronic underhydration [37] where the elder does not adequately replenish fluids and becomes hypernatremic [38,39]. Figure 2 reports pilot data for elderly veterans in long term care who drank four or more 8 ounce glasses of water a day and who were significantly less likely to develop AC than veterans drinking four or less glasses of water per day. In fact, of the 15 veterans who subsequently developed AC, seven consumed less than one liter of fluid per day [9].

Clinical indicators of dehydration in elderly individuals are often subtle. Gross et al. [40] found that the indicators listed in Table 3 were highly correlated with physician dehydration ratings which included physical examination results and laboratory studies, and were unrelated to age. As laboratory results can be affected by many age related changes, laboratory data of elders is most helpful when interpreted as a change from baseline values rather than as a single deviant value [41]. However, standard laboratory data for dehydration are identified in Table 3. Thus measurement of dehydration in the elderly is challenging and needs to be individually assessed as a change from baseline values.

Table 3
Indicators of Dehydration in Acutely Ill Elder

Clinical [40]	Laboratory [39]
sunken eyes	serum sodium > 148 mmol/L
dry tongue with longitudinal furrows	BUN/Creatinine ratio $\geq$ 25
dry mucous membranes of mouth	serum osmolality> 300 mmol/Kg
upper body muscle weakness	
speech difficulties	
confusion	

Figure 2

Fluid intake and probability of developing AC over time based on the number of 8 oz glasses of water consumed per day at the start of follow up [9].

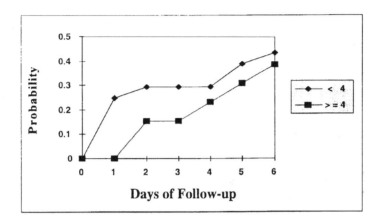

Outcomes

Outcomes for both natural course and for ineffective treatment of AC are depicted in the model. They include death and decreased cognitive and functional status, which often leads to further dependency. However, interventions for AC can alter these natural outcomes. Optimal outcome indicators for preventive care include: the absence of AC and maintenance of baseline functional and cognitive status. Outcome indicators for early intervention include: shortened length of AC, timely treatment of AC, minimization of difficult behaviors, decreased death, and restoration of functional and cognitive status to pre AC baseline. Outcome indicators for rehabilitative care include the stabilization of functional and cognitive status.

In the elderly, AC is a complex, multidimensional phenomenon that has dire consequences if not immediately treated. Additionally, the multiple precipitating factors and individual vulnerabilities of elders further complicates intervention in AC. To date, intervention research has been inconclusive for several reasons, most commonly because of the global application of interventions that were not well matched to the precipitating factors for AC that were set forth in this article. The intervention model provides the needed organization to help guide clinicians in appropriately preventing and treating AC. The model also suggests interventions that will be most effective in preventing AC and curtailing unwanted outcomes, by focusing on preventing one common precipitant of AC, dehydration.

CLINICAL PRACTICE GUIDELINES

Recently, there has been a push to develop multidisciplinary practice guidelines. This increased interest in clinical practice guidelines (CPG) was stimulated by the Agency for Health Care Policy and Research (AHCPR) that was charged with improving the quality and effectiveness of American health care services in 1989 [42]. Thus in an effort to standardize and optimize patient care outcomes, CPGs have been developed for a variety of conditions. AHCPR has issued fifteen such guidelines, other professional organizations and individual healthcare facilities have developed many more [43]. Practice guidelines are defined as, "systematically developed statements to assist practitioner and patient decisions about appropriate health care for specific clinical circumstances" [42]. CPGs may be based on consensus, expert opinion or preferably on research findings [42,44]. As implied by definition, CPGs are broad guidelines that can be tailored for specific local applications; such as use in specialty care [45]. With this in mind, a CPG for hydration management to prevent acute confusion will be outlined.

DEVELOPMENT OF A HYDRATION MANAGEMENT GUIDELINE

It is difficult to standardize care for the elderly, in part, because of the unique interplay of age related changes and comorbidity often found in this population. Classical "geriatric conditions" have been presented in the literature; conditions that are not specific disease states per se, but are so ubiquitous that they could indicate one of many disease states. This taps into the greatest utility of a guideline for managing geriatric conditions like dehydration; its potential to influence multiple disease states simultaneously. Therefore, the remainder of this paper will address specific issues of structure and measurement relevant to the development of a hydration management guideline (HMG).

Target Population

The first step is to identify the target population for the CPG. In this case residents of long term care facilities will serve as the target population. Long term care residents are older, frailer and more dependent in self care than community dwelling residents. In addition to age related changes in thirst perception [46,47], renal function and overall body composition, many LTC residents depend on caretakers for adequate fluid intake, especially elders with Alzheimer's Disease. Problems such as joint pain, fear of incontinence, swallowing problems, communication difficulties, cognitive impairment, and medications further complicate hydration management. Adams [48] noted that community dwelling elders consumed more fluids than LTC elders. In fact, LTC residents have frequently been identified as at risk for dehydration because of inadequate fluid intake [37,38,49,50]. Risk factors for dehydration in this population identified by Lavisso Mourey and colleagues [49] included: female gender, over 85 years of age, more than 4 chronic illnesses, more than 4 medications, and requiring assistance with transfer and ambulation. A study by Gaspar [51] also identified female LTC residents at increased risk. The relationship between functional status and risk for dehydration was further explicated in this study, in that totally dependent and independent LTC residents were more likely to have adequate fluid intake, whereas semi-dependent residents were not. Semi-dependent residents were those individuals who are cognitively unaware of their needs yet have mobility and those who are physically unable to meet their needs but who abandon expressing them [51].

Hydration Assessment

The second step in guideline development involves pinpointing the exact phenomenon of interest, in this case underhydration/dehydration that results in hypernatremic dehydration. Often LTC residents do not consume the required amount of fluids and are, therefore, chronically underhydrated which can significantly damage aged, vulnerable organ systems causing new disease states or complicating chronic ones. Determining dehydration is difficult largely due to age-related changes that make interpretation of laboratory results ambiguous when values are compared to standardized norms for younger adults. Stable, elevated serum osmolality, sodium and BUN/Cr ratios in some LTC residents, without clinical signs of dehydration, highlight the problem with measurement [41]. However, investigators suggest that because of the stability of these indicators, deviations from the resident's baseline laboratory values may be more crucial in overall evaluation of fluid status.

Researchers investigating hydration status in young adults have found that urinary indices (urine color, urine osmolality and specific gravity) and are more sensitive to early dehydration or hypohydration, than hematologic indices [52,53]. Although the subjects of the studies cited above were young, urinary indices may also be diagnostic of hypohydration in the elderly if deviations from the resident's baseline value are used.

Timing is also an important element in evaluation. Gross et al. [40] developed a list of seven clinical indicators that were not correlated with age for the assessment of dehydration in emergency room care. The more indicators observed, the more likely the elderly individual will be dehydrated. It is probable that for accurate detection of dehydration both clinical and laboratory measures will be needed when developing a CPG.

Hydration Intervention

The third step includes developing appropriate intervention strategies based on research findings or expert clinical practice. Research findings are scarce; no universally accepted norms for fluid intake are available for this population. Frail elders' daily fluid requirements are even more variable, taking into consideration, overall health status, fluid restrictions, renal functioning and preferences of the elder. Type of fluid is another consideration; water is considered the best alternative, yet many elderly persons find water bland and therefore limit their intake. In a study of amount, time pattern, and type of fluids consumed by LTC residents and community dwelling residents, Adams [48] determined that LTC residents drank fewer and different types of fluids than community dwelling individuals. Community residents drank more water and hot beverages, like coffee and tea, whereas LTC residents drank more milk and fruit juice. Dietary habits also influence hydration status, with solid food accounting for approximately one third of the total daily consumption of fluids in an average person [54].

Patterns of fluid intake in this population help determine timing of an intervention. Adams [48] found that time patterns for drinking fluids were similar between LTC and community dwelling residents. Both groups consumed 75% of their daily fluid intake between 6:00 AM. and

6:00 PM., with the highest intake in the afternoon. An important difference in pattern of intake was that LTC residents consumed most fluids at mealtime or at medication time indicating that they were dependent on the nursing staff for their fluid intake. Further, they drank the amount that was offered regardless of the amount. Gaspar [51] also found that the more frequently LTC residents were offered fluids, the more likely they were to consume an adequate daily amount of fluids.

Given the constraints of the LTC environment, careful consideration must be given to how the fluids will be provided. The literature has suggested different approaches from the practical; having a fluid cart which is routinely taken to individual residents' rooms [55], to the social; having tea parties or "happy hours" where appropriate fluids and socialization are encouraged [56]. Additional suggestions include, special easy to hold mugs for fluids and use of commercial thickening preparations for individuals with swallowing problems.

Evaluation

Plans for evaluation of the effectiveness of the HMG in preventing acute confusion is the final step in constructing the guideline. It is important to examine both the clinical effectiveness and the practicality of the guideline in the evaluation phase [43]. Several questions form the basis for evaluation of this guideline:
Did the incidence of AC decline?
Was the decline in AC attributable to hydration management?
Is the guideline comprehensive enough to be reproduced in other LTC settings?
Is the guideline sufficiently practical to promote its utilization?
Does the cost of implementing care under the guideline offset the costs incurred by AC?

Because guidelines for "geriatric conditions", such as dehydration, are difficult to develop and implement, pilot testing and revisions are imperative. In addition, clinical knowledge is constantly revised, therefore routine review of the HMG should be implemented.

CONCLUSION

Literature supports that dehydration is a common precipitating factor in the development of AC in the frail elderly. This paper discussed an intervention model for the prevention of AC based on the management of precipitating factors such as, dehydration. The challenges of developing, implementing and evaluating a clinical guideline (HMG) derived from this model was reviewed. Although conceptually complex, the construction of clinical guidelines to prevent "geriatric conditions" like dehydration should be attempted because of the numbers of frail elders who could benefit from such care.

Acknowledgement : The primary author (JM) is grateful to Dr. Kathleen Buckwalter who was instrumental in the formative stages of this article.

REFERENCES

1. Hoffman N. Dehydration in the elderly: Insidious and manageable. Geriatrics 1991; 46(6):35-38.
2. Kositzke J. A question of balance. Dehydration in the elderly. Journal of Gerontological Nursing 1990; 16 (5):4-11.
3. Francis J, Kapoor W. Prognosis after hospital discharge of older medical patients with delirium. Journal of the American Geriatrics Society 1992; 40:601-606.
4. Levkoff S, Safrana C, Cleary P, Gallop J, Phillips R. Identification of factors associated with the diagnosis of delirium in elderly hospitalized patients. Journal of the American Geriatrics Society 1988; 36:1099-1104.
5. Murray A, Levkoff S, Wetle T, Beckett L, Cleary P, Schor J, Lipsitz B, Rowe J, Evans D. Acute delirium and functional decline in the hospitalized elderlypatient. Journal of Gerontology: Medical Sciences 1993; 48:M181-186.
6. Foreman M. Confusion in the hospitalized elderly: Incidence, onset and associated factors. Research in Nursing & Health 1989; 12: 21-29.
7. Lipowski ZJ. Delirium: Acute confusional states. New York: Oxford University Press, 1990.
8. Neelon V, Champagne M. Managing cognitive impairment: The current bases for practice. In: Funk S, Tournquist E, Champagne M , Wiese R, eds. Key aspects of eldercare: Managing falls, incontinence and cognitive impairment. New York: Springer Publishing Co., 1992.
9. Culp K, Tripp-Reimer T, Wadle K, Wakefield B, Aikens J, Mobily P & Kundrat M. Screening for acute confusion in elderly long-term care residents. Journal of Neuroscience Nursing 1997;29:86-100.
10. Foreman M. Acute confusion in the elderly. Annual Review of Nursing Research 1993, 11:3-30.
11. Francis J, Martin D, Kapoor W. Prospective study of delirium in hospitalized elderly. Journal of the American Medical Association 1990, 263: 1097-1101.
12. Inouye S, Viscoli C, Horwitz R, Hurst L,Tinetti M. A predictive model for delirium in hospitalized elderly medical patients based on admission characteristics. Annuals of Internal Medicine 1993; 119: 474-481.
13. Kuroda S, Ishizu H, Ujike H, Otsuki S, Mitsunobu K, Chuda M, Yamamoto M. Senile delirium with special reference to situational factors and recurrent delirium. Acta Medica Okayama 1990; 44: 267-272.
14. Pompei P, Foreman M, Rudberg M, Inouye S, Braund V, Cassel C. Delirium in hospitalized older persons: Outcomes and predictors. Journal of the American Geriatrics Society 1994; 42: 809 815.
15. Rockwood K. The occurrence and duration of symptoms in elderly patients with delirium. Journal of Gerontology: Medical Sciences, 1993; 48: M162-166.
16. Schor J, Levkoff S, Lipsitz L, Reilly C, Cleary P, Rowe J, Evans D. Risk factors for delirium in hospitalized elderly. Journal of the American Medical Association,1992; 267: 827 831.
17. Sirois F. Delirium: 100 cases. Canadian Journal of Psychiatry, 1988;33: 375 378.
18. Levkoff S, Evans D, Liptzin B, Cleary P, Lipsitz L, Wetle T, Reilly C, Pilgrim P, Schor J, Rowe J. Delirium. The occurrence and persistence of symptoms among elderly hospitalized patients. Archives of Internal Medicine, 1992;152: 334-340.
19. Warren J, Bacon E, Harris T, McBean A, Foley D, Phillips C. The burden and outcomes associated with dehydration among U.S. elderly, 1991. American Journal of Public Health, 1994; 84: 1265-1269.
20. Inouye S. The dilemma of delirium: Clinical and research controversies regarding diagnosis and evaluation of delirium in hospitalized elderly medical patients. The American Journal of Medicine, 1994; 97: 278-288.
21. Neelon V, Champagne M, McConnell E, Carlson J, Funk S. The 24 hour effects of pattern–specific

interventions to reduce acute confusion in hospitalized elderly. Gerontologist, 1994; 34: (Abstract).

22. Seymour D, Henschke P, Cape R, Campbell A. Acute confusional states and dementia in the elderly: The role of dehydration/volume depletion, physical illness and age. Age and Ageing, 1980; 9: 137-146.

23. Williams M, Campbel, E, Raynor W, Musholt M, Mlynarczyk S, Crane L. Predictors of acute confusional states in elderly patients. Research in Nursing & Health, 1985; 8: 31-40.

24. Budd S, Brown W. Effect of a reorientation technique on postcardiotomy delirium. Nursing Research, 1974; 23: 341-348.

25. Williams M, Campbell E, Raynor W, Mlynarczyk S, Ward S. Reducing acute confusional states in elderly patients with hip fractures. Research in Nursing and Health, 1985; 8: 329-337.

26. Bay E, Kupfershmidt B, Opperwall B, Speer J. Effect of the family visit on the patient's–mental status. Focus on Critical Care, 1988; 15 (1): 10-16.

27. Chatham M. The effect of family involvement on patient's manifestations of post- cardiotomy psychosis Heart & Lung, 1978; 7: 995-999.

28. Owens J, Hutelmyer C. The effect of preoperative intervention on delirium in cardiac surgical patients. Nursing Research, 1982; 31: 60-62.

29. Nagley S. Predicting and preventing confusion in your patients. Journal of Gerontological Nursing, 1986; 12 (3): 27-31.

30. Gustafson Y, Brannstrom B, Berggren D, Ragnarsson J, Sigaard J, Bucht G, Reiz S, Norberg A, Winblad B. A geriatric anesthesiologic program to reduce acute confusional states in elderly patients treated for femoral neck fractures. Journal of the American Geriatrics Society, 1991; 39: 655-662.

31. Wanich C, Sullivan Marx E, Gottlieb G, Johnson J. Functional status outcomes of a nursing intervention in hospitalized elders. Image,1992; 24: 201-207.

32. Cole M, Primeau J, Bailey R, Bonnycastle M, Masciarelli F, Engelsmann F, Pepin M, Ducic D. Systematic intervention for elderly inpatients with delirium: A randomized trial. Canadian Medical Association Journal, 1994; 151: 965-970.

33. Rockwood K, Cosway S, Stolee P, Kydd D, Carver D, Jarrett P, O'Brien B. Increasing the recognition of delirium in elderly patients. Journal of the American Geriatrics Society, 1994; 42: 252-256.

34. Wakefield B. Acute confusion in hospitalized elderly veterans. Paper presented at the annual research conference of the Midwest Nursing Research Society, Detroit, MI, 1996, April.

35. Lavizzo Mourey R. Dehydration in the elderly: A short review. Journal of the National Medical Association, 1987; 79:1033-1038.

36. Silver A. Aging and risks for dehydration. Cleveland Clinic Journal of Medicine, 1990;57:341 344.

37. Colling J, Owen T, McCreedy M. Urine volumes and voiding patterns among incontinent nursing home residents. Geriatric Nursing, 1994; 15(4): 188-192.

38. Himmelstein D, Jones A, Woolhandler S. Hypernatremic dehydration in nursing home patients. An indicator of neglect. Journal of the American Geriatrics Society, 1983; 31:466-471.

39. Weinberg A, Minaker K, The Council on Scientific Affairs, AMA. Dehydration. Evaluation and Management in older adults Journal of the American Medical Association, 1995; 274:1562-1556.

40. Gross C, Lindquist R, Anthony W, Granieri R, Allard K, Webster B. Clinical indicators of dehydration severity in elderly patients. The Journal of Emergency Medicine, 199210:267-274.

41. Weinberg A, Pals J, McGlinchey Berroth R, Minaker K. Indices of dehydration among frail nursing home patients: Highly variable but stable over time. Journal of the American Geriatrics Society, 1994; 10:1070-1073.

42. Field M, Lohr K. (Eds.). Clinical practice guidelines. Directions for a new program. Washington, D.C.: National Academy Press, 1990.

43. Field M. (Ed). Setting priorities for clinical practice guidelines. Washington, D.C. National Academy Press, 1995.

44. Taler G. Clinical practice guidelines: Their purposes and uses. Journal of the America Geriatrics Society, 1996; 44:1108-1111.

45. Katz P, Ouslander J. Clinical practice guidelines and position statements: The American Geriatrics Society approach. Journal of the American Geriatrics Society, 1996; 44:1123-1124.

46. Phillips P, Rolls B, Ledingham J, Forsling M, Morton J, Crowe M, Wollner L. Reduced thirst after water deprivation in healthy elderly men. New England Journal of Medicine, 1984; 311: 753-759.

47. Phillips P, Bretherton M, Johnson C, Gray L. Reduced osmotic thirst in healthy elderly men. American Journal of Physiology, 1991; 261: R166-R171.

48. Adams, F. How much do elders drink? Geriatric Nursing, 1988; 9 (4): 218-221.

49. Lavisso Mourey R, Johnson J, Stolley P. Risk factors for dehydration among elderly nursing home residents. Journal of the American Geriatrics Society, 1988; 36:213-218.

50. O'Neill P, Davies I, Wears R, Barrett J. Elderly female patients in continuing care: Why are they

hyperosmolar? Gerontology, 1989; 35:205-209.

51. Gaspar P. What determines how much patients drink? Geriatric Nursing, 1988; 9 (4):221–224.

52. Armstrong L, Maresh C, Castellani J, Bergeron M, Kenefick R, LaGasse K, Riebe D. Urinary indices of hydration status. International Journal of Sport Nutrition, 1994; 4:265-279.

53. Francesconi RP, Hubbard RW, Szlyk PC, Schnakenberg D, Carlson D, Leva N, Sils I, Hubbard L, Pease V, Young J, Moore D. Urinary and hematologic indexes of hypohydration. Journal of Applied Physiology, 1987; 62:1271-1276.

54. Reedy D. How can you prevent dehydration? Geriatric Nursing, 1988; 9 (4):224-226.

55. Spangler P, Risley T, Bilyew D. The management of dehydration and incontinence in nonambulatory geriatric patients. Journal of Applied Behavior Analysis, 1984; 17:397-401.

56. Munsson N, Kincaid J, Ryan P, Glussman B, Varone L, Gamarra N, Wilson R, Reefe W, Silverman M. Nature, nurture, nutrition: Interdisciplinary programs to address the prevention of malnutrition and dehydration. Dysphagia, 1990; 5:96-101.

HYDRATION AND AGING

II - RESEARCH

AGING AND THE RENIN-ANGIOTENSIN SYSTEM

L. HORGEN, V. ANDRIEUX, C. BADIER, H. PAGEON, F. GRESSIER, M. REBOUD*, B. CORMAN **.

Université de Marne-la-Vallée, DESS de Biologie et Pharmacologie du Vieillissement, Noisy-le-Grand, 93160, * Institut Jacques Monod, 2 place Jussieu, Paris, 75251 and § Département de Biologie Cellulaire et Moléculaire, CEA, Centre d'Etudes de Saclay, Gif-sur-Yvette, 91191, France. Correspondence should be sent to Bruno Corman, Département de Biologie Cellulaire et Moléculaire, CEA, Centre d'Etudes de Saclay, Gif-sur-Yvette, 91191, France. Tel : 01 69 08 63 99, Fax : 01 69 08 35 70

Abstract : *The decrease in the renin-angiotensin system activity with age is a regular observation in man as in rodents. Different investigators have tried to dissect the underlying mechanisms of this drop in activity and its consequences on the responsiveness of the renal and cardiovascular systems. The age-related decrease in intrarenal renin activity results from a reduce content of renin in individual nephron independently of any loss of nephrons. The constant content of renin mRNA in old kidney suggests that this decrease in renin activity is due to an alteration in translation of renin mRNA or in maturation of the protein. The plasma concentrations of angiotensin I converting enzyme and angiotensinogen are barely modified with age and do not appear to be a limiting factor for the production of angiotensin II. However, it does not preclude a change in local tissue activity of the renin-angiotensin system. Different physiological functions seem to be related to the decrease in renin activity. In the kidney, the intrarenal vascular resistances are increased and the vasodilatory reserve is reduced in senescent rats. The ability of the kidney to retain sodium is impaired and correlates with a decrease in the angiotensin II-dependent aldosterone secretion by the adrenals. The vasocontriction of arteries following stimulation by angiotensin II was maintained with age in rat and rabbit. On the other hand, the coupling between the inositol accumulation, intracellular calcium concentration and contraction are modified in the course of aging. The role of the renin-angiotensin system in the aging processes has been tested by* *lifelong chronic inhibition of converting enzyme activity in normotensive animals. In rats, the inhibition of the renin-angiotensin system lowers the blood pressure by 20 mm Hg but did not affect the lifespan of the colony. Some of the identified age-related changes in renal and cardiovascular systems were delayed, but not supressed, by converting enzyme inhibition. It suggests that the involved basic aging mechanisms are independent of the activation of the renin-angiotensin system, and that variations in arterial blood pressure may accelerate (hypertension) or slow-down (hypotension) the outcome of the aging processes.*

The renin-angiotensin system plays a key role in the regulation of blood pressure and hydromineral balance through the control of vascular resistance, aldosterone secretion and kidney function. With age, the activity of this system is decreased as indicated by the drop in plasma renin activity found in elderly as in senescent animals. This decline was suspected to be partly responsible for the age-related reduced ability of the body to face changes in fluid composition. Several investigations on the relationship between the different components of the renin-angiotensin system and the physiological changes with age have been performed in recent years. These data were recently reviewed in man by Belmin et al. [4]. The present review focuses on the data obtained in different experimental models of senescence and their implications in the aging processes.

I - THE RENIN-ANGIOTENSIN SYSTEM

The renin-angiotensin system is the name of the system of substrates and enzymes that gives rise to a major circulating hormone, the angiotensin II. This system is composed of angiotensinogen, renin, angiotensin converting enzyme and of angiotensin I, II, III and 1-7.

Renin is an aspartic proteinase of 40 kDa. This glycoprotein is formed of inactive pre-pro-renin including a 66 residue amino-terminal pre-pro-peptide. The matured pro-form (prorenin) can follow two different pathways. In the protogranules of the myoepithelial cells of the juxtaglomerular apparatus, it can be activated by a serine protease. Then, active renin is stored in secretion granules. It can also be released into the blood flow in this immature form. Renin mRNA has been detected in different tissues such as kidney, liver, heart, adrenal, brain, spleen, ovary, testis or eye. In mammals, however, the kidney is the main synthesis site and appears to be the only activation site of renin.

Angiotensinogen is a 55 kDa α2-globulin, belonging to the serpin family. It is formed of a 24 amino-acid signal peptide and of a mature protein of 452 or 453 amino acids in human and rats respectively. Angiotensinogen is synthesized in the liver, and locally in the brain, arterial wall, kidney, brown adipose tissue, heart and adrenals. It is released from the liver into the blood stream without previous storage or maturation. Its secretion is regulated at the transcriptional level. Renin cleaves the amino terminal decapeptide from angiotensinogen to yield angiotensin I, an inactive peptide. It is noteworthy that renin, conversely to other aspartic proteinases, have a major enzymatic activity at physiological pH. Another interesting characteristic is its remarkably narrow substrate specificity. Other enzymes such as cathepsins are also able to produce angiotensin I from angiotensinogen.

Angiotensin I converting enzyme is a carboxypeptidase which catalyses the removal of the carboxy terminal dipeptide of angiotensin I to form the active octapeptide angiotensin II (Asp-Arg-Val-Tyr-Ile-His-Pro-Phe). Three forms of angiotensin converting enzyme have been described of 140 (circulatory), 90 (testicular) and 160 kDa (membrane-anchored forms). The membrane converting enzyme is present in most epithelial cells and endothelial cells. It is also found in smooth muscles, fibroblasts, endocrine cells and cardiac tissue. The soluble converting enzyme is secreted by vascular endothelium. Converting enzyme is mostly present in pulmonary capillaries and in smaller amounts in other organs. Angiotensin II is converted to angiotensin III and angiotensin 1-7 by peptidases. Angiotensin III still displays biological activity, but is less efficient than angiotensin II which is thought to have the greatest biological significance.

Two distinct angiotensin receptor subtypes - AT1 and AT2 - have been pharmacologically characterized. They belong to the family of 7 transmembrane domains receptors. AT_{1A} receptors mediate most of the known biological effects of angiotensin II through activation of phospholipase C, release of diacylglycerol and increase in intracellular calcium. AT2 receptor has been localized in blood vessels from immature animals, in brain and adrenals of adults. The angiotensin II concentration is the main factor regulating the membrane density of the receptors.

II - AGE-RELATED CHANGES IN THE DIFFERENT COMPONENTS OF THE RENIN-ANGIOTENSIN SYSTEM.

2.1. Renin

Most of the experimental sudies on aging of the renin-angiotensin system indicate that plasma renin activity (PRA) decreases with age. The origin of this age-related reduction in PRA is still unknown. A decline in PRA could be caused by an increase in renin clearance or a decrease in the ability of the kidney to secrete or synthesize active renin. A change in synthesis may be related to a difference in transcription, translation or maturation of the protein.

One of the first questions which comes to mind is whether the decrease in PRA observed in the course of aging results from a loss of nephrons or from morphological or functional alteration of each juxtaglomerular apparatus. This point was addressed by Hayashi et al. [13] who dissected individual superficial and juxtamedullary glomeruli and determined their renin content. The PRA of the male Wistar rats they used decreased by half from 3-6 months to 13-18 months (fig1). Concomitantly, the mean values of both superficial and juxtamedullary single nephron renin content was reduced in the oldest group (fig1). These results sugests that the low plasma renin activity reported in old animals is related to a reduction in the renin content of each juxtaglomerular apparatus rather than to a reduction in the number of nephrons.

Fig 1

Mean values of plasma renin activity (PRA) and single nephron renin content in 3-6 and 13-18 month-old rats (from Hayashi et al , 13).

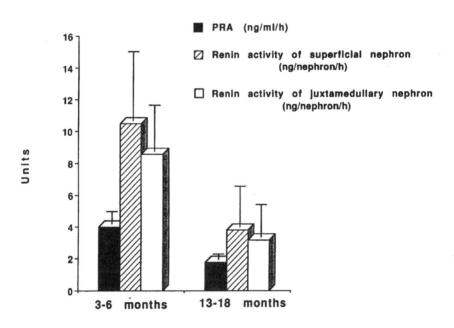

Different mechanisms can be proposed to explain this decrease in single nephron content of renin. One is associated with the glomerulosclerosis frequently observed in aging kidney which would result in the destruction of the glomeruli. The relationship between the extent of this disease and the decrease in plasma renin activity has been investigated by Magro et al. [21]. They exploited the difference in the progression of glomerulosclerosis in two rat strains - Wistar and Fawn-Hooded - to correlate plasma renin activity with the histopathologic score of the kidney. The Fawn-Hooded rats, which developed a significant score as early as 4 months, exhibited a drop in PRA in the first part of life which correlated with renal disease (fig 2). The Wistar rats whose progression of renal disease was delayed compared with the Fawn-Hooded animals, exhibited a later decrease in PRA, and the drop in PRA also correlated with renal histopathologic score. These experiments would suggest that glomerulosclerosis is the cause of the decrease in single nephron renin content in aging rats.

Fig 2

Relationship between histopathologic score and plasma renin activity in aging males Fawn-Hooded and Wistar rats (from Magro et al , 21).

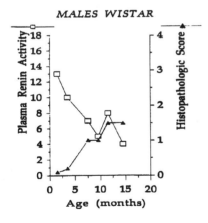 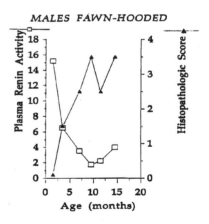

This conclusion was challenged by a study on age-related changes in the activity of the renin-angiotensin system, in which care was taken to obtain senescent animals free of chronic progressive nephrosis [7]. In these normotensive WAG/Rij rats, there was no evidence of glomerulosclerosis until the age of 30 months, and the number of nephrons remained constant. The plasma renin activity and plasma renin concentration of the 30 month-old animals were decreased to one fourth that of the 3 month-old rats. Renal renin content was halved in the same time. These data indicated that the age-related decrease in plasma and renal renin activity may be independent of the development of glomerulosclerosis. The fall in plasma renin activity was commensurate with a reduced plasma concentration of angiotensin II [9].

Some information on the cause of this drop in intrarenal renin content was brought from the quantification of renin mRNA in kidneys of 5 to 37 month-old male c57BL/6J mice performed by Hung and Richardson [16]. These authors found by northern blot analysis that the size of renin mRNA hybridized by a cDNA probe was unchanged with age. The total amount of renin mRNA did not change significantly from 5 to 29 months and decreased thereafter. It was concluded that the drop in renin activity is related to a change in translation up to 29 months and to a fall in transcription at the very end of life between 30 and 37 months.

Such a reduction in renin synthesis can be linked to an unspecific decline in kidney protein synthesis, as reported by Ricketts et al. [25] from the incorporation of radioactive valine by kidney cells isolated from adult and senescent rats. In animals fed ad libitum, a reduction in protein synthesis did correlate with the progression of renal disease in the oldest animals. However, rats which were protected from kidney disease by diet restriction had a preserved capacity for protein synthesis, suggesting that impaired synthesis is associated with kidney disease but not with kidney aging.

The relationship between renin synthesis and renin mRNA in rats free of renal disease, and presumably unchanged synthesis ability, was recently investigated [9]. Intrarenal renin mRNA measured by the reverse transcriptase and polymerase chain reaction was unchanged from 10 to 30 months. Intrarenal renin activity measured in the same kidney decreased by 50% during this period. On the whole, these experiments suggest that the decrease in renin activity reported in the course of aging is due to an alteration in translation of renin mRNA or in maturation of the protein, independently of any glomerular injury.

2.2. Angiotensin I converting enzyme

The activity of converting enzyme in plasma of aging rats has been measured in several conditions. In female WAG/Rij rats, converting enzyme activity was unchanged with age [7]. In males of the same strain, a small (-15%), but significant, decline in plasma converting enzyme activity was noticed [23]. The role of thyroidal status and food intake on converting enzyme activity with age was assessed by Mooridian and Lieberman in male Fisher 344 rats [22]. They failed to find any change in the plasma activity of the enzyme from 6 to 25 months whether the animals were experimentally rendered hypothyroid or hyperthyroid and whatever their food intake. These studies concluded that angiotensin I converting enzyme plasma activity is not a limiting factor for the production of angiotensin II in the course of aging. This, of course, does not preclude a cellular change in tissue activity of converting enzyme.

2.3. Angiotensinogen

Plasma angiotensinogen production is mainly unchanged or slightly reduced with age. Like converting enzyme, the plasma renin substrate angiotensinogen does not appear to be a limiting factor for the production of angiotensin II. Nevertheless, angiotensinogen is also synthesized locally in different tissues where the production of angiotensin II could take place. In this respect, Eggena et al. [10] examined the age-related changes in the production of angiotensinogen in cultured vascular smooth muscle cells derived from 3, 12 and 24 month-old Fischer 344 rats. The production of angiotensinogen was quantified by measurement of angiotensin I production after incubation with homologous rat renin. As shown in fig 3, a two-fold increase in angiotensinogen production by the cells was noted in 24 month-old animals as compared with the 3 and 12 month-old rats. This local rise of the angiotensinogen level could partially compensate the age-related fall of plasma renin and result in greater formation of angiotensin II than anticipated from the plasma concentration. Tissue activation of angiotensinogen synthesis has also been identified in hearts of senescent rats. Heymes et al. [15] quantified the mRNA of angiotensinogen and converting enzyme in the left and right ventricle of 3 and 24 month-old Wistar rats. A specific and parallel activation of the expression of angiotensinogen and converting enzyme gene was found in the left ventricle, while no change was noticed in the right one (fig 4). This specific localisation of gene activation in the left ventricle led to hypothesize a mechanical - such as decreased arterial compliance with age - rather than hormonal origin for this increase in gene expression.

Fig 3

Angiotensinogen production by primary culture of smooth muscle cells isolated from artery of 3-12 and 24 month-old rats (from Eggena et al, 10). * different from 3 and 12 months.

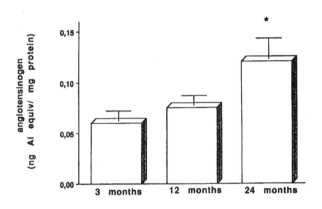

Fig 4

Angiotensinogen and angiotensin converting enzyme mRNA in right and left ventricles of 3 and 24 month-old Wistar rats (from Heymes et al, 15).

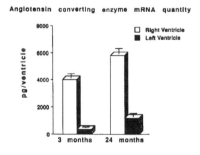

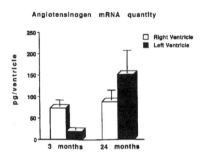

III - THE RENIN-ANGIOTENSIN SYSTEM AND THE CONTROL OF PHYSIOLOGICAL FUNCTIONS

3.1. Kidney hemodynamic

The kidney is one of the target organs for angiotensin II which contributes to the regulation of renal blood flow, glomerular filtration rate and filtration fraction. The perfusion of angiotensin II and the use of antagonists of AT1 receptors have been employed to test the vasoconstrictive response and the vasodilatory reserve of old kidneys. This aspect of renal function was investigated by Tank et al. [26] in 3 and 15 month-old male Sprague-Dawley rats known for their high incidence of glomerulosclerosis with age. In control conditions, glomerular filtration rate and renal blood flow were decreased in old animals according to the extent of proteinuria and glomerulosclerosis. Intrarenal resistance was lower in 15 month-old animals despite a nearly constant mean arterial pressure. Infusion of angiotensin II or endothelin induced comparable pressor response in both young and old rats. By contrast, the decrease in glomerular filtration rate and in renal blood flow with increasing intrarenal resistance following such infusion was larger in old animals. The administration of Losartan, an antagonist of angiotensin II receptor, induced a similar renal vasodilatory response. The authors concluded that old kidneys with evidence of glomerulosclerosis exhibit exaggerated responses to systemic vasoconstrictor stimuli, whereas responsiveness to angiotensin II blockade is preserved but not enhanced.

Somewhat different conclusions were reached by Baylis [3] in comparable experiments performed in conscious chronically catheterized 3-5 and 19-22 month-old Sprague Dawley rats. Acute blockade of endogenous angiotensin II with Losartan or converting enzyme inhibition caused small decreases in blood pressure in both groups and produced significant vasodilatation with increased renal plasma flow in the older rats. Perfusion of a high dose of angiotensin induced significant and similar increases in blood pressure and renal vascular resistance in old and young animals. It was inferred that the renal hemodynamic in the old kidney is controlled by endogenous angiotensin II and that renal vascular sensitivity to the administration of angiotensin II is unaltered with age.

Few data are available on the renal response to angiotensin II in aging rats free of renal disease. Evidence of a reduced vasodilatory reserve of senescent kidney is supported by the lack of postprandial hyperfiltration in 30 month-old animals as compared with the 50 % increase in glomerular filtration rate after food ingestion in adult rats [8]. The role of angiotensin II in maintening baseline renal hemodynamic has been tested by acute inhibition of converting enzyme activity by perindopril in female WAG/Rij rats [7]. In adult animals, the administration of perindopril has a vasodilatory effect resulting in decreased blood pressure and increased renal blood flow and glomerular filration rate. In the 30 month-old animals, in which the activity of the renin-angiotensin system was markedly reduced, the inhibition of converting enzyme activity did not modify the mean blood pressure, renal blood flow or filtration rate. It was concluded that, in aging rats without evidence of chronic progressive nephrosis, the renal vasodilatory reserve is reduced and the baseline renal hemodynamic is no longer controlled by angiotensin II.

3.2. Renal adaptation to sodium restriction

In response to dietary sodium restriction, the renal reabsorption of sodium is increased and its urinary excretion is sharply decreased in a few days. This rapid adjustment is accompanied by the release of aldosterone, which is itself under the control of angiotensin II. The renal response to sodium restriction and the activation of the renin-angiotensin-aldosterone system have been compared in adult and senescent female Wistar rats [18]. The cumulative loss of sodium during the first 6 days of salt restriction was increased by a factor 2 in 30 month-old animals as compared with 10 month-old rats, indicating a reduced renal ability to retain sodium. Plasma renin activity remained lower throughout the restriction period in the senescent animals. Simultaneously, as shown in fig 5, the increase in aldosterone secretion following sodium restriction was blunted in the oldest animals, indicating an impaired stimulation of adrenal cortex by angiotensin II. The hypothesis of a reduced response of adrenal tissue to angiotensin II was tested in vivo by Rakotondrazafy and Brudieux (24) and in vitro by Belloni et al. [5]. In vivo, perfusion of a low dose of angiotensin II elicited a three fold increase in plasma aldosterone of adult female Long Evans rats (table 1). The same dose of angiotensin II failed to induce a significant aldosterone release in 28-32 month-old animals. Perfusion of high doses of angiotensin II was followed by a rise in plasma aldosterone in both adult and senescent rats, but the increment was halved in the oldest group. These results are in agreement with the in vitro data of Belloni et al. who found that the angiotensin II stimulated secretion of aldosterone by isolated adrenal glomerula cells is reduced in aging rats.

Table 1
Age-related changes in plasma aldosterone response to exogenous angiotensin II in 12 adults (8-10 months) and 9 old (28-32 months) rats. (from Rokatondrazafy and Brudieux, 23)

	Basal conditions pmol/l	20 ng/min of AII pmol/l	300 ng/min of AII pmol/l
adults	203 ± 39	619 ± 114	2617 ± 400
old	266 ± 42	408 ± 86	1102 ± 158

Fig 5
Effect of salt restriction on urinary aldosterone excretion in 10, 20 and 30 months old rats (from Jover et al , 18). * different from the aldosterone values in normal sodium diet.

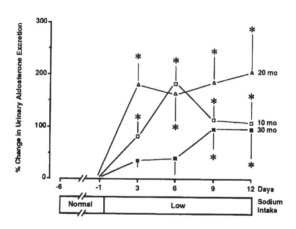

3.3. Vascular reactivity

The effect of aging on the reactivity of ear and skeletal muscle arteries has been tested in vitro in 6 to 48 month-old female rabbits [20]. The life span of this rabbit colony was 5 to 6 years. At rest, in the absence of agonist, there was no difference in strip length for a constant 100 mg tension. The addition of angiotensin II induced a similar maximum developed force from 6 to 48 month-old animals. The mean values of the dose reponse curve showed that the concentration required to reach half maximum tension was constant for each age group. The author concluded that there were no consistant age-related changes in the reactivity to angiotensin II of small vessel from female rabbit .

Similar parameters were tested in aortic strips of 4 and 22 month-old male Wistar rats [27]. The vasoconstrictive response to angiotensin II was not altered in the aging rats. The relationship between vascular response and inositol phosphate accumulation by angiotensin II was further compared in male Fischer 344 rats. The contraction of rings isolated from the thoracic aorta was similar between 6 and 24 months for all angiotensin II concentrations tested [6]. By contrast, inositol phosphate accumulation for a maximal dose of angiotensin II was one third lower in the aorta of 24 month-old rats as compared with 6 month-old rats (fig 6). On the other hand, a high concentration of angiotensin II induced an identical contraction and inositol accumulation in the tail artery of adult and old animals. This tends to indicate that the coupling between inositol phosphate and vasoconstriction is modified with age in large arteries such as the thoracic aorta.

Fig 6

Inositol phosphate accumulation induced by 1 µM of angiotensin II. The values are expressed as a % of the values from unstimulated aortic segments (from Cai et al , 6). The basal counts for unstimulated aortic segments of 6 and 24 months old rats are 1721 ± 320 and 1134 ± 373 counts per minute, and for tail artery 1424 ± 132 and 1115 ± 267 counts per minute respectively. *: significantly different from 6 months.

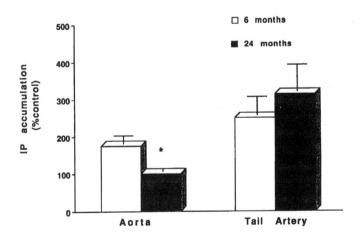

IV - EFFECT OF CHRONIC INHIBITION OF THE RENIN-ANGIOTENSIN SYSTEM ON AGING PROCESSES

The positive effect of chronic converting enzyme inhibition (CEI) on survival and age-related changes in renal and cardiovascular systems has been well documented in different models of hypertension, heart failure and renal disease, whereas the influence of CEI on normal aging was just recently investigated. At least three studies dealing with the effect of lifelong CEI are available.

In normotensive mice, Ferder et al. [11, 12, 17] reported that treatment by enalapril from weaning to 24 months increased the lifespan of the animals. The survival was 15% at 24 months in the control group and reached 70% in the treated group. The main effects of enalapril on the heart and kidney were a lowering of cardiac weight, a decrease in myocardial and glomerular sclerosis, and an increase in the number of mitochondria in myocardiocytes. No difference was found in the diameter of the internal arteries, but the media thickness was reduced in the experimental group.

The effect of long term CEI in renal function of normotensive male Munich-Wistar rats has been studied by Anderson et al.[1]. In this strain of rats, glomeruli are accessible at the surface of the kidney, allowing determination of single glomerular hemodynamic. The animals were treated from 3 to 29 months and functional and morphological determinations were performed at the end of the experiments. Chronic CEI by enalapril markedly delayed the rise in albumin excretion as compared with the untreated control group. The reported age-related increase in glomerular capillary hydraulic pressure and the reduction in filtration coefficient were normalized by chronic CEI. The development of glomerulosclerosis, which was moderate in this strain (8% of the glomeruli at 29 months) was also prevented by CEI.

A comparable protocol was designed in normotensive male WAG/Rij rats with perindopril as a converting enzyme inhibitor [2, 14, 19, 23]. The treatment was started at 6 months and changes in the structure and the function of renal and cardiovascular systems were checked at 12, 24 and 30 months. Chronic CEI inhibited the plasma activity of the converting enzyme and lowered the blood pressure by 20 mm Hg throughout the treatment. The mean survival ages of treated and untreated rats were similar and close to 27 months. The most interesting result was that the actual aging processes were not modified by CEI and reduction in blood pressure, but the consequences of these processes were frequently postponed. Some of this beneficial effect of CEI on different organs are shown in table 2 and in fig 7 for intrarenal vascular resistance. This shift in the age-related changes of heart, vessel and kidney suggest that the involved basic aging mechanisms are independent of the activation of the renin-angiotensin system and blood pressure. However, variations in arterial pressure can accelerate (hypertension), or slow-down (hypotension), the outcome of these aging mechanisms.

Table 2

Examples of age-related changes of the renal and cardiovascular systems which are postponed by chronic converting enzyme inhibition (from 2, 14, 23).

Kidney
     rise in intrarenal vascular resistance
     deposit of albumin droplet in podocytes
     expansion of mesangial domain
     proteinuria
     progression of focal and segmental glomerulosclerosis

Cardiovascular system
     decrease in endothelial function
     reduction in carotid compliance
     increase in medial and intimal thickening
     increase in the lower limit of cerebral blood flow autoregulation
     cardiac hypertrophy

Fig 7

Effect of chronic converting enzyme inhibition by perindopril on the age related changes in intra-renal vascular resistance. Experiment were performed on male WAG/Rij rats (from Heudes et al., 14).

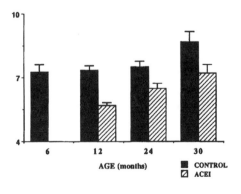

INTRA-RENAL VASCULAR RESISTANCE (mm Hg/ml/min)

In conclusion, the available experimental data on aging of the renin-angiotensin system indicate that the renal and plasma activity of renin decreases with age. This reduced activity is not due to a loss of nephrons or to the incidence of renal disease, but appears to be related to an intrinsic aging mechanism. A change in renin mRNA translation or in the maturation of active renin may be the cause of this drop. The consequence is a reduced plasma concentration of angiotensin II. However, local up-regulation of angiotensinogen or converting enzyme activity may partially compensate for the reduction in plasma renin activity in some tissues. The reduced activity of the renin-angiotensin system may contribute to the loss of adaptation to sodium restriction, the decreased functional reserve of the kidney and the decrease control of vasoreactivity. Data on chronic converting enzyme inhibition in normotensive animals indicated that intrinsic aging of the renal and cardiovascular system is independent of the renin-angiotensin system, but that its inhibition may postpone the consequences of the normal aging.

REFERENCES

1. Anderson S., H.G. Rennke, R. Zatz. Glomerular adaptations with normal aging and with long-term converting enzyme inhibition in rats. Am. J. Physiol. F35-42, 1994.
2. Atkinson J., T. Rabelais, B. Corman. Effect of chronic ANG I-converting-enzyme inhibition on aging processes. III: endothelial fonction of mesenteric arterial bed of rat. Am. J. Physiol.: 267:R136-R143, 1994.
3. Baylis C. Renal responses to acute angiotensin II inhibition and administered angiotensin II in the aging, conscious, chronically catheterized rat. Am. J. Kidney Dis. 22(6):842-50, 1993.
4. Belmin J., B.I. Lévy, J.B. Michel. Changes in the renin angiotensin-aldosterone axis in the laterlife. Drugs and Aging 5(5):391-400:1994
5. Belloni A.S., P. Rebuffat, L.K. Malendowicz, G. Mazzocchi, S. Rocco, G.G. Nussdorfer. Age-related changes in the morphology and function of the zona glomerulosa of the rat adrenal cortex. Tissue and Cell.: 24(6): 835-842, 1992.
6. Cai G., H. Gurdal, T.M. Seasholtz, M.D. Johnson. Age related changes in angiotensin II-stimulated vascular contraction and inositol phosphate accumulation in Fisher 344 rats. Mech. Ageing Dev.: 76:125-133, 1994.
7. Corman B., J.B. Michel. Renin-angiotensin system, converting-enzyme inhibition, and kidney function in aging female rats. Am. J. Physiol.: 251: R450-R455, 1986.
8. Corman B., S. Chami-Khazraji , J. Shaeverbeke , J.B. Michel . Effect of feeding on glomerular filtration rate and proteinuria in conscious rats. Am. J . Physiol: 255: F250-F256 ,1988
9. Corman B., M.B. Barrault , C. Klingler , A.M. Houot , J.B. Michel , R. Della Bruna , F. Pinet , F. Soubrier. Renin gene expresion in the aging kidney :effect of sodium restriction. Mech. Ageing Dev. 84, 1-13, 1995.
10. Eggena P. , A.M. Morin , J.D. Barett., J.F. Krall. The influence of aging on angiotensinogen production by rat vascular smooth muscle cells in vitro. Clin. and Exp. Hyper. : A10(4): 597-603, 1988.
11. Ferder L., F. Inserra, L. Romano, L. Ercole, V. Pszenny. Effects of angiotensin converting enzyme inhibition on mitochondrial number in the aging mouse. Am. J . Physiol.: 65:C215-C218, 1993.
12. Ferder L., F. Inserra, L. Romano, L. Ercole, V. Pszenny. Decreased of glomerulosclerosis in aging by angiotensin-converting-enzyme inhibition. J. Am. Soc. Nephrol.: 5:1147-1152, 1994.
13. Hayashi M., T. Satura, R. Nakamura, W. Kitajima, E. Kato. Effect of aging on single nephron renin content in rats. Renal Physiol.: 4:17-21, 1981.
14. Heudes D., O. Michel, J. Chevalier, E. Scalbert, E. Ezan, J. Bariety, A. Zimmerman, B. Corman. Effect of chronic ANG I converting enzyme inhibition on aging processes. I: kidney structure and

function. Am. J. Physiol.: 266: R1038-R1051, 1994.

15. Heymes C. , B. Swinghedauw , B. Chevalier. Activation of angiotensinogen and angiotensin-converting enzyme gene expression in the left ventricle of senescent rats. Circulation : 90(3):1328-1333, 1994.

16. Hung L. , A. Richardson. The effect of aging on the genetic expression of renin by mouse kidney. Aging Clin. Exp. Res.: 5:193-198, 1993.

17. Inserra F. , L. Romano., L. Ercole., E.M.V. De Cavanagh , L. Ferder. Cardiovascular changes by long term inhibition of the renin -angiotensin sytem in aging . Hypertension :25(3) :437-442:1995

18. Jover B., M. Dupont, G. Geelen, W. Wahba, A. Mimram, B. Corman. Renal and systemic adaptation to sodium restriction in aging rats. Am. J Phys.: 265 (33)R833-R838, 1993.

19. Kreher P., M.T. Ristori , B. Corman, J. Verdetti. Effects of chronic angiotensin I - converting enzyme inhibition on the relation between ventricular action potential changes and myocardial hypertrophy in aging rats. J. Cardiovasc. Pharmacol.: 25:75-80, 1995.

20. Lon Owen T..Reactivity of small vessels from mature to senescent female rabbits . Blood Vessels 22:172-178: 1985

21. Magro A.M., U.H. Rudofsky. Plasma renin activity decrease precedes spontaneous focal glomerular sclerosis in aging rats. Nephron : 31:245-253 , 1982.

22. Mooradian A.D. , J. Lieberman. Age related decrease in serum angiotensin-converting enzyme activity: the role of thyroidal status and food intake. J. Geront.: 45:B24-B27, 1990.

23. Michel J.B., D. Heudes, O. Michel, P. Poitevin, M. Philippe, E. Scalbert, B. Corman, B.I. Levy. Effect of chronic ANG I-converting-enzyme inhibition on aging processes. II: large arteries. Am. J. Physiol.: 267:R124-R135, 1994.

24. Rakotondrazafy J., R. Brudieux. Age related change in plasma aldosterone response to exogenous angiotensin II in the rat. Horm. Res.: 76: 125-133, 1994.

25. Ricketts W.G., M.C. Birchevall-Sparks, J.P. Hardwick, A. Richardson. Effect of age and dietary restriction synthesis by isolated kidney cells. J. Cell. Physiol.: 125: 492-498, 1985.

26. Tank J.E., J.P. Vora, D.C. Houghton, S. Anderson. Altered renal vascular responses in the aging rat kidney. Am. J. Physiol.: 266:(35) F942-F948, 1994.

27. Wakabayashi, K. Sakamoto, K. Hatake, S. Yoshimoto, M. Kurahashi. Effect of age on contractile response to angiotensin II in rat aorta. Life Science. 47 (9):771-779, 1990.

PATHOPHYSIOLOGY OF HYPODIPSIA
IN THE ELDERLY

M. H. HORANI, J. E. MORLEY

Geriatric Research Education and Clinical Center St Louis University Health Center 1402 South Grand Bvd, Room M236 St Louis MO 631041028 USA

INTRODUCTION

Water has multiple functions in our body including transport, removal of metabolic waste products, normal cell functions and maintenance of normal body temperature. And it is so much part of our life that we can't survive without the natural defense mechanisms which maintain balance between water input and output. These mechanisms are consist predominantly of a balance maintained between thirst, antidiuretic hormone, and the kidney. The integration of these safety devices tends to decease with normal aging process as many other adaptive performances do with age (Coper et al 1986).

I - PHYSIOLOGY OF THIRST

Thirst is a motivational state in which there is a sensation of a need for water because of changes in body fluid. This sensation leads to a motivated behavior of drink. But thirst is not the only drive to drink, there are other urges to drink even if we are not thirsty. A clear example for this, is the craving for water we experience after eating spicy food or after excessive speaking or smoking. We may divide drinking into primary or regulatory drinking, when there is a relative or absolute deficit in water in one of body compartments, and secondary or nonregulatory drinking when there is no immediate need for water. The later kind of drinking enables the animal to shorten the time of its exposure to predators, by drinking in anticipation of future need for water while eating [1]. The physiological stimuli for thirst are divided into osmotic and nonosmotic:

a- Osmotic thirst: Thirst is regulated largely by plasma tonicity. This control appears to be mediated by a collection of osmosensitive neurons located in the ventromedial and anterior hypothalamus. These osmoreceptors are very close but not identical to those that mediate vasopressin secretion [2- 3] .The regulatory systems for both thirst and vasopressin secretions are very alike except for the osmolar threshold which activate each of them, this threshold is higher for thirst (290 mosm/kg) than for vasopressin secretion(280mosm/kg) [4].

The usual sensation of thirst in a normal person is the result of a 1 to 2 percent contraction of total body water, with a considerable rise in the osmolality of body fluids and slight cellular dehydration.The changes intracellular volume of osmosensitive neuron produce an electrical impulse which, in turn generates thirst and stimulates vasopressin secretion. This stimulation follows the rise in osmolality caused by solutes that do not freely penetrate the cell. The integration of vasopressin release and thirst is essential to assure the maintenance of a normal water contents and osmolality in the body fluid.

b- Nonosmotic Thirst: Thirst may also result from nonosmotic stimuli, some of which also stimulate vasopressin secretion. At the top of the list of these stimuli is hypovolemia and/or hypotension. This hemodynamic stimulation is mediated by a neural baroregulatory system that consists of left atrial and arterial baroreceptor and the renin - angiotensin system [5-6]. We see this kind of stimulation even in iso- osmotic contractions of the extracellular fluids, such as hemorrhage, vomiting, diarrhea, and rapid accumulation of the fluids in the third space (ascites) [7].

Another significant drive for Thirst is renin- angiotensin system which can cause thirst even when normal osmolality exists and the blood pressure is normal or elevated. This seen clearly in severe thirst in patients with malignant hypertension or chronic renal failure in which the thirst can be relieved by nephrectomy [8]. Researchers have found intrinsic renin- angiotensin system in the brain, which appears to be the reason why not only angiotensin II acts as dipsogen but also the other components of this system (renin, Angiotensin I). [9,10]

II - THIRST IN TH ELDERLY

Characteristic of the normal aging process are changes in the hemostatic system that increase the elderly individuals risk for dysfunction. With age, total body water falls, (17% decrease in women from third to eighth decade, 11% decrease in men in the same period). This decrease primarily reflects a decline in intracellular water, as extracellular water remained constant [11].

Several animal studies have been conducted to investigate the effect of aging on water ingestion and thirst. Davies et al [12] found no changes in water intakes in 24 month- old mice compared to 6 month- old mice under periods of deprivation or when challenged with hypertonic saline. Silver et al [13] found that after water deprivation, 20 and 24- month- old rats drank less than three and 12- month - old rats, and the water intake associated with food ingestion was also significantly depressed with advancing age. Nevertheless, this finding was difficult to interpret as there was also a decrease in food ingestion in older rats. In contrast to previous findings Beck et al [14] found that old Fischer rats to be polydipsic compared with younger rats, this discrepancy may be interpreted that there is between strain variability in rats.

It is known that food and water intakes in rodents are entrained to the light /dark cycle, and ingestive behaviors are predominantly nocturnal . Some investigators were interested in the effect of aging on this cycle. Silver et al [13] found that old mice ingested less fluid during the dark period of the circadian cycle compared to younger mice, old mice also consumed less water in response to 18h fluid deprivation. A similar finding was reported by Burwell et al [15] who described a blunted rhythm (decrease amplitude), and an altered time of peak activity in older rats, however, these findings exist in only a subset of aged rats. And like other studies (De koning - Verest et al, gallagher Burwawall et al, peng et al) there was no age difference in over all water consumption. Also the researchers confirmed the results of Gallagher- Burwel (1989) study, that the cognitive decline in aged rats, as determined by the ability to learn a spatial task, was not predictably related to disruption of the diurnal rhythm of drinking.

In human studies, it was shown by Philips et al [16]that water deprived elderly persons did not drink sufficiently to replace their fluid deficit, as young subjects did, in spite of the fact that elderly persons have higher levels of plasma osmolality and a higher plasma sodium concentration, also elderly subjects reported lower levels of thirst and mouth dryness after water deprivation than the younger controls. Crowe et al found that elderly subjects, unlike the young, showed little change in subjective thirst over a 7- hour period following the water load [17].

Thirst in response to heat stress and thermal dehydration was reduced in the older persons [18]. The investigators found also that older men thermoregulated less well than younger men when put in a hot dry chamber for 240 minutes, this occured despite the fact that the sweating was similar in both groups.

Infusion of hypertoni saline has also been used as a stimulus to study thirst and fluid intake in the elderly, Phillips et al reported that older subjects were significantly less thirsty than younger subjects after a 2-hour infusion of hypertonic saline despite similar increases in plasma sodium and osmolality, and the older subjects drank less during 30- min rehydration period. Th concluded that older subjects have a lower thirst sensitivity to hypertonicity and a tendency toward an increased thirst threshold, compared to young subjects [19].

III - THE ETIOLOGY OF HYPODIPSIA IN THE ELDERLY

3.1. Arginine Vasopressin(AVP) Secretion

Administration of AVP into the third ventricle stimulates the intake of water in normally hydrated dogs[20], and the concentration of AVP in cerebrospinal fluid changes in parallel to body fluid osmolality [21, 22]. Several studies have demonstrated the changes of basal levels of AVP with aging, These studies have contradictory results, Some investigators reported a rise in basal AVP in the elderly [23][15][24]. Others found no change[16, 18] or decrease in AVP in the elderly [25,26].

These discrepancies may reflect differences in age distribution, and the lack of standardization of the preexpremental conditions in respect of access to fluid and the amount of fluid ingested.

Also studies concerning the change with aging in AVP response to dehydration have demonstrated contradictory results. Some found that there is a diminished response in the elderly [26] while others found an unchanged [17] .or enhanced response [16]. This disparity may be attributed to differences in prehydration, ages of the subjects, and medical condition of the subjects.

Thirst depends on the normal function of the osmoreceptors to detect dehydration of the cells. So far no study has been conducted to test the change in thirst osmoreceptors with aging, but there are several studies which tested the response of AVP osmoreceptors to hypertonic saline in the elderly. All these studies [27, 28, 29, 30] (except Phillips et al [19]) agree that there is enhanced AVP secretion in the elderly in response to infusion of hypertonic saline, indicating greater sensitivity of the AVP osmoreceptors in old people.

Levels of AVP in the elderly were found by Asplund et al [31] to change according to a seasonal rhythm with highest levels during fall in the elderly males, and during the fall and winter in the elderly females. Hofman and Swaab [32] reported that biosynthesis of AVP in human supra chiasmatic nucleus exhibits a seasonal rhythm that becomes disrupted, and with reduced amplitude in the elderly compared to young people. A circadian rhythm of AVP has also been demonstrated with AVP levels rising at night . In older persons this circadian rhythm is no longer present , resulting in the nocturia commonly seen in older persons [33].

3.2. Renin Angiotensin System

Angiotensin II is a potent dipsogen in a wide variety of species when infused intravenously or when injected into the brain [34]. It is thought to increase the fluid intake, following depletion of extracellular fluid, peripherally (via the vagus nerve) as well as via a direct central effect (on the circumventricular region). Silver et al found that three - month - old rats drank more fluid, after angiotensin was administered, than did 12,20, and 24- month- old rats [35].

Water deprivation enhances plasma renin activity (PRA) in young adults [36] and thirst can be severe when PRA is elevated in association with chronic renal failure. In old persons, despite normal levels of a plasma renin substrate or inactive renin [37, 38], levels of plasma renin and renin activity have been noted to be decline by 30 - 50 %. The renin response to salt restriction, diuretics, and/or upright posture is also impaired in the elderly [39, 40]. It may be concluded that with age there is a decline in the conversion from inactive renin to active renin, which might be, in part, responsible for the decrease in PRA in the elderly.

Weidman et al found slight lower plasma renin activity and aldosterone concentrations in the old age group compared to young in the supine position when receiving normal sodium diet. There was an increase of both renin activity and aldosterone in both groups under the stimuli by upright posture and sodium depletion. However, the mean values were significantly lower in the aged group.

Yamamoto [41] and colleagues demonstrated impaired angiotensin II production in elderly hypernatremic patients. They theorized that this in turn impairs thirst and causes dehydration.

And that the decrease in angiotensin II production is responsible for impaired vasopressin release and renal concentrating capacity. Several studies showed, in contrast to Yamamoto study that there is no change in angiotensin II blood levels with age [42, 43]. A decrease in baroreceptors sensitivity has also been observed in the elderly [24, 44] but it is unknown whether hypovolemic stimuli such as hemorrhage evokes normal thirst in the elderly.

3.3. Hypodipsia and Opioid system

The opioid system plays a role in the physiologic control of the thirst. It seems that opioids exert their effects centrally, particularly at the level of the paraventricular and supra optic hypothalamus [45]. Animal studies showed that opioid agonists increase fluid and food intake while opioid antagonists have the opposite effect. In rodents, the opioid antagonist, naloxone has been effective in decreasing water intake stimulated by hypertonicity,[46] ,hypovolemia [47] , angiotensin II [48], exercise [49], palatable liquids [50], and water deprivation [51]. In addition naloxone, has been shown to decrease plasma renin activity and certain angiotensin II activities [52].

There are few studies about the changes of the opioid system with aging and its effect on the drinking behavior. Kavaliers and Hirst [53] found that naloxone significantly decreases the fluid intake in young mice after 24 - hour - fasting while the intake was only slightly decrease in older mice under same conditions. Similar results were reported by Silver et al [13] in older mice after 18 hour water deprivation.

In their human study Silver et al [54] found that older subjects drank less water, after overnight deprivation, than younger subjects. In the second stage of the study, administration of naloxone led to 51% decrease of water intakes in the younger group, while there was only 10% decrease in older subjects. Stomach fulness was less affected in the old group compared to the young one, which may explain why naloxone caused less decline in the water intake in the old subjects.The researchers suggested that hypodipsia in the elderly may be due to a deficit in the opioid drinking drive. This decline in the sensitivity to suppressive effect of naloxone with age, reflects an actual decrease in brain levels of opioid peptides [55] and opioid receptors [56]

3.4. Oropharyngeal Factors

It is well established that some preabsorbtive factors, such as oropharyngeal stimulation or gastric distension are important in early termination of drinking and contribute to a rapid reduction in thirst and AVP secretion during drinking, before correction of water deficit [57, 58]. These mechanisms are surprisingly quantitative and they ensure that the amount of water drunk does not exceed the amount of water needed.

Sensations arising from the oropharyngeal cavity can be categorized as taste, thermal, and tactile. In addition there is a perception of dryness and wetness.

Elderly persons demonstrate a similar oropharyngeal inhibition of thirst after drinking but a reduced oropharyngeal inhibition of AVP secretion compared to younger group [23, 57].

Some oropharyngeal factors such as a dry mouth, have long been associated with thirst [1, 32, 34, 59,60] ,and it may be that old people are insensitive to these changes. Phillips et al found that the elderly group, after water deprivation had nonsignificant and less well- defined change in mouth dryness as compared with young group [15]. Older persons may also have less pleasure (hedonic satisfaction) with fluid intake as taste perception changes with aging [61]. The temperature of the water may play a role in the amount of fluid intake, this concept was confirmed by animal studies, which showed the volume of water intake by water deprived animals positively correlated with temperature of the water up to body temperature (kapatos and Gold 1972, Deauxand Englrom 1973). Carlisle (1973) reported the same results in schedule - induced drinking (without deprivation). Gold and co-workers (1973) observed that even in the first few minutes of a test session the intake of cool water was suppressed in rats, and concluded that tongue cooling during drinking acts as a short - latency satiation mechanism that anticipates cellular and extracellular hydration. Whether fluid temperature effects human drinking, and whether there is a change in the perception of water temperature with aging, still needs to be investigated [62].

Taste of the fluid is deemed to be non homeostatic modulator of drinking, which neither initiates nor terminates it, but instead increases or decreases the amount drunk in response to given arousal. (Adolph 1967, Adolph et al 1954).

Studies have consistently shown that the threshold for tastei ncreases with age, and that bitter and sour stimuli are the most affected [63- 64]. De Castro [65] Asked 139 males and 123 females (ages 20- 80), to record their daily intake of foods and fluids for a week, and he observed that elderly subjects drank more coffee and tea than younger subjects, who drank significantly more diet soda. But these results seemed to be due to cohort effects rather than effect of aging. De Castro confirmed what has been shown in a previous study (Lowick et al 1989) that elderly drank less alcohol than the younger groups. He also noticed that the elderly tend to ingest fluids earlier in the day than the younger groups and there was a reduction in the amplitude of diurnal variation with aging which is consistent with the finding in rats (Peng, Jiangand Hsu 1980, Peng and Kang 1984). There was no difference in the amount of fluids intakes or in the food associated drinking between old and younger groups in this study Olfaction also contributes to the flavor of food and beverages. Most studies indicate that there is a dramatic decline in sensitivity to air born chemical stimuli with aging. The decline in both taste and smell may contribute to an inadequate intake of food and fluids in old people [66, 67].

3.5. Central Nervous System Impairment

Some researchers have suggested that occult central nervous system disease is a possible explanation for hypodipsia in the elderly. Miller et al [68] studied six patients ages 68 - 9) who had had previous cerebrovascular accidents and had a history of recurrent dehydration and hypernatremia. Despite the ability to obtain water, none of the patients complained of thirst, and he suggested that this hypodipsia might have been due to cerebral cortical dysfunction.

Other investigators tried to correlate the impaired thirst in the elderly with the deterioration in cognitive function. After overnight fluid restriction, patients with Alzheimer disease were found to have a greater degree of dehydration and diminished thirst as measured by water ingested in one hour of ad libitum intake. In addition, levels of plasma AVP were subnormal for serum osmolalities in those patients [69, 70]. There was also a direct correlation between the water intake and the mini mental status examination score in Alzheimer patients, However, little is known about the subjects or their fluid status on entry, so it is not possible to generalize these finding to all persons with Alzheimer disease. Studies evaluating plasma norepinphrinenorepinephrine in the normal elderly have found significant increases as compared to the young and middle age individuals [71,72,73]. Norepiniphrine Norepinephrine is a potent antidipsogenic. It decreases drinking produced by carbachol, angiotensin II, hypertonic saline [74,75].

Tumors and other lesions involving certain anatomical sites of the CNS, such as the anterior wall of the third ventricle can lead to hypodipsia and impaired release of AVP.

3.6. Hypodipsia Associated with Anorexia

There is a high correlation between food and water intake under a variety of conditions in rats. It was demonstrated that rats drink 73% of their total daily water intake within 10 minutes before or after eating (Kiissilef 1969).

Anorexia is a common finding in the elderly, and it is a multifactorial entity [76, 77]. Whether hypodipsia in older people is related to this anorexia, has not been proven. Silver et al found that the water intake associated with food was significantly depressed in the old rats group compared to young one. But there was also a decrease in total food ingestion, which made his finding difficult to interpret. Studies have found that neuropeptide Y has a potent stimulating effect on food and fluid intake when injected into the paraventricular hypothalamic nucleus (PVN). It has been postulated that there is a relationship between the aging - related anorexia and diminished function of neuropeptide Y containing systems in the aged rats [78]. Pich et al found that feeding and drinking responses elicited by injection of neuropeptide Y into PVN , were significantly attenuated in the aged rats compared to young rats. The volume of the water intake associated with food ingestion was found in animals to be dependent on the components of the food. Fitzmans and Le Magnen (1969) found a delay in the reassociation of drinking with meals following a change in diet from high carbohydrate to high protein.Whether the change of the pattern of nutrient selection in the elderly [79] plays a role in age- related hypodipsia is not clear.

3.7. Other Causes of Hpodipsia in The Elderly

Medications may have direct or indirect effect on thirst and fluid intake. Drugs Such B–adrenergic agonists increase drinking, whereas alpha - adrenergic agonists decrease drinking [80].

Drugs effect the systems that control thirst and fluid intake, by interfering with opioid system (Benzodiazepines), AVP secretion (Chlorpropamide), or by changing taste (D-Penicillamine [81], phenadione [82]) or olfaction. (Isotretinoin [83]).

Some elderly try to limit their fluid intake, thinking that will solve urinary incontinence problems.

CONCLUSION

The sensation of thirst is basic to our existence. Among the different age groups, older persons are extremely susceptible to dehydration, even with mild stresses. Hypodipsia and reduced renal concentrating ability are important factors in predisposing the elderly to dehydration.

Prevalence of dehydration has been found to as high as 25% among the residents at nursing homes [84]. Those elderly living in continuing - care - units with the highest osmolality have been shown to have a significantly reduced survival rate [85].

Age related changes must be considered during assessment of the elderly, and the complaints of thirst cannot be relied on as an indicator of fluid needs in this group. The fluid offered needs to be palatable, acceptable to the person, and should be offered in larger rather than smaller containers, as there is a tendency to drink what is offered [86]. Drugs that cause hypodipsia should be eliminated or replaced when it is possible.Teaching the family and older person about age- related changes in hydrational needs, is also advisable.

There is a need for more studies to understand the mechanisms of hypodipsia in the elderly. Such studies are vital for prevention of the disturbances of fluid balance in the elderly, and for development of appropriate therapeutic interventions.

REFERENCES

1. Fitzimons Thirst and sodium appetite in the regulation of the body fluid". Control Mechanisms of Drinking ,Springer- Haefeli, p1- 7, 1975.
2. Andersonyy B , "Polydipsia caused by intra hypothalamic injections of hypertonic NaCl solution". Expereintia 8: 157 ,1952.
3. Andersonyy B ,McCann S M : A further study of polydipsia evoked by hypothalamic stimulationy y in the goat .Acta physiol Scand 33:333 ,1955.
4. Zerbe RL ,Robertson GL : Osmoregulation of thirst and vasopressin secretion in man : The effectyy of various solutes. Am J Physiol 244 : E607 ,1983 .
5. Fitzimons JT : The physiology of thirst and sodium appetite .Monogr Physiol Soc # 35 ,1979.
6. Fitzimons JT, Moore - Gillon MJ : Drinking and antidiuretic in response to reduction in venous return in the dog :neural and endocrine mechanism .J Physio 308 : 403 , 1980.
7. Zerbe RL ,Robertson GL "Osmotic and nonosmotic regulation of thirst and vasopressin secretion". Maxwell & Kleeman,s Clinical disorders of fluid and electrolyte metabolism. 5th ed, NY : McGraw- Hill. 1993.
8. RichardE.Weitzman , Charles R. Kleeman. "The clinical physiology of water metabolism PartI : The physiologic regulation of arginine vasopressin secretion and thirst (Medical Progress).West J Med 131 :373 - 400 Nov 1979.
9. Fischer - Ferraro C, Nahmod VE ,Goldstein DJ, et al." Angiotensin and renin an rat and dog brain". J Exo Med 133 :353 - 361, 1971.
10. Ganten D, Marquez Julio A ,Granter P, et al. "Renin in dog brain" , Am J Physiol 221 : 1733- 1337, 1971.
11. Laurel A Pfeil, Paul R Katz, and Paul J Davis " Water metabolism" Geriatric Nutrition Second Edition, Raven Press ,Ltd,NY 1995.
12 Davis I, Goddard A.B, Fotheringham B, et al. "The effect of age on the control of water conservation in the laboratory mouse - metabolic studies". Exp. Gerontol 20 : 53- 66 ; 985.
13. Silver A J, Flood J F, Morley J E "Effect of aging on fluid ingestion in Mice". J .Gerontol ;46 : B117- 121 , 1991.
14. Beck N, Yu B.P " Effect of aging on urinary concentrating mechanisms and Vasopressin- dependent cAMP in rats". Am J Physiol 243: F121- 125; 1982 .
15. Burwell R , Whealin J, and Gallagher M. "Effects of aging on the diurnal pattern of water intake in rats". Behavioral and Neural Biology ; 58 : 196- 203 , 1992.
16. Phillips PA, Rolls BJ, Ledingham JG, et al. "Reduced thirst after water deprivation in healthy elderly men". N Eng J Med ; 311(12) : 753- 9, 1984.
17. Crowe MJ, Forsling ML, Rolls BJ, et al ."Altered water excretion in healthy elderly men. Age Ageing ;16 : 285- 93. 1987.
18 Miescher E, Fortney S." Responses to dehydration and rehydration during heat exposure in young and older men". Am J Physiol; 257; 1050- 6 .1989.
19. Phillips PA., Bretherton Mjohnston CI, and Gray L ., " Reduced osmotic thirst in healthy elderly men". Am J Physiol 261(1 Pt 2) ; R166- 71 ,1991.

20. Szczepanska- Sadowska E, Sobocinska J, and Sadowski B. "Central dipsogenic effect of vasopressin". Am. J. Physiol. ;242: R372 .1982

21. Szczepanska- Sadowska E ,Gray D , and Simon- Opperman Ch. "Vasopressin in blood and third ventricle CSF during dehydration , thirst, and hemorrhage '. Am. J. Physiolo ;245:R549, 1983.

22. Szczepanska- Sadowska E, Simon- Opperman Ch, Gray D, and Simon E. "Plasma and cerebrospinal fluid vasopressin and osmolality in relation to thirst' Pflugers Arch ; 400:294   (1984)

23. Kirkland J L, Lye M , Goddard E, et al . "Plasma arginine vasopressin in dehydrated elderly patients "Clin Endocrinol ;20:451- 6, 1984.

24. Vargas E, Lye M, Faragher EB, et al Cardiovascular hemodynamics and the response of vasopressin , aldosterone , plasma renin activity , and plasma catecholamines to head - uptilt in young and old healthy subjects . Age Ageing ; 15: 17- 28 . 1986.

25. Rowe JW, Minaker KL , Sparrow D, et al . " Age related failure of volume - pressure - mediated vasopressin release . J Clin Endocrinol Metab ; 54 : 661- 4, 1982.

26. Li HC, Hsieh S M , Nagai I . "The response of plasma arginine vasopressin to 14 - h water deprivation in the elderly" Acta Endocrinol ; 105 : 314- 17 . 1984.

27. Helderman J H, Vestal RE, Rowe JW, et al ."The response of arginine vasopressin to intravenous ethanol and hypertonic saline in man : the impact of aging ' J Gerontol ; 33 : 39 - 47, 1978.

28. Bevilacqua M, Norbiato G,Chebat E, et al ."Osmotic and non- osmotic control of vasopressin release in the elderly - effect of metoclopramide" J Clin Endocrinol Metab;65: 1243- 7, 1987.

29. Thompson CJ , Bland M , Burd J, and Baylis PH. "The osmotic threshold for thirst and vasopressin are similar in healthy man ' Clin Sci ; 71:651- 6 ,1986.

30. Davis Joan , O'Neill PA, McLean KA, et al. "Age - associated alteration in thirst and arginine vasopressin in response to water and sodium load". Age and Ageing ;24: 151- 9, 1995

31. Asplund R, Aberg H, Wetterberg L. "Seasonal changes in the levels of antidiuretic hormone and melatonin in the elderly". J OF Pineal Res ;18 : 154- 158 , 1995.

32. Hofman M ,and Swaab DF ."Influence of aging on the seasonal rhythm of the vasopressin - expressing Neurons in the human suprachiasmatic nucleus" Neurobiology of Aging ;16 (6) : 965- 71 , 1995

33. Asplund R, Aberg H. "Diurnal variation in the levels of antidiuretic hormone in the elderly" J Int Med ; 299: 131 , 1991.

34. Rolls BJ ,Rolls ET . Thirst .Cambridge : Cambridge University Press, 1982.

35. Silver AJ, Morley JE,Ishimaru- Tseng TV, and Morley PMK. " Angiotensin II and fluid ingestion in old rats 'Neurobiology of Aging ;14: 519- 22, 1993.

36. Rolls BJ, Wood RJ , Rolls ET , and Lind H."Thirst following water deprivation in humans" Am J Physiol ; 239 :R476- 82.1980

37. Noth R , Lashman M, Tan S, et al" Age and the renialdosterone system ' Arch Intern Med ; 137 : 1414- 17, 1977.

38. Tsunoda K ,Abe K ,Toshikasu G, et al " Effect of age on renin - angiotensin aldosterone system in normal subjects : simultaneous measurement of active and inactive renin, renin substrate an aldosterone in plasma " J Clin Endocri Metab ; 62 : 384- 9, 1986

39. Wiedmann P , De Myttenaere- Bursztein S, Maxwell MH, and deLima J. " Effect of aging on plasma renin and aldosterone' Kidney Int 8(5) : 325 - 33 , 1975 Nov .

40. Crane MG,Harris JJ " Effect of aging on renin activity and aldosterone excretion" J Lab Clin Med 87 (6) ; 947- 59 , 1976 Jan.

41. Yamamoto T, Harada H, Fukuyama J, et al ."Impaired arginine vasopressin secretion associated with hypoangiotensinemia in hypernatremic dehydrated elderly patients" JAMA ; 259(7) : 1039- 42, 1988.

42. Fitzimons JT' Pathology and pathophysiology of thirst and sodium appetite .In: Physiology and Pathophysiology (Seldin DW , Giebisch G,eds) . New York : Raven Press . 2;885- 910, 1985.

43. Skott P , Ingerslev J , Neilsen D, and Geise J. " the renin- angiotensin- aldosterone system in normal 85 yr - old people " Scan J Clin Lab Invest ;33:87- 94, 1974 .

44. Gribbin B,Pickering TG, Sleight P, et al . " Effect of age and high blood pressure on baroreflex sensitivity in man" . Circ Res ; 29: 424- 31 , 1971 .

45. Grossman A, Moult PA, Cannah D, Besser M. "Different opioid mechanisms are involved in the modulation of ACTH and gonadotropin release in man".Neuroendocrinology ;42:357- 60, 1986.

46. Morley JE " Neuroendocrine effect of endogenous opioid peptides in human subjects : A review". Psychoneuroendocrinology ; 8 : 361- 79 ,1983.

47. Ostrowsky NL ,Rowland N , Foley TL, et al . "Morphine antagonist and consummatory behaviors. Pharmacol Biochem Behav ;14: 549- 559.

48. Rowland N ."Comparison of suppression by naloxone of water intake induced in rats by hyperosmolality , Hypovolemia , and angiotensin. Pharmacol Biochem Behav ; 16 : 87- 91 ,1982 .

49. Fishman SM ,Carr DB "Naloxone blocks exercise - stimulated water intake in the rats" Life Sci ;32 :

2523- 2527, 1983.

50. Siviy SM ,Calcagretti DJ, Reid LD ." Opioid and palatability". In: Hoebel BJ, Novin D, eds"The neural basis of feeding and reward . Brunswick : Haer Institute ; pp 517- 30 , 1982 .

51. Holtzman SG. "Effects of narcotic antagonists on fluid intake in the rat" Life Sci ; 16 : 1465 - 1470, 1975.

52. Summy - long JY , Keil LC, Deen K, et al " Endogenous opioid peptide inhibition of the central actions of angiotensin". J Pharmacol Exp Ther : 217 : 619- 29 , 1981

53. Kavaliers M, Hirst M " The influence of opiate agonist on day- night feeding rhythm in young and old mice". Brain Res ; 326 : 160- 7 , 1985.

54. Silver AJ, Morley JE." Role of opioid system in the hypodipsia associated with aging ".JAGS ; 40: 556- 560, 1992.

55. De Wied D , Van Ree JM. " Neuropeptide , mental performance and aging '. Life Sci ; 31 : 709 - 19 , 1982.

56. Messing RB , Vasques BJ , Saminiego B . " Alteration in Dehydromorphin binding in cerebral hemispheres of aged male rats". J Neurochem ; 36 : 784- 89, 1981

57. Phillips PA ,Bretherton M, Risvanis J, et al. " Effect of drinking on thirst and vasopressin in dehydrated elderly men". Am J Physiol. 264; R 877- R881, 1993.

58. Thrasher T N, Nistel- Herrera J F, Keil C , and Ramsay DJ."Satiety and inhibition of vasopressin secretion after drinking in dehydrated dogs". Am J Physiol ; 240(4) E394- 401, 1981 Apr.

59. Wolf AV. "Thirst: Physiology of the urge to drink and problems of water lack" Springfield, Ill. : Charles C Thomas, 1958

60. Adolphyy EF.' "PhisiologyPhysiology of man in the desert" New York: Interscience, 1947.

61. Cowart BJ, " Development of taste perception in humans : sensitivity and preference throughout life sp"'. Psychol Bull ; 90 : 43- 73, 1981.

62. Weijnen J. A. W. M ." Lingual stimulation and water intake ".Control mechanisms of drinking ,Springer- Haefeli, p9- 13, 1975.

63. Frank ME, Hettinger TP, Mott AE. "The sense of taste : neurobiology ,aging, and medication effects". Critical Reviews in oral Biology and Medicine; 3 (4) : 371- 93 , 1992.

64. Cowart BJ : Relationships of taste and smell across the adult life span .Ann N Y Acad Sci ; 561 : 39 - 55 .1989.

65. De Castro J M . " Age related changes in natural spontaneous fluid ingestion and thirst in humans". J of Geront. ;47 (5) : 321- 30 , 1992

66. Weiffenbach JM , and Bartoshuk L M, " Taste and smell ' Clin in Ger Med ; 8 (3) 543-55, 1992.

67. Schifffman . " Perception of taste and smell in the elderly persons". Critcal Critical Rev in Food Sci & Nutr. ;33(1): 17- 26, 1993.

68. Miller PD Kerbs RA, Neal BJ, et al. "Hypodipsia in geriatric patients'Am J Med ; 73 : 344- 6 , 1982

69. Albert SG, Nakara BRS, Grossberg GT, et al. " vasopressin response to dehydration in Alzheimer diseas" '. J AM Geriatr Soc ; 70 : 619, 1989.

70. Albert SG , Nakara ,Grossberg GT, et al. " Drinking behavior and vasopressin to hyperosmolality in Alzheimer diseas". Int Psychogeriatrics ;6 : 79 , 1994.

71 Byrsztyn M, Bresnhan M, Gavras I, Gavras H. "Effect of aging on vasopressin , catecholamine , and alpha 2- adrenergic receptors". J Am Ger Soc; 38(6) : 628- 32, 1990.

72 Jensen E W, Eldrup E, Kelbaek H , et al . "Venous plasma noradrenaline increases with age : correlation to total blood volume and long - term smoking habits".Clin Physiol; 13(1): 99-109, 1993.

73 Hetland ML, Eldrup E, Bratholm P, Christensen NJ. " the relationship between age and venous plasma ,cocentration,concentration of noradrenaline , catecholamine metabolite s, DOPA and Neuropeptide Y- Like immunoreactivity in normal human subjects". Scan J Clin & Lab inv; 51(3): 219- 24, 1991.

74. Leibowitz SF .:In :Handbook of Hypothalamus, Vol3, edited by P.J Morgane and J Panksepp, pp 299- 437.1980.

75. Rowland N :In:Analysis of IMotvationalIMotivational Processes , edited by FM Toates and TR Halliday, pp39- 59. Academic Press, London.

76. Morley JE. " Anorexia in older persons : epidimiologyepidemiology and optimal treatme". Drugs & aging ; 8(2) : 134- 55 , 1996

77. Morley JE, Silver AJ . " Anorexia in the elderly' . Neurobiology of aging ; 9(1) : 9- 16 ,1988

78. Pich E M , Messori B ,Zoli M, et al ." Feeding and drinking responses to neuropeptide Y injections in the paraventricular Hypothalamic nucleus of aged rats '.Brain Res ;575 : 265 · ·71 ,1992

79. Elahi VK,Elahi D,Andres R, et al " A longitudinal study of nutritional intake in men". J Gerontol ; 38 :162- 180,1983.

80. Morley JE " Behavioral pharmacology for eating and drinking " Psychopharmacology : The Third Generation Of Progress, Raven Press, NY , PP 1267- 72, 1987.

81. Henkin RI, Keiser HR, Jaffe IA, et al. " Decreased taste sensivitysensitivity after D- Penicillamin

reversed by copper administration" Lancet; 2: 1268- 1271, 1967.

82. Scott PJ . "Glossitis with complete loss of taste sensation during Dindevon treatment. Report of case". New Zeal Med J ;59 : 296, 1960.

83. Heise E, Schnuch A. " taste and olfactory disturbances after treatment for acne with istretinoin, a 13-cis- isomer of retinoic acid"'. Euro Arch of Oto- Rhino- Laryngolgy; 247(6): 382- 3, 1990.

84. Spangler PF, Risle TR, and Bilyew DD. " The management of dehydration and inconteinence incontinence in nonambulatory geriatric patient" J. App. Behav.Anal; 17 :397- 401, 1984.

85. O'Neill PA, Davis I , " Reduced survival with increasing plasma osmolality in elderly continuing-care patients" Age and ageing; 19 (1) 68- 71 .1990.

86. Adams F ," Fluid intake , how much do elders drin" . Geriatric Nursing. July/August , pp 218 - 221, 1988.

OSMOTIC AND VOLUME RECEPTORS: CONTROL OF FLUID HOMEOSTASIS IN AGING

N. S. STACHENFELD

Address for correspondence: Nina S. Stachenfeld, Ph.D. The John B. Pierce Laboratory 290 Congress Avenue New Haven, CT 06519 TEL: 203-562-9901 FAX: 203-624-4950

Abstract : *Disturbances in body fluid balance initiate adjustments, such as drinking and renal sodium and water retention, which act to restore fluid homeostasis. Restoration of fluid homeostasis is slower in older compared to younger people following exercise-induced dehydration and water deprivation. The slower recovery in older individuals has been attributed to a deficit in thirst sensitivity to osmotic stimuli and a reduced renal concentrating capacity. However, these changes may not represent deficits per se, but changes in the operating point for the regulation of body fluids. For example, older subjects restored fluid losses effectively following ~ 2.4 % dehydration, despite a rightward shift in the osmotic threshold for the onset of thirst sensation. Furthermore, the stimulus-response characteristics of osmotic control of free water (CH_2O) were similar in older and younger subjects, although the older subjects operated on a steeper portion of the plasma osmolality - CH_2O curve. These data suggest a shift in the operating point for control of body fluid balance in older people following dehydration. The reported deficits in thirst in dehydrated older subjects may be due either to diminished sensitivity of cardiac mechanoreceptors that sense changes in central volume or to diminished sensitivity of central osmoreceptors that sense changes in plasma osmolality. Studies that employed hypertonic saline infusion to provide a stimulus for drinking found that the osmotic sensitivity of thirst was unaffected by age. Renal handling of free water and sodium was also unaffected by age during recovery from hypertonic saline infusion. To test the hypothesis that the inhibitory action of central blood volume expansion on thirst and renal fluid* *regulation is attenuated with aging, we monitored the drinking and renal responses of dehydrated older and younger subjects during 195 min of head-out water immersion, which shifts blood centrally and increases plasma volume. Head-out water immersion restored plasma volume in older and younger subjects, but suppressed thirst rating and fluid intake younger subjects only. We concluded that the inhibitory influence of central volume expansion on thirst and drinking behavior is diminished with aging. These findings indicate that a deficit in the sensitivity of central volume receptors is an important mechanism for the reported thirst deficit and altered body fluid regulation following dehydration in older people.*

The maintenance of body fluid homeostasis requires a balance between intake, controlled by thirst and sodium appetite, and output, controlled by renal water and osmo-regulation. Disturbances in body fluid balance initiate reflex adjustments, such as stimulation of central osmoreceptors, unloading of atrial low-pressure (volume) baroreceptors, and increases in arginine vasopressin (AVP), all of which contribute to increased thirst and water retention [12, 25, 31].

Older people have a blunted thirst response to dehydration. The mechanism of this deficit is not easily identified because body fluid regulation requires the integration of a number of physiological systems. Body water loss induces a hyperosmotic hypovolemia, so any deficit in body fluid regulation could reflect a specific problem in either the osmo- or volume reflexes. Hypertonic saline infusion stimulates thirst and renal osmoregulation by increasing plasma osmolality (Osm_p), but also expands plasma volume, resulting in simultaneous, opposing inputs from osmo- and volume reflexes [4, 28]. Therefore, studies using dehydration or hypertonic saline infusion cannot distinguish whether a specific deficit exists in either the osmotic or volume sensing pathways. In contrast, head-out water immersion, forces blood into the intrathoracic cavity and expands central blood volume without altering plasma composition [7], so can be used. We have used this technique to isolate the contribution of central volume receptors in the control of in thirst and drinking behavior. Using this technique, we have demonstrated a role for these receptors in the diminished thirst response in older people [27].

CONTROL OF THIRST AND ARGININE VASOPRESSIN (AVP)

Thirst and AVP, the major fluid regulating hormone, are highly sensitive to changes in plasma tonicity. Strong and positive correlations

(> 0.90) exist between plasma osmolality (Osm_p) and both thirst and plasma concentration of AVP ($[AVP]_p$). The slopes of these relationships are used to assess osmotic control of thirst and AVP release; a steeper slope is interpreted as heightened sensitivity of central osmoreceptors that stimulate the cognitive sensation of thirst and cause the release of AVP. Osmoreceptors are very sensitive, responding to alterations in Osm_p of as little as 1% (~ 3 mosmol/kg H_2O). Thirst and AVP also are sensitive to decreases in plasma volume through unloading of low-pressure baroreceptors, although ~ 8% plasma volume loss is needed to induce these responses. Therefore, under conditions of high plasma tonicity and body water deficit, restoration of body water is achieved through a combination of thirst-induced drinking and vasopressin-mediated renal water retention. In addition, a number of substances, e.g. angiotensin II may play an important role in of body fluid regulation by acting on structures in the anterior hypothalamus (paraventricular and supraoptic nucleii) and altering thirst and AVP release [12] (See ref # 12 for a more in depth review of central control of body fluid regulation).

Measurement of cognitive thirst sensation.

Perceptions of thirst described in this paper are assessed by a visual-analogue rating scale [16, 24]. The subjects respond to the question "how thirsty do you feel right now?" on a scale 180 mm in length with intersecting lines at 0 mm "not at all" and at 125 mm "extremely thirsty". This scale has been used extensively for psychophysical assessments in both older and younger subjects and corresponds well to physiological determinants of thirst, such as plasma osmolality [24].

BODY FLUID HOMEOSTASIS FOLLOWING DEHYDRATION

Older people are considered more susceptible to dehydration than younger people [13, 24] because they have greater resting Osm_p and are slower to restore body fluid following water loss [15, 21]. This slower recovery has been attributed to deficits in thirst sensation [19, 21] and renal osmo- [15] and fluid regulatory [3, 5] responses, and has been interpreted by some investigators as a loss of homeostatic capacity. However, it has also been proposed that that the altered adjustments to body fluid do not represent age-associated deficits in homoestatic mechanisms per se, but rather a shift in the operating point around which these control systems regulate body water balance [15].

Phillips et al. [21] examined the thirst, hormonal and renal water and electrolyte responses of healthy, older (71 yr) and younger (23 yr) men following 24 hr water deprivation. As expected, Osm_p increased and plasma volume decreased in all subjects following the water deprivation. Older subjects consistently rated their thirst sensation lower than the younger subjects, and did not drink enough during a 120 min ad libitum rehydration period to restore Osmp to pre-deprivation levels, whereas their younger counterparts restored Osm_p in 60 min. Urine osmolality (Osm_u) was lower in the older subjects following dehydration, suggesting a deficit in renal concentrating capacity. Because the $[AVP]_p$ responses were similar between older and younger subjects, the authors interpreted the lower Osm_u as a deficit in intrarenal function, rather than the result of hormonal factors. However, pre-dehydration levels of Osm_u were very high (over 900 mosmol/kg H_2O in the younger and ~ 700 mosmol/kg H_2O in older subjects), while the rise in Osm_u appeared similar between the age groups, which calls into question the conclusion that renal concentrating response to water deprivation is diminished in older age.

More recently, Mack et al. [15] demonstrated that given enough time, older people adequately restore body fluids following thermal dehydration, indicating appropriate, if sluggish, osmotic control of body fluids. Mack et al. [15] compared the responses to exercise-induced dehydration and a prolonged (180 min) rehydration period in older (65 yr) and younger (22 yr) men. Older subjects had greater pre-exercise Osmp than younger subjects (288 versus 283), and urine osmol and sodium excretion were similar between the groups. In response to dehydrating exercise, Osmp increased and plasma volume decreased similarly in the older and younger subjects. Although thirst ratings and fluid intake were reduced markedly in the older subjects, they restored fluid and electrolyte status to the expected isotonic level and restored Osm_p to its pre-dehydration level, demonstrating appropriate reflex control of osmotic homeostasis, albeit at a higher Osm_p (Fig. 1). The stimulus- response curve for Osm_p and free water clearance (CH2O) was not affected by age, although osmotic regulation of CH_2O occurred at a higher Osm_p in the older people, as it did with osmotic control of thirst. Taken together, these findings indicate appropriate osmolar control over CH_2O and thirst, but at a higher operating point, and that the greater basal Osm_p in older people is not the result of chronic hypohydration.

Figure 1

Relationship between plasma osmolality and perceived thirst. Data points represent means ± SEM for each group at rest before dehydration; after 1 h of dehydration, 2 h dehydration, and 30 min recovery from dehydration (no fluid ingested); and at 1,2, and 3 h of rehydration [15]. Reprinted with permission from the American Physiological Society.

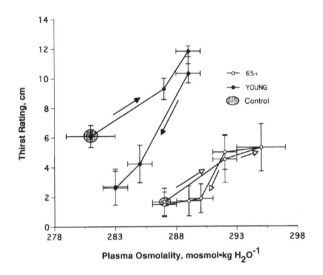

CONTROL OF THIRST AND FLUID INTAKE

Osmotic regulation of thirst and fluid intake

Older people may possess appropriate reflex control of body water deficits during dehydration [15], but thirst and renal concentrating deficits are still evident in older people. The infusion of hypertonic saline is used to examine the specific role of osmoreceptors in the control of thirst and drinking because hypertonic saline infusion induces a strong osmotic stimulus, but without extracellular fluid volume depletion. The results of the few studies that have used this method are conflicting, but in general suggest that osmotic sensitivity of thirst remains intact with aging.

In the first study [19], hypertonic (5.0 % NaCl) saline was infused at 0.06 ml·kg⁻¹·min⁻¹ for 120 min in older (70 yr) and younger (25 yr) subjects to compare their thirst and $[AVP]_p$ responses to osmotic stimuli. This study is the only one to find that thirst and drinking responses to given elevations of Osm_p were blunted in older, compared to younger subjects. Surprisingly, there was no effect of age on changes in $[AVP]_p$, indicating a maintenance of AVP osmoreceptor function in aging. More recent studies have not supported the findings of a diminished osmotic thirst perception in older people [4, 28]. For example, Davies et al. [4] infused hypertonic (3.0% NaCl) saline at 0.1 ml·kg^{-1}·min^{-1}, and demonstrated similar thirst responses to elevations in Osm_p in older and younger subjects, although $[AVP]_p$ was enhanced in the older subjects.

The reason for the contradictory results between these two studies is unclear, but may have been due to differences in baseline hydration or health status of the study groups. We therefore addressed this question again [28], taking care to ensure adequate and similar hydration levels in the older and younger subjects. We tested our subjects in the upright position and provided water at its most palatable temperature (15°C) to maximize drinking responses. Hypertonic (3.0% NaCl) saline was infused into older (72 yr) and younger (26 yr) men and women at a rate of 0.1 ml·kg^{-1}·min^{-1} body weight for 120 min [28]. A 30 min seated equilibration period followed the infusion, after which time the subjects drank water ad libitum for 180 min.

Hypertonic saline infusion increased Osm_p (~19 mosmol/kg H_2O) and plasma volume (~ 17 %) similarly in the older and younger subjects, indicating similar osmotic and volume stimuli to both groups; older and younger people had similar thirst, drinking and $[AVP]_p$ responses. These findings extended our earlier conclusions that older people maintain adequate control of fluid balance after dehydration [15], but were in direct contrast to the conclusions of Phillips et al. [19] that older people have attenuated thirst and drinking responses to osmotic stimulation. An explanation for this apparent contradiction may lie in a close examination of the role of volume receptors in the regulation of thirst. The volume expansion (~ 17 %) produced in our study was greater than that produced by Phillips et al. [19] (~ 13 %), and was a sufficient stimulus to load cardiopulmonary baroreceptors. Loading cardiopulmonary baroreceptors, sends a contradictory signal concerning fluid status to that of elevated Osm_p [23], and reduces the thirst drive [25, 31]. We speculated that the greater plasma volume expansion in our study led to a greater modulating signal for thirst in the younger subjects [25, 31], and had little impact in the older subjects, thus inducing similar thirst responses between the two groups. This led us to the hypothesis that osmotic thirst sensitivity is intact, but atrial receptors sensitive to changes in blood volume are attenuated in aging [2, 6].

The seemingly contradictory findings of attenuated dehydration- [15, 21], but not osmotically-induced thirst sensation [28] in older people supports the hypothesis of a decline in volume sensitivity. Figure 2 compares the thirst responses to thermal dehydration (hyperosmotic, hypovolemia) and hypertonic saline infusion (hyperosmotic, hypervolemia) in younger (top) and older (bottom) subjects. In the younger subjects, the plasma volume expansion from hypertonic saline infusion attenuated the thirst response at any given osmolality. In other words, the thirst response was greater during dehydration because of the extracellular volume loss. In contrast, the older people responded similarly, regardless of extracellular volume status. Taken together, these two studies suggested that older people maintain osmotic sensation with aging, but do not appear to be as sensitive to changes in central blood volume.

Figure 2
Thirst responses to increased plasma osmolality (Posm) during i3%
saline nfusion (J) and dehydration exercise (E) [15] in younger (A) and
older (B) subjects [28]. Reprinted with permission from the American
Physiological Society.

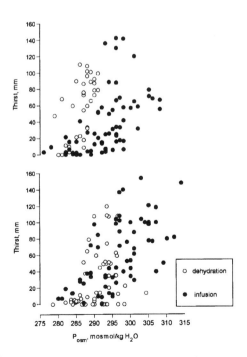

Central volume (atrial stretch) receptors and the control of thirst and fluid intake

To test the hypothesis that the sensitivity of the central volume (stretch) receptors is attenuated with aging, we directly examined the role of central volume expansion in the thirst and drinking behavior in older individuals. Head-out water immersion (HOI) is an ideal method to isolate the individual contributions of osmotic and volume stimuli because during this procedure, hydrostatic pressure drives blood into the intrathoracic cavity, and expands central blood volume without altering plasma osmolality [7]. In dehydrated younger people the increased central volume activates cardiac volume (stretch) receptors, which reduces thirst [31] and drinking [25], despite continued high Osm_p. We hypothesized that if the age-related deficit in thirst sensation was a diminished sensitivity of these central volume-sensors, HOI-induced central volume expansion would have little impact thirst sensation and fluid intake in dehydrated older people.

To induce thirst and AVP release, older (70 yr) and younger (24 yr) men and women were dehydrated by exercise in the heat followed by overnight water deprivation. The following morning, the subjects sat for 195 min either immersed to the neck (HOI) in tap water or in a water perfused suit (time control, TC). After 15 min of HOI or TC, the subjects were allowed to drink water ad libitum for the remaining 180 min.

Exercise and overnight water deprivation increased Osmp (6 and 6 mosmol/kg H_2O) and decreased plasma volume (8 % and 12 %) similarly in older and younger subjects, so the osmotic and volume stimuli for thirst were the same for both groups prior to HOI or TC. Nonetheless, older subjects rated their thirst (69 mm) significantly lower than younger (94 mm) subjects prior to HOI and TC. Within 15 min, HOI led to a plasma volume expansion of (~ 239 ml and (~ 226 ml in older and younger subjects, respectively, which predict an increase in central venous pressure of (~ 4.12 mm Hg and 3.90 mm Hg [8] and is sufficient to load cardiopulmonary baroreceptors. In the younger subjects, despite elevated Osm_p, this signal significantly reduced thirst sensation relative to pre-HOI and to TC levels (Fig. 3); however, the older subjects' thirst ratings were unchanged during the first 15 min of HOI and were similar to those during TC (Fig. 3). Thus, thirst sensation in older subjects was insensitive to the increased central venous pressure. In addition, cumulative water intake was lower during HOI compared to TC (6.1 ± 1.1 and 14.3 ± 2.2 ml/kg , HOI and TC, respectively, p < 0.05) in younger subjects, but was unaffected by HOI in older subjects (6.7 ± 2.1

and 8.4 ± 3.3 ml/kg, for HOI and TC, respectively). Because the input from high and low pressure baroreceptors is one of the signals for thirst and drinking [22], the older subjects' lack of response with baroreceptor loading was consistent with the finding of a reduced cardiopulmonary baroreceptor sensitivity in older people [2], and supported our hypothesis that a reduced ability to sense changes in volume status contributes to the deficit in thirst sensation in older subjects under dehydrated conditions.

Figure 3
Subjective ratings of thirst sensation following dehydration, and through 30 minutes of head-out water immersion (HOI) or time control (TC). The arrow connotes the beginning of ad libitum drinking (at 15 min). *Different from corresponding HOI value. ‡ Different from older subjects. § Differnt from pre-immersion value. Note only thirst ratings in the younger subjects are significantly reduced prior to the beginning of drinking.

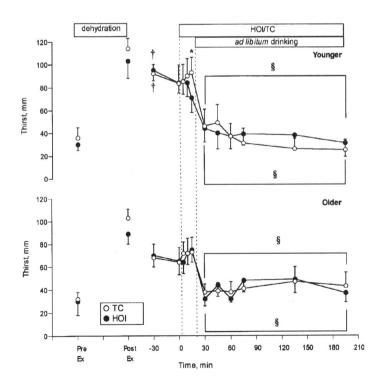

ARGININE VASOPRESSIN RESPONSE AND BODY WATER BALANCE

The linear relationship between AVP and thirst has been demonstrated during hypertonic saline infusion [4, 19, 28] and dehydration [21]. Aging does not appear to affect the magnitude or the slope of these responses [4, 19, 20, 28]. However, during both of these modes of body fluid disturbance, thirst and $[AVP]_p$ responses in older people appear dissociated [4, 19, 21], indicating that pathways regulating thirst and AVP release during body fluid regulation may indeed be independent in older people. It seems unlikely, however, that sensory pathways emanating from volume and osmo-receptors which control thirst and AVP release would be affected differentially by age. Therefore, AVP may be controlled by a peripheral mechanism, such as by increased plasma concentration of atrial natriuretic peptide ($[ANP]_p$), since intravenous ANP infusion suppresses osmotically-induced AVP release in younger and older people [1]; or AVP may be influenced by a central mechanism, such as angiotensin II [12].

RENAL OSMOL AND VOLUME REGULATION

Renal Osmoregulation

In general, osmotic (primarily sodium) regulation appears to remain intact with aging, but is achieved at a slower pace [14, 17]. Sodium excretion in response to an isotonic saline infusion (2000 ml) was markedly reduced in subjects over 40 yr over the 4 hours following infusion [14]. Sodium excretion increased in these subjects overnight however, suggesting delayed, rather than insufficient, sodium handling. In subjects over 65 yr, sodium excretion was not compromised during a 3 hr infusion of isotonic saline [17]. Resting glomerular filtration rate (GFR) was 20 % lower in older, compared to younger, subjects, and the infusion was accompanied by an increase in mean arterial pressure only in older subjects. Most of the sluggish responses to osmotic challenges can be accounted for by the age-associated reduction in GFR, which can be attributed to a progressive fall in the number of functioning nephrons in aging. The rise in mean arterial pressure may be a necessary compensatory mechanism to preserve sodium balance in older people because the diminished GFR may compromise renal tubule sodium delivery. Other factors, such as a decline in the activity of the renin-angiotensin-aldosterone system, may also play a role in sluggish renal concentrating capacity.

We found intact osmotic regulation in older people [28] with hypertonic saline infusion, which provides a much greater challenge to sodium (i.e., osmotic) regulation than isotonic saline infusion. Older and younger subjects were in positive fluid balance at the end of a hypertonic saline infusion and 180 min of ad libitum drinking. The increased water reabsorption in the kidney was mediated by continued elevation of $[AVP]_p$. The stimulus-response curve for $[AVP]_p$ and CH_2O was similar between older and younger subjects indicating intact renal sensitivity to AVP with aging. Plasma osmolality and $[AVP]_p$ were greater in older subjects during the early period of ad libitum drinking, so water retention (negative CH_2O) was greater in the older subjects. These findings are noticeably different from those during dehydration and isotonic saline infusion [14], which is associated with a sluggish urine concentrating response [15, 20].

The fractional excretions of sodium and potassium were also increased to the same extent in older and younger subjects following the hypertonic saline infusion. Despite our older subjects' universally lower levels of plasma renin activity (PRA) and plasma concentration of aldosterone ($[ALD]_p$), the similar renal handling of sodium and potassium suggested intrarenal compensation in the older subjects. Plasma concentration of ANP did not change markedly in either group, which indicates that the primary control of sodium and water balance is due to altered $[AVP]_p$, PRA and $[ALD]_p$ [32] as well as intrarenal mechanisms.

Isotonic volume expansion

The reports of renal responses to isotonic volume expansion are conflicting, and depend on the method of inducing volume expansion as well as initial hydration status. A series of studies have demonstrated a delayed and/or reduced diuresis following an oral water load in healthy older men [3-5], associated with a reduction in peak renal diuresis and CH_2O. After correcting for creatinine clearance (i.e. estimated GFR), these differences in renal diluting capacity disappear. This suggests that the slower renal response following water expansion is a function of the reduced GFR, perhaps by limiting the rate of sodium and chloride delivery to the loop of Henle and distal convoluted tubule.

The intravenous infusion of isotonic (0.9 % NaCl) saline, which induces an isotonic plasma volume expansion of ~ 8 % in older and younger subjects so is also used to test hypotheses concerning renal responses to volume stimuli [28]. In the presence of this plasma volume expansion, CH_2O increased dramatically in younger subjects (265 ± 98 ml) but only slightly in the older subjects (44 ± 26 ml) following 60 min of ad libitum drinking. The older subjects did not compensate for the early sluggish increase in CH_2O, resulting in a net fluid retention and plasma hypotonicity (fall of 6 mosmol/kg H_2O compared to baseline) by 120 min of drinking. This blunted renal diluting response was not explained by differences in PRA, $[AVP]_p$, $[ANP]_p$ or $[ALD]_p$, all of which responded similarly between the two groups, but was likely due to the reduced renal function in the older group, because the difference disappeared when CH_2O was corrected for GFR [28].

An investigation by Tajima et al. [29] found iso-osmotic volume expansion induced by HOI stimulated urine output and sodium excretion in older and younger subjects, but the increase in older people was greater and more rapid. Glomerular filtration rate increased transiently only in older subjects, and fractional sodium excretion was similar between the two groups, so again, much of the difference in sodium excretion may have been due to differences in renal function, not tubular handling of sodium. Mean arterial pressure (MAP) also increased only in the older group during HOI, which probably increased atrial pressure and stimulated the exaggerated atrial natriuretic peptide (ANP) response, which was two-fold greater in the older people.

We did not find age differences in renal water or sodium excretion or fluid balance during HOI, and we did not observe an increase in GFR in older subjects [27]. Although the overall renal fluid control during HOI was similar between older and younger subjects, it is doubtful the mechanisms for this control are the same. It is generally accepted that the renal water and sodium responses to HOI are the result of low pressure (cardiopulmonary) baroreceptor loading through a fall in renal sympathetic nerve activity [7]. The increase in MAP in older people suggests that the natriuresis may not have been entirely mediated by cardiopulmonary baroreceptor loading, but involved arterial baroreceptor activation as well, perhaps through renal sympathetic nerve activity suppression [11] or through a pressure diuresis mechanism. The relative contribution of arterial versus cardiopulmonary baroreceptors to the natriuresis during central volume expansion in older people has not been determined, but cardiopulmonary baroreceptor control of renal sympathetic nerve activity has been shown to be diminished in older dogs [9] and low pressure baroreceptor sensitivity maybe reduced in older humans [2].

Arterial baroreflex function also declines with age [10], as does the integration of high and low baroreceptors [26], suggesting additional factors, such as ANP, also contribute to HOI-induced natriuresis in older adults. The increase in $[ANP]_p$ in older compared to younger subjects during HOI was three-fold greater in our study, and was two-fold greater in the investigation by Tajima et al. [29] and there is evidence for a role of ANP in the peripheral vasoconstrictive response during cardiopulmonary baroreceptor unloading in patients with left ventricular hypertrophy [30]. The role of ANP in the HOI-induced natriuresis is not at all clear because other neural and hormonal (e.g., PRA and $[ALD]_p$) stimuli also influence the overall fluid and sodium regulatory responses. However, the exaggerated $[ANP]_p$ increase only in the older subjects suggests a significant role for this hormone in the HOI-induced natriuresis.

SUMMARY

Body fluid regulation involves the integration of a number of physiological systems. Alterations in any of these control systems can contribute to a delayed rehydration in older people following a deficit in total body water. Reported differences in thirst and body water regulatory responses between older and younger people is dependent on the manner by which body water is manipulated (i.e., exercise, water deprivation or hypertonic saline infusion). Relative to younger people, older people adequately restore body fluids and Osm_p, but do so more slowly and at an elevated Osm_p operating point. In younger subjects, a delay in fluid restitution is caused, in part, by the early restoration of plasma volume, and removal of a volume-dependent drive for drinking [18]. However, we have demonstrated that in aging, changes in extracellular volume have little effect on thirst sensation and water intake, while osmotic thirst sensitivity remains intact, suggesting osmotic thirst stimulation may be the most effective method to stimulate thirst and drinking, and restore body fluids in older individuals.

REFERENCES

1.   Clark, B. A., D. Elahi, L. Fish, M. McAloon-Dyke, K. Davis, K. L. Minaker, and F. H. Epstein. Atrial natriuretic peptide suppresses osmostimulated vasopressin release in young and elderly humans. Am. J. Physiol. 261: (Endocrinol. Metab. 24): E252-E256, 1991.
2.   Cleroux, J. C., C. Giannattasio, G. Bolla, C. Cuspidi, G. Grassi, C. Massola, L. Sampieri, G. Seravalle, M. Valsecchi, and G. Mancia. Decreased cardiopulmonary reflexes with aging in normotensive humans. Am. J. Physiol. 257 (Heart Circulatory Physiol. 26): H961-H968, 1989.
3.   Crowe, M. J., M. L. Forsling, B. J. Rolls, P. A. Phillips, J. G. G. Lindingham, and R. F. Smith. Altered water excretion in healthy elderly men. Age Ageing 16: 285-293, 1987.
4.   Davies, I., P. A. O'Neill, K. A. McLean, J. Catania, and D. Bennett. Age-associated alterations in thirst and arginine vasopressin in response to a water or sodium load. Age and Ageing 24: 151-159, 1995.

5. Dontas, A. S., S. G. Marketos, and P. Papanayiotou. Mechanisms of renal tubular defects in old age. Postgrad. Med. J. 48: 295-303, 1972.
6. Ebert, T. J., V. Hughes, F. E. Tristani, J. A. Barney, and J. J. Smith. Effect of age and coronary heart disease on the circulatory responses to graded lower body negative pressure. Cardiovascular Res. 16: 663-669, 1982.
7. Epstein, M. Renal effects of head-out water immersion in humans: a 15-year update. Physiol. Rev. 72: 563-621, 1992.
8. Gauer, O. H., J. P. Henry, and H. O. Sieker. Changes in central venous pressure after moderate hemorrhage and transfusions in man. Circ. Res. 4: 79-84, 1956.
9. Hajduczok, G., M. W. Chapleau, and F. M. Abboud. Increase in sympathetic activity with age. II. Role of impairment of cardiopulmonary baroreflexes. Am. J. Physiol. 260 (Heart Circulatory Physiol. 29): H1121-H1127, 1991.
10. Hajduczok, G., M. W. Chapleau, S. L. Johnson, and F. M. Abboud. Increase in sympathetic activity with age. I. Role of impairment of arterial baroreflexes. Am. J. Physiol. 260 (Heart Circulatory Physiol. 29): H1113-H1120, 1991.
11. Hajduczok, G., K. Miki, S. K. Hong, J. R. Claybaugh, and A. Krasney. Role of cardiac nerves in response to head-out water immersion in conscious dogs. Am. J. Physiol. 253 (Regulatory, Integrative, Comp. Physiol. 22): R235-R241, 1987.
12. Johnson, A. K. Brain mechanisms in the control of body fluid balance. In: Fluid Homeostasis During Exercise, edited by C. V. Gisolfi and D. T. Lamb. Carmel, Indiana: Brown and Benchmark, 1990, p. 347-424.
13. Leaf, A. Dehydration in the elderly. N. Engl. J. Med. 311: 791-792, 1984.
14. Luft, F. C., M. H. Weinberger, N. S. Fineberg, J. Z. Miller, and C. E. Grim. Effects of age on renal sodium homeostasis and its relevance to sodium sensitivity. Am. J. Med. 82 (Suppl. 1B): 9-15, 1987.
15. Mack, G. W., C. A. Weseman, G. W. Langhans, H. Scherzer, C. M. Gillen, and E. R. Nadel. Body fluid balance in dehydrated healthy older men: thirst and renal osmoregulation. J. Appl. Physiol. 76: 1615-1623, 1994.
16. Marks, L. E., J. C. Stevens, L. M. Bartoshuk, J. F. Geny, B. Rifkin, and V. K. Stone. Magnitude-matching: the measurement of taste and smell. Chem. Senses 13: 66-87, 1988.
17. Mimran, A., J. Ribstein, and B. Joyer. Aging and sodium homeostasis. Kidney Inter. 41: S107-S113, 1992.
18. Nose, H., G. W. Mack, X. Shi, and E. R. Nadel. Role of osmolality and plasma volume during rehydration in humans. J. Appl. Physiol. 65: 325-331, 1988.
19. Phillips, P. A., M. Bretherton, C. I. Johnston, and L. Gray. Reduced osmotic thirst in healthy elderly men. Am. J. Physiol. 261 (Regulatory Integrative Comp. Physiol. 30): R166-R171, 1991.
20. Phillips, P. A., B. J. Rolls, and J. G. G. Ledingham. Body fluid changes, thirst and drinking in man during free access to water. Physiol. Behav. 33: 357-363, 1984.
21. Phillips, P. A., B. J. Rolls, J. G. G. Ledingham, M. L. Forsling, J. J. Morton, M. J. Crowe, and L. Wollner. Reduced thirst after water deprivation in healthy elderly men. N. Engl. J. Med. 311: 753-759, 1984.
22. Quillen, E. W. J., I. A. Reid, and L. C. Keil. Cardiac and arterial baroreceptor influences on plasma vasopressin and drinking. In: Vasopressin: Cellular and Integrative Functions, edited by A. W. Cowley, J. F. Liard and D. A. Ausiello. New York: Raven, 1988, p. 405-411.
23. Robertson, G. L., and S. Athar. The interaction of blood osmolality and blood volume in regulating plasma vasopressin in man. J. Clin. Endocrinol. Metab. 42: 613-620, 1976.
24. Rolls, B. J., and P. A. Phillips. Aging and disturbances of thirst and fluid balance. Nutr. Rev. 48: 137-144, 1990.
25. Sagawa, S., K. Miki, F. Tajima, F. Tanaka, J. K. Choi, L. C. Keil, K. Shiraki, and J. E. Greenleaf. Effect of dehydration on thirst and drinking during immersion in men. J. Appl. Physiol. 72: 128-134, 1992.
26. Shi, X., K. M. Gallagher, R. M. Welch-O'Connor, and B. H. Foresman. Arterial and cardiopulmonary baroreflexes in 60- to 69- vs. 18- to 36-yr-old humans. J. Appl. Physiol. 80: 1903-1910, 1996.
27. Stachenfeld, N. S., G. W. Mack, L. DiPietro, and E. R. Nadel. Mechanism for attenuated thirst in older adults: role of central volume receptors. Am J. Physiol. 272 (Regulatory, Integrative, Comp. Physiol. 41) : R148-R157, 1997.
28. Stachenfeld, N. S., G. W. Mack, A. Takamata, L. DiPietro, and E. R. Nadel. Thirst and fluid regulatory responses to hypertonicity in older adults. Am. J. Physiol. 271 (Regulatory Integrative Comp. Physiol. 40): R757-R765, 1996.
29. Tajima, F., S. Sagawa, J. Iwamoto, K. Miki, J. R. Claybaugh, and K. Shiraki. Renal and endocrine responses in the elderly during head-out water immersion. Am. J. Physiol. 254 (Regulatory Integrative Comp. Physiol. 23): R977-R983, 1988.
30. Trimarco, B., G. Lembo, N. De Luca, M. Volpe, B. Ricciardelli, G. Condorelli, G. Rosiello, and M. Condorelli. Blunted sympathetic response to cardiopulmonary receptor unloading in hypertensive

patients with left ventricular hypertrophy. Circulation 80: 883-892, 1989.

31. Wada, F., S. Sagawa, K. Miki, K. Nagaya, S. Nakamitsu, K. Shiraki, and J. E. Greenleaf. Mechanism of thirst attenuation during head-out water immersion in men. Am. J. Physiol. 268 (Regulatory Integrative Comp. Physiol. 37): R583-R589, 1995.

32. Wazna-Wesly, J. M., D. L. Meranda, P. Carey, and Y. Shenker. Effect of atrial natriuretic hormone on vasopressin and thirst response to osmotic stimulation in humans. J. Lab. Clin. Med. 125: 734-742, 1995.

RELATIONSHIP OF DEHYDRATION AND CHRONIC RENAL INSUFFICIENCY WITH FUNCTION AND COGNITIVE STATUS IN OLDER US BLACKS

D. K. MILLER, H. M. PERRY, III, J. E. MORLEY

From the Division of Geriatric Medicine, St. Louis University Health Sciences Center; and the Geriatric Research, Education, and Clinical Center, St. Louis Veterans Affairs Medical Center; St. Louis, MO. Supported by Grant No. 5 RO1 AG10436 from the National Institute on Aging's Minority Physical Frailty program. Address correspondence to Douglas K. Miller, M.D., Division of Geriatric Medicine, 1402 S. Grand, Rm. M238, St. Louis, MO 63104. Tel : (314) 577-8462. Fax: (314) 771-8575, email: millerdk@wpogate.slu.edu.

Dehydration is the most common fluid and electrolyte disorder seen in older persons [1]. Older persons are particularly susceptible to dehydration [2], and dehydration commonly results in hospitalization of these individuals [3,4]. Dehydration can lead to delirium, orthostatic hypotension, and falls [5-7]. An increased serum urea nitrogen to creatinine ratio and an elevated serum sodium are acceptable markers of dehydration but can be due to other causes in older persons, such as renal failure [8]. Altered renal function with or without an increase in serum creatinine is not rare with aging [2].

There is surprisingly little literature on the community prevalence of dehydration in older persons and its effects on function and cognitive status. Our group has had the opportunity of studying an inner-city population of older African Americans [9]. In view of the paucity of literature on the effects of dehydration in older persons, we have analyzed our data to determine these effects and their relationship to chronic renal insufficiency.

METHODS

Subjects: All subjects were noninstitutionalized, living in a five-square mile catchment area in north St. Louis, and self-described as black or African American. The basic study design, described in detail previously [9], will be reviewed briefly here. A sample frame of all persons aged 70 years and older living in the catchment area was developed using lists from the Health Care Finance Administrations Medicare Enrollment Eligibility File, and those persons who either lived in a nursing home or identified themselves as white (2%) were removed. Six-hundred twelve persons were selected at random from the sample frame and approached for participation, of whom 416 (68%) were recruited and interviewed. An additional 230 subjects were recruited from senior citizen apartments and from programs associated with a community service organization that worked in the catchment area. From these participants 168 persons were recruited into a physical evaluation focused on their strength, balance, body habitus, and nutritional status. Blood tests were obtained on 174 subjects; 134 of these had received the strength and balance evaluation, and 40 had not. Therefore analyses involving historical data and laboratory tests usually included 174 subjects, while those analyses that also involved strength and balance variables included 134 subjects.

Approval was obtained from the St. Louis University (SLU) Health Sciences Center's Institutional Review Board for all research procedures. Informed consent was obtained from all recruited participants in conformance with the assurance given by SLU to the Department of Health and Human Services to protect the rights of human subjects.

Measurement: Independent variables included the following. Creatinine, blood urea nitrogen (BUN), ratio of BUN to creatinine (BUN/Cr), and serum sodium were measured by a reliable commercial laboratory. The laboratory's published upper limit of normal was accepted as the highest normal value for each test (1.5 mg/dl for creatinine, 20 mg/dl for BUN, 18 for BUN/Cr, and 146 meq/L for serum sodium). Creatinine was used as an indicator of renal function, and BUN/Cr and sodium were used as indicators of dehydration.

All frailty dependent variables were obtained without knowledge of the laboratory tests. Dependent variables based on the interview included the following. Basic activities of daily living (ADLs) were measured using the six-item Katz scale [10], and intermediate ADLs were measured using the eight-item Lawton and Brody scale [11]; both scales were scored as the number of items requiring personal assistance. Subjects were asked whether they had fallen to the floor in the prior three months. If the subject sought medical attention or cut down on usual activities after the fall, it was considered injurious. Interviewers also obtained the Geriatric Depression Scale (GDS) [12] and a structured form [13] of the Mini-Mental State Examination (MMSE) [14]. The modified Rosow-Breslau scale was determined using the method of Guralnik et al. [15] and scored 0 to 3 as inability to (a) walk up and down a full flight of stairs, (b) walk one-half mile, or (c) do heavy work around the house without assistance.

Frailty dependent variables based on the strength and balance examination included the following. Speed of cognitive processing was measured using the Trails A test and the standard protocol [16]. Balance was evaluated using the timed one-leg stand with eyes open, as described and validated by Bohannon [17] and a standing-balance scale developed by Guralnik et al. [18], which ranges from 0 (worst) to 4 (best). Ability to perform walking tasks was measured using the timed "Up & Go" test of Podsiadlo and Richardson [19]; in this test the subject arises from a firm chair, walks three meters, turns around, returns to the chair, and sits down again as quickly as possible. Overall physical capabilities were measured with the 7-Item Physical Performance Test (PPT-7) of Reuben and Siu [20]. This test involves lifting a moderately heavy book to shoulder height, writing a sentence, simulated eating using beans and a tin can, donning/doffing a jacket, picking a penny off of the floor, turning 360 degrees while standing, and usual walking speed. During the physical assessment, subjects was also queried regarding their overall subjective quality of life using the QL-index Uniscale developed and validated by Spitzer and colleagues [21].

Each of the dependent variables was coded such that a higher number represented greater frailty. For the MMSE, Guralnik Stance, PPT-7, and quality of life variables, this required reversing the direction of the originally described measure.

Comparison of participants and non-participants: Compared to untested subjects, those receiving blood tests were in slightly better health, reporting fewer basic ADL dependencies (.18 vs .38, P < .001), fewer intermediate ADL dependencies (1.06 vs 1.88, P < .001), higher MMSE (25.2 vs 24.0, P = .002), better Rosow-Breslau functioning (1.06 vs 1.31, P = .015), and a lower percentage being in poor health (4.6% vs 11.7%, P = .007). However, there were no significant differences in age, gender, number of falls or injurious falls, GDS score, Trails A time, one-leg stand time, quality of life, Guralnik stance performance, get "Up & Go" time, or reported fair health.

Statistical Analysis: The relationship between dehydration and renal function independent variables and the frailty dependent variables were tested in two stages. First, each independent variable was regressed against each dependent variable using ordinary least squares linear regression. Second, this regression was repeated, this time controlling for age and sex potential confounding variables. In the case of MMSE, years of formal education was also included because of its strong influence on cognitive testing in general and the MMSE in specific [22,23]. Standardized betas are reported rather than the unstandardized betas to permit an evaluation of the comparative influence of each independent on each dependent variable [24]. (Unstandardized beta results are available from the first author upon request.) Inspections of residuals indicated acceptable distributions for all dependent variables except the one-leg stand, for which the log-normal transformation was used to produce a more acceptable distribution of residuals.

To evaluate which of the independent variables were most strongly associated with each dependent variable, stepwise linear regression was used, again in two stages. In the first stage, only creatinine, BUN/Cr, and sodium were included (denoted the 3-item MLR), because BUN reflects both renal insufficiency and dehydration while the others generally reflect only one or the other. In the second stage (denoted the 4-item MLR), BUN was added to the other three variables and the stepwise linear regression was repeated. Analyses involving the one-leg timed stand again used the log-normal transformed value. Summary R2 for the model are reported.

RESULTS

Pertinent characteristics of the study sample are noted in Table I. Participants were rather older, with mean and median ages near 80, and more than two-thirds was female. Slightly more than a quarter reported fair or poor health, not unusual for this age group. About one-fifth had some degree of renal insufficiency by standard criteria of increased creatinine, and one-tenth appeared somewhat dehydrated with an increased BUN/Cr ratio. Only 1% had in increased serum sodium level. Although this study group has somewhat increased disability and risk for progressive frailty compared to age-sex matched controls [9], they are still in a reasonable range for a noninstitutionalized group of this age (bottom section of Table 1).

Table I
Salient Characteristics of Study Sample

Independent Variables	Result	
Age	79.7	(6.00; 70-97)
Female (%)	67.8	
Self-reported health (%)		
Excellent, very good	50.6	
Good	22.4	
Fair	22.4	
Poor	4.6	
Creatinine	1.28	(0.40; 0.7-3.9)
Cr > 1.5 mg/dl (%)	19.0	
BUN	17.3	(7.99; 6-64)
BUN > 20 mg/dl (%)	23.0	
BUN/Cr	13.4	(3.92; 5.5-29.1)
BUN/Cr > 18 (%)	10.3	
Sodium	141.9	(2.15; 135-147)
Sodium > 146 meq/L	1.1	
Dependent Variables		
Basic ADL Dependencies	0.184	(.469; 0-3)
Intermediate ADL Dependencies	1.06	(1.63; 0-8)
Falls in past 3 mo	0.247	(0.638; 0-4)
Falls > 1 (%)	16.7	
Injurious falls in past 3 mo	0.115	(0.414; 0-3)
Injurious falls > 1 (%)	8.6	
Geriatric Depression Scale	5.10	(4.69; 0-23)
Independent Variables		
Mini-mental State Exam Score	25.2	(3.63; 14-30)
Modified Rosow-Breslau Scale	1.06	(1.07; 0-3)
Trail A time (sec)	107	(77.2; 29.2-514.6)
One-leg stand (sec)	4.61	(6.80; 0-30)
Guralnik Stance Score	2.51	(1.30; 0-4)
Time up and go (sec)	22.3	(25.2; 6.3-110.0)
7-item PPT (0-28)	15.0	(5.26; 3-25)
Quality of life (0-100)	81.4	(19.2; 10-100)

Notes: Results represent mean (standard deviation; range), unless noted. BUN denote blood urea nitrogen, Cr denotes creatinine, and PPT denotes Physical Performance Test.

Table II reports the two stages of regression of each independent variable against each dependent variable. Several patterns of association are worth noting. First, frequently BUN/Cr, creatinine, and BUN were all three significantly associated with each dependent variable, while serum sodium essentially never was. Second, control for age and sex (and for age, sex, and education in the case of MMSE) generally resulted in modest changes at best in the standardized betas (e.g., never did it change by more than 25%). In only two cases did control for covariates change a significant finding into an insignificant finding (creatinine vs Trails A and creatinine vs PPT-7), and even in these cases the changes were modest. Third, standardized betas for BUN were consistently higher than those for both BUN/Cr and creatinine. Fourth, BUN/Cr and creatinine seemed to have approximately similar influence on basic and intermediate ADL dependencies, the modified Rosow-Breslau scale, trails A time, timed "Up & Go", and PPT-7, while dehydration (BUN/Cr) had the more important impact on the GDS, balance (one-leg stand time and Guralnik stance score), and quality of life and renal function (Cr) had the more important influence on number of injurious falls and MMSE result.

The stepwise linear regression results reflected similar findings (Table III). The 3-item regressions indicate the same patterns of association of BUN/Cr and creatinine with the frailty outcome variables and lack of association of sodium with the outcome variables as noted in the prior analyses. The most important finding of the 4-item regressions was that BUN was the only predictive independent variable remaining in the model for nine of the twelve dependent frailty variables; that is, BUN appeared to capture the combined explanatory power of both the BUN/Cr (dehydration) and creatinine (renal function). The only exceptions were the predominant influence of BUN/Cr (dehydration) on the two balance variables and that of creatinine (renal function) on MMSE score. Although the P-values for the independent variables were often highly significant, the total model R2s tended to be modest. The largest model R2s were for intermediate ADL dependencies followed by timed "Up & Go," Trails A time, PPT-7, and Rosow-Breslau functioning. Stepwise linear regression models were also run adding age and gender to both the 3-item and 4-item models. The two new independent variables never changed the significant relationships between the dehydration/renal variables and the frailty dependent variables, although in several cases the total model R2s increased moderately (usually due to the addition of age).

Table 2
Bivariable Relationships Between Dehydration/Renal Function Measures and Measures of Frailty

Frailty Variable	BUN/Cr Ratio		Sodium		Creatinine		BUN	
	Stand. β	P-value	Stand. β	P-value	Stand. β	P-value	Stand. β	P-value
Basic ADL dependencies	0.180	0.018	-0.130	0.086	0.187	0.0136	0.291	0.0001
Control: age, sex	0.175	0.027	-0.148	0.057	0.214	0.0069	0.292	0.0001
IADL dependencies	0.315	0.0001	0.0038	0.960	0.317	0.0001	0.457	0.0001
Control: age, sex	0.293	0.0001	-0.060	0.426	0.317	0.0001	0.422	0.0001
No. of injurious falls	0.110	0.148	-0.093	0.191	0.188	0.013	0.243	0.001
Control: age, sex	0.104	0.188	-0.116	0.138	0.208	0.009	0.242	0.002
Geriatric Depression Scale	0.203	0.008	0.081	0.289	0.0918	0.230	0.213	0.005
Control: age, sex	0.181	0.021	0.060	0.442	0.119	0.113	0.205	0.0075
Mini-Mental State Exam	0.045	0.556	-0.062	0.417	0.274	0.0003	0.221	0.0034
Control: age, sex, & education	-0.007	0.927	-0.089	0.212	0.216	0.003	0.149	0.034
Rosow-Breslau Scale	0.274	0.0002	0.066	0.388	0.198	0.0087	0.330	0.0001
Control: age, sex	0.254	0.001	0.031	0.685	0.221	0.0046	0.314	0.0001

Table 2
Bivariable Relationships Between Dehydration/Renal Function Measures and Measures of Frailty (Cont.)

Frailty Variable	BUN/Cr Ratio		Sodium		Creatinine		BUN	
	Stand. ß	P-value	Stand. ß	P-value	Stand. ß	P-value	Stand. ß	P-value
Trails A time (sec)	0.258	0.004	0.022	0.807	0.189	0.0365	0.357	0.0001
Control: age, sex	0.232	0.010	-0.038	0.666	0.165	0.0769	0.302	0.0005
One-leg stand time (sec)	0.274	0.002	0.034	0.702	0.0694	0.431	0.235	0.0068
Control: age, sex	0.246	0.005	-0.015	0.869	0.0652	0.474	0.203	0.0195
Guralnik Stance Score	0.325	0.0002	0.057	0.522	0.094	0.289	0.314	0.0003
Control: age, sex	0.274	0.002	-0.014	0.871	0.108	0.238	0.276	0.0013
Timed "Up & Go" (sec)	0.260	0.002	0.106	0.224	0.235	0.0062	0.391	0.0001
Control: age, sex	0.250	0.005	0.079	0.373	0.250	.0057	0.377	0.0001
7-item PPT	0.260	0.002	0.128	0.140	0.220	0.0107	0.333	0.0001
Control: age, sex	0.265	0.002	0.098	0.255	0.169	0.0555	0.295	0.0004
Quality of life	0.215	0.014	0.030	0.737	0.158	0.0723	0.230	0.0085
Control: age, sex	0.231	0.010	0.021	0.818	0.120	0.200	0.211	0.0176

Notes: BUN denotes blood urea nitrogen, Stand. b denotes standardized beta from the ordinary least squares regression, ADL denotes activities of daily living, IADL denotes intermediate ADL, and PPT denotes Physical Performance Test.

Table 3
Results of Three-Item and Four-Item Stepwise Multiple Linear Regression

Frailty Variable	3-Item MLR Variable(s) Entered	R2	4-Item MLR Variable(s) Entered	R2
Basic ADL Dependencies	Cr, BUN/Cr	066	BUN	085
IADL Dependencies	Cr, BUN/Cr	195	BUN	209
No. of Injurious Falls	Cr	035	BUN	059
Geriatric Depression Scale	BUN/Cr	041	BUN	045
MMSE	Cr	075	Cr	075
Rosow-Breslau Scale	Cr, BUN/Cr	112	BUN	109
Trails-A Time	Cr, BUN/Cr	097	BUN	127
One-leg Stand Time	BUN/Cr	075	BUN/Cr	075
Guralnik Stance Score	BUN/Cr	106	BUN/Cr	106
Timed "Up & Go"	Cr, BUN/Cr	123	BUN	153
7-Item PPT	Cr, BUN/Cr	115	BUN	111
Quality of Life	BUN/Cr	046	BUN	053

Notes : MLR denotes multivariable stepwise linear regression, ADL denotes activities of daily living, IADL denotes intermediate activities of daily living, MMSE denotes Mini-Mental State Exam, and PPT denotes Physical Performance Test, variable(s) entered denotes those variables found to be significantly associated with the outcome variable after controlling for the other variables in the model, Cr denotes creatinine, and BUN denotes blood urea nitrogen. The 3-item MLR model included BUN/Cr, Cr, and sodium. The 4-item MLR models included the prior three items plus BUN alone.

DISCUSSION

This study has identified that both dehydration (as measured by an increased BUN/creatinine ratio) and renal insufficiency (elevated creatinine) are associated with a number of indicators of frailty, deteriorating mental status, and poorer quality of life. Because of these dual associations (i.e., with both dehydration and renal insufficiency), a BUN alone is a particularly strong predictor of function as measured by the IADL scale explaining more than 20% of the variance in IADL dependencies. Only in areas related to balance was the dehydration index a better prediction of poor performance. This may be related to the propensity of dehydration to produce orthostasis. Overall these findings highlight the importance of fluid imbalance in the pathogenesis of functional impairment in older persons. The modest size of the total model R2s is not surprising for these dependents variables as the different components of frailty usually have multiple significant contributors, often without dominance by one or two explanatory variables [25].

Our previous studies have identified inner city African Americans as being at particular risk for the development of functional impairment [9]. For this reason there is an acute need to identify the factors involved in the pathogenesis of this functional decline. Identification of specific factors that are highly predictive of functional decline should allow the design of specific prevention programs to delay the onset of frailty in this population. The role of renal insufficiency in producing frailty and the well recognized relationship of renal insufficiency to hypertension and diabetes mellitus in this population support the need for aggressive screening for and management of these conditions. Increased community education concerning the putative relationship of these conditions to functional decline is indicated as an important starting point for this effort.

Dehydration has been associated with greater likelihood of hospitalization [3,4], increased hospital costs [2], and higher mortality [4,26]. Our results further support the role of dehydration in placing older persons at increased risk for poor outcomes.

In conclusion this study has suggested that both renal insufficiency and mild degrees of dehydration are important markers for functional decline in older persons. BUN appears to have reasonable power as a possible predictor of poor functional status in older, inner city African Americans.

REFERENCES

1. Lavizzo-Mourey R, Johnson J, Stolley P. Risk factors for dehydration among elderly nursing home residents. J Am Geriatr Soc 1988; 36:213-8.
2. Weinberg AD, Minaker KL. Dehydration. Evaluation and management in older adults. Council on Scientific Affairs, American Medical Association. JAMA 1995; 274:1552-6.
3. Vital and Health Statistics from the Centers for Disease Control and Prevention/National Center for Health Statitistics. Detailed Diagnoses and Procedures, National Hospital Discharge Survey 1991. Washington, DC: US Dept of Health and Human Services, 1994.
4. Warren JL, Bacon WE, Harris T, McBean AM, Foley DJ, Phillips C. The burden and outcomes associated with dehydration among US elderly, 1991. Am J Public Health 1994; 84:1265-9.
5. Seymour DG, Henschke PJ, Cape RD, Campbell AJ. Acute confusional states and dementia in the elderly: the role of dehydration/volume depletion, physical illness and age. Age Ageing 1980; 9:137-46.
6. Francis J, Martin D, Kapoor WN. A prospective study of delirium in hospitalized elderly. JAMA 1990; 263:1097-101.
7. Inouye SK, Viscoli CM, Horwitz RI, Hurst LD, Tinetti ME. A predictive model for delirium in hospitalized elderly medical patients based on admission characteristics. Ann Intern Med 1993; 119:474-81.
8. Gross CR, Lindquist RD, Woolley AC, Granieri R, Allard K, Webster B. Clinical indicators of dehydration severity in elderly patients. J Emerg Med 1992; 10:267-74.

9. Miller DK, Carter ME, Miller JP, et al. Inner-city older blacks have high levels of functional disability. J Am Geriatr Soc 1996; 44:1166-73.

10. Katz S, Ford AB, Moskowitz RW, Jackson BA, Jaffe MW. Studies of illness in the aged. The index of ADL: a standardized measure of biological and psychosocial function. JAMA 1963; 185:914-9.

11. Lawton MP, Brody EM. Assessment of older people: self-maintaining and instrumental activities of daily living. Gerontologist 1969; 9:179-86.

12. Yesavage JA, Brink TL, Rose TL, et al. Development and validation of a geriatric depression screening scale: a preliminary report. J Psychiatr Res 1982-3; 17:37-49.

13. Molloy DW, Alemayehu E, Roberts R. Reliability of a standardized Mini-Mental State Examination compared with the traditional Mini-Mental State Examination. Am J Psychiatry 1991; 148:102-5.

14. Folstein MF, Folstein SE, McHugh PR. "Mini-mental state." A practical method for grading the cognitive state of patients for the clinician. J Psychiatr Res 1975; 12:189-98.

15. Guralnik JM, LaCroix AZ, Branch LG, Kasl SV, Wallace RB. Morbidity and disability in older persons in the years prior to death. Am J Public Health 1991; 81:443-7.

16. Reitan RM. Trail Making Test. Manual for Administration and Scoring. Tucson, Arizona: Reitan Neuropsychology Laboratory, 1986.

17. Bohannon RW, Larkin PA, Cook AC, Gear J, Singer J. Decrease in time balance test scores with aging. Phys Ther 1984; 64:1067-70.

18. Guralnik JM, Simonsick EM, Ferrucci L, et al. A short physical performance battery assessing lower extremity function: association with self-reported disability and prediction of mortality and nursing home admission. J Gerontol 1994; 49:M85-94.

19. Podsiadlo D, Richardson S. The timed "Up & Go": a test of basic functional mobility for frail elderly persons. J Am Geriatr Soc 1991; 39:142-8.

20. Reuben DB, Siu AL. An objective measure of physical function of elderly outpatients: the physical performance test. J Am Geriatr Soc 1990; 38:1105-12.

21. Spitzer WO, Dobson AJ, Hall J, et al. Measuring the quality of life of cancer patients: a concise QL-Index for use by physicians. J Chron Dis 1981; 34:585-97.

22. Murden RA, McRae TD, Kaner S, Bucknam ME. Mini-Mental State Exam scores vary with education in blacks and whites. J Am Geriatr Soc 1991; 39:149-55.

23. Crum RM, Anthony JC, Bassett SS, Folstein MF. Populaiton-based norms for the Mini-Mental State Examination by age and educational level. JAMA 1993; 269:2386-91.

24. SAS Institute Inc. SAS/STAT User's Guide, Version 6, Fourth Edition, Volume 2. Cary, NC: SAS Institute Inc., 1990.

25. Fried LP, Guralnik JM. Disability in older adults: evidence regarding significance, etiology, and risk. J Am Geriatr Soc 1997; 45:92-100.

26. Weinberg AD, Pals JK, Levesque PG, Beal LF, Cunningham TJ, Minaker KL. Dehydration and death during febrile episodes in the nursing home. J Am Geriatr Soc 1994; 41:968-71.

HYDRATION AND AGING

III - INTERVENTION

CHARACTERISTICS OF FLUDROCORTISONE ACETATE-RESPONSIVE HYPONATREMIA IN ELDERLY PATIENTS

S.-E ISHIKAWA, T. SAITO

Division of Endocrinology and Metabolism, Department of Medicine, Jichi Medical School, Tochigi 329-04 Japan.Mail Proofs to: San-e Ishikawa, M. D., Division of Endocrinology and Metabolism, Department of Medicine, Jichi Medical School, 3311-1 Yakushiji Minamikawachi-machi, Tochigi 329-04 Japan.Phone: 81-285-44-2111 Fax: 81-285-44-8143

INTRODUCTION

Hyponatremia may occur in association with increased, decreased or normal amounts of body fluid [1]. Dilution of extracellular sodium (Na) by increased body fluid appears to lead to hyponatremia in most clinical setting. Hypovolemic hyponatremia results from renal or extrarenal loss of Na, but it is a minor cause of hyponatremia. Syndrome of inappropriate secretion of antidiuretic hormone (SIADH) is classified in euvolemic hyponatremia. In most clinical setting of hyponatremia, arginine vasopressin (AVP) release is augmented either primarily or secondarily. In the present review, we describe hyponatremia in the elderly patients, and discuss regarding the pathophysiological role of AVP in hyponatremia and the efficacy of fludrocortisone acetate therapy.

MECHANISM OF AVP SECRETION

AVP is the peptide hormone of the pituitary gland and synthesized in both magnocellular and parvocellular neurosecretory neurons of the hypothalamus [2]. Cell bodies of these neurons reside in the supraoptic nuclei (SON) and paraventricular nuclei (PVN). The major projection of magnocellular neurosecretory neurons is to the posterior pituitary. AVP is released from the posterior pituitary to the blood vessels in response to osmotic and nonosmotic stimuli and controls body water homeostasis and blood pressure. The axon terminals of paraventricular neurons reach the zona externa of the median eminence of the hypothalamus, and act as a neurotransmitter, possibly involved in a variety of functions.

Osmotic and nonosmotic stimuli are the two major factors that control AVP release. Osmoreceptors reside in the anteroventral third ventricle (AV3V) region of the hypothalamus, particularly in the organum vasculosum of the lamina terminalis (OVLT), where is located outside the blood-brain barrier, and are sensitive to changes in plasma osmolality (Posm). There are neural inputs from the osmoreceptors to the PVN and SON.

There is a close correlation between Posm and plasma AVP levels in normal subjects and in patients with various states of hydration [3]. Linear regression analysis yielded the osmotic threshold for AVP secretion and the sensitivity of the osmoreceptors. There is a linear relationship between Posm and plasma AVP levels in the physiologic range of Posm. The osmotic threshold for AVP secretion is the point of the intercept on the horizontal axis, that is 280 mOsm/kg H_2O. Several factors potentially affect the osmotic threshold [4]. There seems likely to be a species difference in osmotic threshold for AVP secretion: osmotic threshold ranges from 285 to 292 mOsm/kg H_2O in the rat, dog and monkey. Posm decreases 8 - 10 mOsm/kg H_2O during the prenancy, which is accompanied by a decrement in the osmotic threshold for AVP secretion. In addition, nonosmotic stimuli influence the osmotic threshold. Decreases in circulating blood volume and blood pressure enhance the release of AVP by osmotic stimuli, which shift the osmotic threshold to the left without any change in the sensitivity. The slope of the linear regression line may be affected by several factors, including the nature of solutes, the rate of change in Posm, age and drinking behaviour.

There are other pathways to the magnocellular neurosecretary neurons of SON and PVN from the brain stem [4]. These pathways are based on catecholaminergic neurons. Afferent fibers from arterial baroreceptors terminate in the nucleus of the solitary tract of the dorsomedial medulla oblongata (NTS), mediated through vagal nerve. The A1 adrenergic cell group of the ventrolateral medulla is suggested to be involved in the afferent pathway from the NTS to neurosecretory AVP cells of the SON and PVN. Bilateral cervical vagotomy caused an AVP-mediated antidiuresis. This effect of vagotomy was due to the interruption of tonic baroreceptor-mediated inhibition of AVP secretion.

Decreases in arterial blood pressure and circulating blood volume are the potent nonosmotic stimuli to AVP secretion, mediating the high-pressure and low-pressure (left atrial) baroreceptors. It has been generally accepted that a decrement in blood pressure or blood volume of the order of 8% to 10% is necessary to stimulate AVP secretion [5]. Several additional factors, including low cardiac output, left atrial distention, atrial tachycardia, nicotine and hypoxia are also evident as the nonosmotic stimuli of AVP secretion [4].

RENAL TUBULAR ACTION OF AVP

AVP receptors at the basolateral membranes of renal collecting duct cells are functionally coupled to the Gs protein, leading to the activation of adenylate cyclase (Fig. 1) [6]. The AVP receptors are classified as V2 receptors. Lolait et al. [7] and Birnbaumer et al. [8] independently cloned AVP V2 receptors in kidney of rat and human, respectively. The human V2 receptor cDNA encodes a 371-amino acid protein, a characteristic of G protein-coupled receptors. Receptor occupancy with AVP leads to a conformational change of GDP to GTP in the -subunit of Gs, which allows it to stimulate adenylate cyclase of catalytic unit. Cyclic AMP is a cellular second messenger, and activates cAMP-dependent protein kinase. Cyclic AMP is catabolized by cAMP-dependent phosphodiesterase.

Fig. 1

Cellular action of AVP in renal collecting duct cells. R: AVP V2 receptor, Gs: guanine nucleotide-binding protein, C: catalytic unit, AdC: adenylate cyclase, and PDE: phosphodiesterase

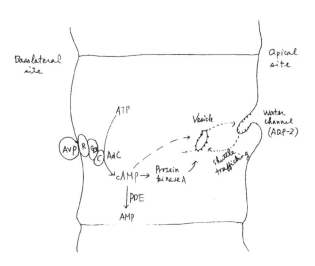

It has been suggested that microtubules and microfilaments are involved in the initiation of intramembranous aggregations and water flow, dependent on AVP. In 1993, a cDNA of apical collecting duct water channel, aquaporin-2, was cloned by Sasaki et al. [9]. The expression of aquaporin-2 mRNA is increased by AVP. Aquaporin-2 are present in the membranes of cytoplasmic vesicles of collecting duct cells, and are translocated to the apical plasma membranes when the cells are stimulateed by AVP. The 5′-flanking region of the aquaporin-2 gene contains cAMP-responsive element. Therefore, cAMP induced by AVP probably plays a key role in regulating the transcriptional rates of the aquaporin-2. Aquaporin-2 on the apical plasma membrane act as water channel and produce water permeability. These findings may exclude the involvement of microtubules and microfilaments in shuttle trafficking of aquaporin-2 in collecting duct cells.

URINARY CONCENTRATION AND AVP SECRETION IN ELDERLY

We studied urinary concentrating ability and secretion of AVP from the posterior pituitary gland in elderly subjects [10]. The studies were carried out in two groups of healthy volunteers, including the elderly group aged 65 to 80 years and the young group with age of 20 to 34 years. (a) Fishberg test: Water drinking was prohibited at least 12 h after the last supper, and in the early morning three urine collections were made at 1-h intervals. The maximal urinary osmolality (Uosm) was 620.6 ± 74.1 mOsm/kg H_2O in the elderly group, which was significantly less than that of 904.4 ± 48.5 mOsm/kg H_2O in the young group (P<0.05). (b) 1-Deamino-8-D-arginine vasopressin (DDAVP) test: After urine and blood collections were made, water (15 ml/kg body weight) was given orally for 30 min. Ten ug DDAVP was given intranasally, and thereafter 1-h urine collection was made for 4 h to measure urine volume and Uosm. Water drinking was forced in the same volume as urine volume at each time when urine was collected. The changes in urine volume and Uosm is shown in Fig. 2. Uosm was reduced to 115.2 ± 22.6 mOsm/kg H_2O in the young group after the oral intake of water. In the elderly group, however, Uosm decreased to only 315.3 ± 69.2 mOsm/kg H_2O, a value significantly greater than that of the young group. After the administration of DDAVP, Uosm increased to 828.7 ± 55.7 mOsm/kg H_2O at 4 h in the young group. Uosm only elevated to 487.8 ± 82.5 mOsm/kg H_2O in the elderly. These results indicate that both urinary concentrating and diluting ability were diminished in the elderly subjects. The reduced urinary concentrating is based on the impaired renal response to AVP. This is supported by the in vitro study showing that the AVP-induced production of cAMP is less in collecting duct of the aged rats than in the young ones [11]. (c) Hypertonic saline test: After urine and blood collections were made, hypertonic saline (5% NaCl) was infused intravenously at a rate of 0.05 ml/kg/min for 120 min. Blood was collected at 30 min intervals for 120 min to measure Posm and plasma AVP levels. The changes in Posm and plasma AVP levels are shown in Fig. 3. Posm increased comparably by 13 mOsm/kg H_2O in both two groups of subjects, which is sufficient to stimulate osmotic release of AVP. An increase in Posm caused a significant increase in plasma AVP levels in both the elderly and the young groups of subjects. The secretion of AVP seemed great in the elderly subjects as compared to that in the young ones, though no significant difference was seen between the two groups. (d) Tilting test: All the subjects had had a Na intake of 8 g/day for a week. They were placed in the supine position on a tilt table, and a venous catheter was inserted through a cubital vein. Thirty min later, the subjects were kept in place at 60° head-up tilt for 20 min, and thereafter they were placed in the supine position again. During the 90 min observation period, blood pressure and heart rate were determined at 5 min intervals. Also, plasma AVP levels and plasma renin activity (PRA) were determined before the head-up tilt and 10, 20, 30 and 60 min after the 60° head-up tilt. These results are shown in Fig. 4. A twenty min head-up tilt produced significant increase in heart rate and mean arterial pressure (MAP) in the young group of subjects. In contrast, there was no significant change in heart rate and MAP in response to the head-up tilt in the elderly subjects. Plasma AVP levels significantly increased following the head-up tilt in both groups. The magnitude was greater in the elderly group than in the young group. Head-up tilt also caused a significant increase in PRA in both two groups, and there was no difference in PRA between the elderly and young groups (data not shown).

Fig. 2

Response of Uosm to 10 ug nasal administration of DDAVP. Open circles show the elderly subjects. Closed circles show the young ones. Values are means ± SEM, n = 6.

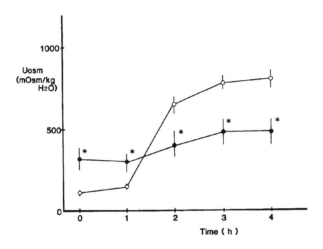

Fig. 3

Changes in Posm and plasma AVP levels in response to hypertonic saline test (5% NaCl at a rate of 0.05 ml/kg/min). Open circles show the elderly subjects, and closed circles show the young ones. Values are means ± SEM, n=6.

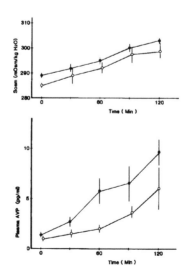

Fig. 4

Changes in heart rate (HR) and mean arterial pressure (MAP) and plasma AVP levels following 60° head-up tilt. Open circles show the elderly subjects, and closed circles show the young ones. *P<0.05 vs. the value before the head-up tilt. +P<0.05 vs. the respective value of the young subjects. Values are means ± SEM, n=6 (cited from ref. 10)

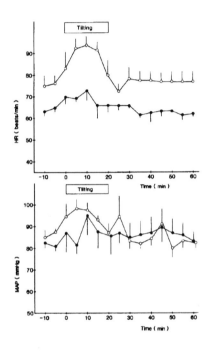

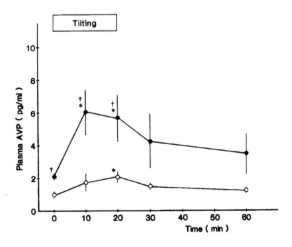

CLASSIFICATION OF HYPONATREMIA

Serum concentration of Na is originated from the composition of water and Na in extracellular fluid, and it ranges from 135 to 146 mEq/l. Hyponatremia can be classified into three types of hyponatremia, including hypovolemic, euvolemic and hypervolemic hyponatremia [1]. Physical finding plays a key role in differentiating hyponatremia. Hypovolemic hyponatremia, due to a primary loss of Na and associated loss of water (Fig. 5), shows dehydration. We can find the dryness of skin and a tongue, hypotension and tachycardia, and the latter two findings are dependent on its severity of dehydration. There are two subgroups of renal and extrarenal loss of Na (Fig. 6). Urinary excretion of Na persistently increased despite of hyponatremia in patients with hypovolemic hyponatremia dependent upon renal loss of Na. Urinary excretion of Na markedly reduced in patients with hypovolemic hyponatremia dependent on extrarenal loss of Na. Hypervolemic hyponatremia appears in patients with edematous diseases, including congestive heart failure, decompensated liver cirrhosis and nephrotic syndrome (Fig. 6) [12, 13]. The underlined diseases have their features of history, physical findings and laboratory data, and so the diagnosis is not so hard. Urinary excretion of Na is usually less than 10 mEq/l. The third type of hyponatremia is euvolemic hyponatremia. This includes syndrome of inappropriate secretion of antidiuretic hormone (SIADH), glucocorticoid deficiency and hypothyroidism (Fig. 6). The diagnostic criteria for SIADH includes hyponatremia, hypoosmolality, exaggerated urinary excretion of Na, hypertonic urine, no edema, no dehydration, and normal functions of kidney and adrenal gland [14]. Recent development of laboratory analysis revealed additional criteria for SIADH, that includes low PRA, low concentration of serum uric acid and relatively high concentration of plasma AVP compared with hypoosmolality. However, we have recognized that it is difficult to diagnose SIADH dependent simply on the above-mentioned criteria, particularly, in elderly patients. As mentioned in detail later, hyponatremia in elderly, which has not associated with particular disease, should be included in euvolemic hyponatremia. Clinical entity of hyponatremia in elderly is distinct from that of SIADH, and these differential diagnosis is very important because of the appropriate treatment indicated.

Fig. 5

Schema of relation between extracellular Na content and fluid in three types of hyponatremia.

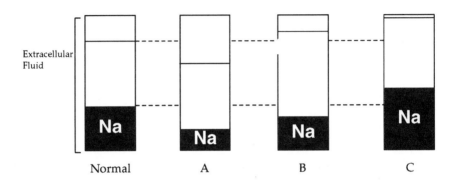

Fig. 6

Classification of hyponatremia (cited from ref. 1)

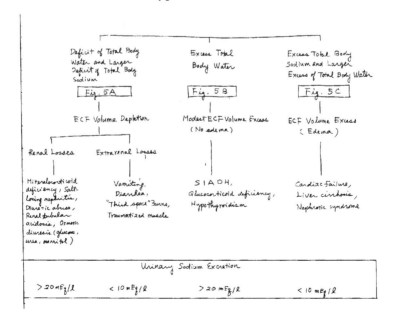

HYPONATREMIA RESPONSIVE TO FLUDROCORTISONE ACETATE

A 70 year-old man fractured his skull after falling off a bicycle [15]. A serum electrolyte analysis showed normal concentrations of Na, 141 mEq/l; K, 3.6 mEq/l; and chloride (Cl), 94 mEq/l. Approximately 2 weeks later he developed tinnitus, gait disturbance and loss of recent memory. The serum level of Na had decreased to 105 mEq/l. He was diagnosed as having SIADH; treatment consisted of hypertonic saline infusions and restriction of water intake. The Na level did not return to within the normal range, however. Physical findings were blood pressure, 130/90 mmHg without postural changes; and pulse rate, 88/min with regular rhythym. His reactions were sluggish and he had dry skin and a dry tongue. Neurologic examination showed cerebral dysfunction that included diminished bilateral deep tendon reflexes and an ataxic gait.

Laboratory studies showed serum concentration of Na at 127 mEq/l; K, 4.2 mEq/l; and Cl, 91 mEq/l. Serum creatinine was 0.6 mg/dl, and serum uric acid, 0.6 mg/dl. Posm was 259 mOsm/kg H_2O and Uosm, 460 mOsm/kg H_2O. Urinary excretion of Na and K were 324 and 32 mEq/day, respectively. Creatinine clearance was 84.4 ml/min. PRA measured 0.34 ng/ml/h and plasma aldosterone concentration was 5.5 ng/dl. The PRA and aldosterone level did not increase after the intravenous administration of furosemide, 1 mg/kg body weight, and after the patient had been in an upright position for 2 h. The plasma aldosterone level increased normally in response to the intravenous administration of ACTH. Plasma AVP level was 6.8 pg/ml.

Clinical course (Fig. 7): After hospitalization, the infusion of hypertonic saline was stopped and the patient began an alternating dietary Na regimen of 153 and 258 mEq/day. Mean serum levels of Na and K were 122 and 4.8 mEq/l, respectively. Urinary excretion of Na increased to between 200 and 300 mEq/day, however, and resulted in a Na deficit. Posm decreased to below 260 mOsm/kg H_2O, but Uosm persisted at levels of 450 to 700 mOsm/kg H_2O. Fludrocortisone acetate treatment was begun to compensate for the elevation in the serum K level and the reduction in the serum Na level. This treatment led to a decrease in urinary excretion of Na. The serum Na level promptly increased to the normal value and, conversely, the serum K level decreased. However, in mid-April the drug administration was stopped, and resulted in appearing hyponatremia and hyperkalemia within 10 days again (Fig. 8). The reinstitution of treatment with fludrocortisone acetate was effective. The return to normal of serum Na levels improved his higher cerebral function.

Fig. 7

Clinical course of hyponatremia before and after therapy with fludrocortisone acetate (cited from ref. 15)

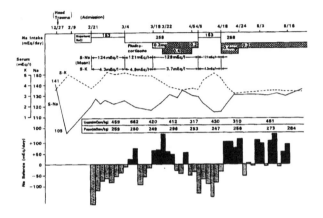

Fig. 8

Relationship between Posm and plasma AVP levels in two groups of elderly patients with SIADH (closed circles) and central salt-wasting syndrome (open circles). Shaded area shows the normal range (cited from ref. 10)

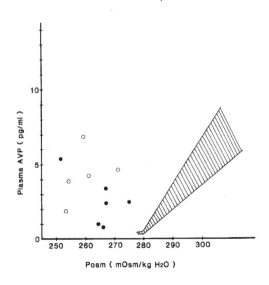

173

Before admitting to our hospital, he was diagnosed as SIADH. However, we indicated a different pathophysiological condition of hyponatremia, which is fit to the criteria for SIADH except for the presence of mild dehydration. Hyponatremia was extremely responsive to fludrocortisone acetate, and we diagnosed so-called "central salt-wasting syndrome" [16,17]. After this case, we have experienced additional cases, and recognized that SIADH in elderly seemed unlikely to differ from central salt-wasting syndrome.

Eleven elderly patients with SIADH and central salt-wasting syndrome were admitted to our hospital, whose serum Na levels were less than 130 mEq/l after examining the initial case described above. They were 7 males and 4 females whose ages were 65 years or older [10]. Six patients with SIADH had hyponatremia, hypoosmolality, exaggerated urinary excretion of Na, hypertonic urine and normal renal and adrenal functions (Table 1). And physical findings showed neither edema nor dehydration. SIADH occurred in 3 patients after cerebral infarction, in 2 patients after head trauma and in one patient in whom the cause was considered idiopathic. Serum Na levels ranged from 107 to 125 mEq/l when hyponatremia was discovered.

Table 1
Laboratory data of six elderly patients with SIADH

		Patient					
		1	2	3	4	5	6
Age, Sex		66M	79F	77M	65M	72M	65F
Serum Na	mEq/l	119	124	109	109	125	124
Serum K	mEq/l	4.5	4.4	3.3	4.0	3.8	4.0
Serum Cl	mEq/l	87	88	69	68	86	91
Blood urea nitrogen	mg/dl	8	19	8	7	13	12
Serum uric acid	mg/dl	2.9	3.5	1.1	2.6		1.7
Plasma osmolality	mOsm/kg H_2O	257	266		238	268	267
Urinary sodium	mEq/day	214	201	132	169		143
Urinary potassium	mEq/day	32	34	30	42		44
Plasma renin activity	ng/ml/h	3.20	1.01	1.41	1.37	0.89	1.48
Plasma aldosterone	ng/dl	5.7	10.5	2.8	4.2	2.4	4.9
Plasma arginine vasopressin	pg/ml	3.4	0.7	1.9	2.4	1.0	2.4

In five patients with central salt-wasting syndrome, hyponatremia was associated with hypoosmolality, hypertonic urine and persistently increased urinary excretion of Na (Table 2). It is unlikely that renal and adrenal functions were poor to have caused a massive renal loss of Na. Physical findings including dry skin, a dry tongue and decreased body weight, suggested the presence of dehydration in four of 5 patients. Three of 5 patients had had head injury 1 - 4 weeks before hyponatremia was manifested. Such accidents were closely related to the onset of hyponatremia, because two patients were confirmed to have had normal values of serum Na when they got head trauma. In two patients there was no particular matter related to the occurrence of hyponatremia.

Table 2
Laboratory data of five patients with central salt-wasting syndrome

		Patient				
		1	2	3	4	5
Age, Sex		86M	71F	79M	71M	78F
Serum Na	mEq/l	117	106	129	105	109
Serum K	mEq/l	5.1	4.7	4.0	4.2	3.9
Serum Cl	mEq/l	82	66	93	67	71
Blood urea nitrogen	mg/dl	10	15	6	8	15
Serum uric acid	mg/dl	2.5	0.3	1.6	0.6	1.1
Plasma osmolality	mOsm/kg H_2O	254	234	271	228	247
Urinary sodium	mEq/day	225	240	177	324	132
Urinary potassium	mEq/day	14	66	29	53	32
Plasma renin activity	ng/ml/h	0.1	0.5	0.4	0.3	1.4
Plasma aldosterone	ng/dl	1.5	2.8	4.2	5.5	2.8
Plasma arginine vasopressin	pg/ml	4.2	3.9	4.6	6.8	1.9

As shown in Tables 1 and 2, plasma AVP levels of the SIADH patients were comparable to those of 1. 4 ± 0.2 pg/ml of the control subjects, and they seem to be less than those of patients with central salt-wasting syndrome. Plasma AVP levels were detectable by RIA in all the patients, though serum Na levels were reduced as mentioned earlier. Figure 8 shows the relationship between Posm and plasma AVP levels. The shaded area means the normal relationship of the control subjects. All the plots shifted to the left. Plasma AVP levels were not sufficiently suppressed despite hypoosmolality in the two groups of patients.

Therapy for hyponatremia: Since dehydration was present in the patients with central salt-wasting syndrome, whose other clinical manifestations were compatible with SIADH, water restriction was not done. They were given 15 - 20 g/day of dietary NaCl for 14 - 154 days, but serum Na levels remained low, in association with the increased renal loss of Na. The patients whose serum Na levels were less than 120 mEq/l were given hypertonic saline intravenously, and the serum Na levels were kept above 120 mEq/l. Thereafter, fludrocortisone acetate at a dose of 0.1 - 0.4 mg/day was given orally. Within a week serum Na levels were elevated above 135 mEq/l, and serum K levels conversely decreased from the high-normal to the low-normal value (Fig. 9). Also, urinary excretion of Na was diminished. Hematocrit levels decreased after the drug administration and indicated approximately 8% decrease in circulating blood volume during the episode of hyponatremia. The dose of fludrocortisone acetate was thus reduced to 0.1 mg/day, and serum Na levels normalized. However, this therapy could not discontinue at least 6 months after the start of therapy, because hyponatremia occurred again.

Fig. 9
Changes in serum Na and K levels after the fludrocortisone acetate therapy in 5 patients with central salt-wasting syndrome. Closed circles and open circles show serum Na and K levels, respectively. Values are means ± SEM. (cited from ref. 10)

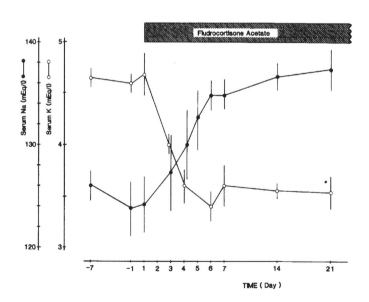

The patients with SIADH restricted water intake of less than 20 ml/kg body weight. In three of 6 patients serum Na levels gradually normalized in approximately 30 days. In contrast, hyponatremia remained unchanged in the other 3 patients. Fludrocortisone acetate (0.1 mg) was given orally to the latter 3 patients who were not sensitive to water restriction. Urinary excretion of Na was reduced, and serum Na levels normalized in 9 days.

Here, we show hyponatremia responsive to fludrocortisone acetate in the elderly patients. This group of patients have been diagnosed as central salt-wasting syndrome. Hyponatremia was associated with hypoosmolality, hypertonic urine and persistently increased urinary excretion of Na. It is unlikely that renal and adrenal functions were poor enough to have caused a massive renal Na excretion. Plasma AVP levels were relatively high despite hypoosmolality. Since AVP secretion is greater in the elderly subjects than in the young, the influence of age on AVP secretion may be involved in the development of hyponatremia. The reduced concentrating ability may also contribute to the augmented secretion of AVP in the elderly subjects. These findings are not inconsistent with the pathological state of SIADH. Only differences are dry skin and a dry tongue in physical finding, and fluctuation in hematocrit values and body weight during the hospital course, suggesting the presence of dehydration. Therefore, we had to distinguish the disorder from SIADH. Such a category is also supported by the following evidences. There are the findings of conversely proportional changes in serum electrolytes, that is, a reduction in Na and an increase in K and the prompt normalization of serum electrolytes in response to fludrocortisone acetate. In addition, hyponatremia persisted because the patients could not maintain normal serum Na levels, even more 6 months after the start of fludrocortisone acetate therapy, without the drug administration.

Low renin activity and concomitant low concentration of plasma aldosterone were not expected in the dehydration. These alterations are not infrequently found in the elderly, whether they were accompanied by hyponatremia or not [18, 19]. The therapy with fludrocortisone acetate dramatically improved hyponatremia, and thus hyponatremia may have a close relation with the disorder of renin-aldosterone system. Elevation of plasma AVP and hypoaldosteronism appear to have been involved in the pathogenesis of hyponatremia in the patients with central salt-wasting syndrome. The increase in plasma AVP might have interrupted the compensatory mechanisms to maintain Na balance, that resulted in the increased renal loss of Na and hyponatremia. Elevation of plasma AVP seems frequent in the elderly subjects, and it is not simply noted that the increase in plasma AVP levels is a secondary phenomenon due to the reduced circulating blood volume. The enhanced release of AVP may rather be a causitive factor for initiating hyponatremia, in association with latent disorder of renal sodium handling , in patients with central salt-wasting syndrome.

As mentioned above, only three of 6 patients with SIADH were responsible to the restriction of water intake less than 20 ml/kg, and serum Na levels normalized. In other 3 patients the signs of hyponatremia were not alleviated after the therapy. Hyponatremia remained unchanged in association with the exaggerated renal loss of Na. The treatment with fludrocortisone acetate normalized serum Na levels in 9 days. We could not distinguish the elderly patients with SIADH who responded to the water restriction therapy from those who did not respond to it, before the start of the therapy. Since AVP secretion is greater in the elderly subjects than in the young, we can not evaluate that SIADH in the elderly subjects is an equal situation to that in the non-elderly. The causes of hyponatremia may be multifactorial in the elderly patients who are diagnosed as SIADH. Hyponatremia is clinically based on SIADH, but the therapy by water restriction is not simply decided. There may be hyponatremia responsive to fludrocortisone acetate in the elderly patients with SIADH, and SIADH in the elderly patients seems unlikely to be distinguished from the disorder of central salt-wasting syndrome. Taken together, the criteria for SIADH in the elderly patients may have to reevaluated carefully.

REFERENCES

1. Berl, T., Schrier, R. W.: Disorders of water metabolism. IN: Renal and Electrolytes Disorders. Third Ed., (ed) Schrier, R. W., Little, Brown and Company, 1986, pp. 1-77.
2. Ishikawa, S., Okada K., Saito, T.: Vasopressin secretion in health and disease. IN: The Pituitary Gland, Second Ed., (ed) Imura, H., Raven Press, New York, 1994, pp. 331-350.
3. Robertson, G. L., Mahr, E. A., Athar, S., Sinha, T.: Development and clinical application of a new method for the radioimmunoassay of arginine vasopressin in human plasma. J. Clin. Invest. 52: 2340-2352, 1973.
4. Schrier, R. W., Berl, T., Anderson, R. J.: Osmotic and nonosmotic control of vasopressin release. Am. J. Physiol. 236: F321-F332, 1979.
5. Robertson, G. L.: The regulation of vasopressin function in health and disease. Recent Prog. Horm. Res. 23: 333-385, 1977.
6. Ishikawa, S.: Cellular actions of arginine vasopressin in the kidney. Endocrine J. 40: 373-386, 1993.
7. Lolait, S. J., O'Carroll, A. M., McBride, O. W., Konig, M., Morel, A., Brownstein, M. J.: Cloning and characterization of a vasopressin V2 receptor and possible link to nephrogenic diabetes insipidus. Nature 357: 336-339, 1992.
8. Birnbaumer, M., Seibold, A., Gilbert, S., Ishido, M., Barberis, C., Antaramian, A., Brabet, P., Rosenthal, W.: Molecular cloning of the receptor for human antidiuretic hormone. Nature 357: 333-335, 1992.
9. Fushimi, K., Uchida, S., Hara, Y., Hirata, Y., Marumo, F., Sasaki, S.: Cloning and expression of apical membrane water channel of rat kidney collecting tubule. Nature 361: 549-552, 1993.
10. Ishikawa, S., Fujita, N., Fujisawa, G., Tsuboi, Y., Sakuma, N., Okada, K., Saito, T.: Involvement of arginine vasopressin and renal sodium handling in pathogenesis of hyponatremia in elderly

patients. Endocrine J. 43: 101-108, 1996.

11. Goddard, C., Davidson, Y. S., Moser, B. B., Davies, I., Faragher, E. B.: Effect of aging on cyclic AMP output by renal medullary cells in response to arginine vasopressin in vitro in C57BL/Icrfa mice. J. Endocrinol. 103: 133-139, 1984.

12. Schrier, R. W.: Pathogenesis of sodium and water retention in high-output and low-output cardiac failure, nephrotic syndrome, cirrhosis and pregnancy. N. Engl. J. Med. 319: 1065-1072, 1988.

13. Schrier, R. W.: Pathogenesis of sodium and water retention in high-output and low-output cardiac failure, nephrotic syndrome, cirrhosis and pregnancy. N. Engl. J. Med. 319: 1127-1134, 1988.

14. Bartter, F. C., Schwartz, W. B.: The syndrome of inappropriate secretion of antidiuretic hormone. Am. J. Med. 42: 790-806, 1967.

15. Ishikawa, S., Saito, T., Kaneko, K., Okada, K., Kuzuya, T.: Hyponatremia responsive to fludrocortisone acetate in elderly patients after head injury. Ann. Intern. Med. 106: 187-191, 1987.

16. Welt, L. G., Seldin, D. W., Nelson, W. P., German, W. J., Peters, J. P.: Role of the central nervous system in metabolism of electrolytes and water. Arch. Intern. Med. 90: 355-378, 1952.

17. Al-Mufti, H., Arieff, A. I.: Hyponatremia due to cerebral salt-wasting syndrome: combined cerebral and distal tubular lesion. Am. J. Med. 77: 740-746, 1984.

18. Crane, M. G., Harris, J. J.: Effect of aging on renin activity and aldosterone secretion. J. Lab. Clin. Med. 87: 947-959, 1976.

19. Zadik, Z., Kowarski, A. A.: Normal integrated concentration of aldosterone and plasma renin activity: Effect of age. J. Clin. Endocrinol. Metab. 50: 867-869, 1980.

THE MANAGEMENT OF DEHYDRATION
IN THE NURSING HOME

M-M. G. WILSON

Division of Geriatric Medicine, St louis University Health Sciences Center and The GRECC, V.A. Medical Center, St Louis, MO

"Water ... not necessary to life, but rather life itself ..."
Saint - Exupery; Wind, Sand and Stars. (1939), 8, Tr. Lewis Galantiere

The syndrome of dehydration in older persons receives relatively scant attention from health professionals, despite the fact that existing data highlights the relatively high prevalence, morbidity and mortality associated with this syndrome. Data from Medicare Provider Analysis and Review files, compiled in 1991 by the Health Care Financing Administration (HCFA), identify dehydration as one of the 10 most common diagnoses reported for Medicare Hospitalizations [1]. In that year, among Medicare beneficiaries aged 65 - 99 years, 6.7% had a diagnosis of dehydration with 1.4% bearing dehydration as the primary diagnosis. The mortality rate within thirty days of admission was 18%, approximately three times the comparative rate for hip fractures. Increasing age was highlighted as a major risk factor for dehydration, with persons older than 85 years being six times more likely to develop dehydration. Higher mortality rates were also identified in older persons. Race and gender were other risk factors identified as African-Americans and men were more likely to be hospitalized with dehydration. [2].

There is limited data pertaining to dehydration in older nursing home residents. However, available studies highlight dehydration as a common problem in nursing homes with a prevalence as high as 35% [3]. Additionally, within the long term care setting dehydration may have more ominous implications as, left untreated, this has been shown to result in a mortality rate exceeding 50% [4]. The financial burden associated with dehydration within nursing homes has not been accurately estimated. However, a review of comparative figures, obtained in 1991, within the acutely hospitalized older population reveal HCFA reimbursement in excess of $446 million for the treatment of dehydration in Medicare beneficiaries [2].

Increased awareness by health professionals of the significant impact of dehydration on medical expenditure and health outcomes is crucial. This will serve to facilitate the appropriate institution of preventive measures and forestall the development of dehydration in community dwelling and institutionalized older persons. Early clinical recognition and effective intervention will also serve to reduce the negative impact of dehydration on morbidity and mortality in older adults.

I - AGE RELATED CHANGES IN FLUID AND ELECTROLYTE HOMEOSTASIS

In humans renal and neuroendocrine mechanisms interact to maintain fluid and electrolyte homeostasis. Tonicity is the most significant factor responsible for the maintenance of normal extracellular fluid volume. Hypertonicity results in the stimulation of hypothalamic osmoreceptors located adjacent to the ventral aspect of the third ventricle. Impulses are subsequently transmitted to the supraoptic and paraventricular nuclei also located within the hypothalamus. The latter nuclei are responsible for the secretion of arginine vasopressin (AVP) which acts on the collecting ducts of the kidney to increase the reabsorption of water. Hypovolemia is a less potent stimulus in the restoration of fluid and electrolyte balance. A reduction in extracellular fluid volume stimulates the baroreceptors located within the aortic arch and carotid sinus. These transmit impulses through the glossopharyngeal and vagus nerves to the hypothalamic osmoreceptors resulting in secretion of AVP and a fall in the levels of plasma atrial natriuretic peptide (ANP). The latter hormonal changes act to limit renal water loss. In severe hypovolemia angiotensin II is secreted and further enhances this neuroendocrine pathway [5,6].

The human is driven to replace lost fluids by drinking. However, the neurophysiology of thirst is poorly understood. It has been well demonstrated that hypertonicity acting via hypothalamic osmoreceptors is one of the major factors that controls thirst perception [7]. The urge to drink is also affected by other factors such as social convenience, hedony and palatability. Generally, over hydration does not occur in normal humans as following adequate correction of the water deficit and hypertonicity, the neuroendocrine mechanisms are aborted [8,9]. Furthermore, fluid intake is carefully regulated as the act of drinking activates preabsorptive oropharyngeal reflexes which inhibit the perception of thirst and the release of AVP. Cold liquids have been found to be more effective at eliciting these oropharyngeal reflexes [8,10]. The sensitivity of these reflexes are unaffected by the tonicity of the fluid ingested [11].

Several age related factors place the older subject at increased risk for dehydration. It is well recognized that age related renal changes reduce the maximal urine concentrating capacity of the kidneys [12]. The reduction in glomerular filtration rate that occurs with aging also serves to further impair the excretory function of the kidneys [13]. Animal studies suggest that these changes may result from decreased responsiveness of the aging kidneys to AVP [14]. This is supported by human studies which demonstrate elevated plasma vasopressin levels in older adults resulting from increased sensitivity of the hypothalamic osmoreceptor system. These findings indicate that the reduction in urine concentrating ability in the aging kidney is an end-organ manifestation of impaired renal tubular function [15].

There is convincing evidence to show that older persons respond to dehydration and thermal stimuli with less thirst and fluid replacement than younger subjects. Older persons have been shown to display a striking lack of thirst and discomfort after water deprivation for 24 hours, when compared to younger adults. This occurred despite notably higher increases in plasma sodium concentration and serum osmolality. Subsequently, when offered water, older persons drank less and were unable to rehydrate themselves to pre-deprivation status [15]. Thirst perception and fluid intake have been found not to vary with the palatability of the fluid offered [16]. The exact mechanisms underlying age related hypodipsia are not clearly understood. Several theories involving neuroendocrine pathways have been proffered to explain the occurrence of a thirst deficit in older adults. These include alterations in the efferent thirst pathways that subserve osmoreceptor function and decreased low and high pressure baroreceptor sensitivity [17,18]. It has also been suggested that increased levels of ANP in older persons may be partially responsible for the blunting of thirst perception with aging, as it is well recognized that ANP inhibits thirst [19]. The findings of Silver and Morley indicate that age related hypodipsia may result from a deficit in the opioid drinking drive [20]. Animal studies have demonstrated an increase in fluid consumption in younger animals following administration of opioid agonists. This effect can be negated by the administration of opioid antagonists. Reduced concentrations of met-enkephalin and a lower density of opioid receptors have been identified in older rats. Animal studies have also identified a failure of naloxone to inhibit fluid intake with aging. Current evidence suggests that defects in the opioid system may contribute to the genesis of hypodipsia in older animals [21,22,23,24]. Similar studies in animals indicate that the angiotensin and histaminergic systems may also be involved in thirst regulation [25].

Alterations in neurotransmitter secretion have also been implicated. Dopamine acetylcholine and noradrenergic systems, all of which are subject to age related changes, have been identified as potential modulators of vasopressin function. Animal studies highlight the role of dopamine in the modulation of drinking behavior. Depletion of dopamine levels with aging may therefore result in a maladaptive behavioral response to thirst [25,26].

The findings of Miller et al demonstrated the increased propensity of older persons with cerebrovascular disease to recurrent episodes of hypernatremic dehydration, suggesting that age related hypodipsia may be a manifestation of neurological cortical dysfunction [27]. Peripheral neurological pathways have also been implicated. Impaired pre absorptive oropharyngeal reflexes and decreased oropharyngeal perception in older adults may act to reduce the sensation of thirst and consequently decrease the drinking drive [28].

II - RISK FACTORS AND CAUSES OF DEHYDRATION IN OLDER PERSONS

The majority of dehydrated older nursing home residents do not have the usual causes of dehydration identified in younger persons, such as diabetes insipidus and protracted diarrhea and vomiting. A common factor in most cases is impaired access to water. Some workers , justifiably, maintain that dehydration in the nursing home should be considered an index of poor care [4]. Several readily identifiable medical conditions render the nursing home resident vulnerable to dehydration see Table 1). Older persons with acute infections or cerebrovascular disease appear to be at the highest risk for dehydration. Residents with more than four chronic diseases or who take more than four different medications constitute a high risk group for dehydration. Functional status is also an important index of dehydration risk, with persons requiring skilled care and maximal assistance for transfers and ambulation being at high risk for dehydration. Female residents over the age of 85 years also constitute a high risk group. This has been attributed to their relatively low lean body mass and subsequent higher surface area, in comparison to male residents. Impaired cognitive function is yet another factor which may predispose nursing home residents to dehydration. Lavizzo Mourey and others identified dehydration in about two-thirds of their population of nursing home residents. Dementia and delirium may contribute to a reduction in fluid intake, either through impaired communication or behavioral disorders which may have a negative impact on feeding and drinking [3]. These findings indicate that a great proportion of nursing home residents fall into high risk categories for dehydration, underscoring the importance of close surveillance to ensure optimal hydration status in all residents.

Table 1
Risk Factors for Dehydration in the Elderly

Age > 85 years
Female gender
Polypharmacy
Acute infections:
Urosepsis
Pneumonia
Viral syndromes
Cerebrovascular disease
Multiple Chronic Illnesses
Impaired cognitive Function
Depression / dysphoria
Restricted mobility / manual dexterity
Reduced functional status
Enteral tube feedings
Urinary incontinence

Infections and fevers are common problems in nursing home residents [29]. It is well recognized that fever increases the risk of dehydration. The majority of clinical diagnoses associated with febrile episodes include, urosepsis, lower respiratory tract infections, and viral syndromes [30]. Himmelstein et al in a study of nursing home patients identified underlying infection as the primary cause of hyernatremic dehydration in 82% of all dehydrated residents [4].

The ability of the resident to obtain and drink fluids may also be impaired by diseases which reduce manual dexterity. These include cerebrovascular disease which may manifest not only with paretic features but also with dyspraxia. Parkinson's disease, essential tremor and other neurological conditions manifesting with involuntary movements may impair fluid intake.

Major depression often remains undetected within the nursing home setting. Morley and Kraenzle identified dysphoric features in 30% of their nursing home residents [31]. Weight loss resulting from anorexia was a prominent associated feature [31]. Fluid intake may also be compromised resulting in an increased risk of dehydration in untreated depression. The high prevalence of urinary incontinence among nursing home residents is well recognized. Affected residents often feel that the frequency of incontinence will be exacerbated by fluid intake. This may result in voluntary restriction of fluid intake to avoid the social embarrassment of incontinent episodes.

Iatrogenesis is a frequent contributory cause of dehydration in long term care settings. The injudiscious prescription of diuretics and laxatives often precipitates dehydration. Adverse drug effects, such as delirium and gastrointestinal distress and over-sedation can also compromise fluid intake. Despite the proven increase in morbidity and mortality associated with the use of physical restraints, several health professionals continue to utilize these measures in older persons who are confused or high fall risks [32]. Enforced immobility by these measures has been shown even in young healthy persons to severely restrict fluid intake.

Environmental factors may contribute to the increased risk of dehydration. Such factors include inadequate supervision at meal times, insufficient time and staff allocated to assist residents with feeding or drinking at meals and the failure to provide appropriately adapted cutlery and tableware. Social circumstances during meals have been shown to have a positive impact on fluid and food intake. The failure to provide pleasant social interaction during meals and lack of attention to patient comfort and dignity may detract from the hedonic quality of meals and compromise intake.

The high mortality associated with dehydration in nursing home residents mandates early recognition and therapeutic intervention. To this end, the Omnibus Budget Reconciliation act of 1987 and 1990 defined risk factors for dehydration and established fluid maintenance triggers to prompt early intervention in residents of long term care facilities (see Table 2) [33]. It must be emphasized that the majority of causes of dehydration are readily reversible. Furthermore, appropriate and prompt intervention prevents most of the complications associated with dehydration (see Table 3).

Table 2

OBRA 1987 / 1990 Minimum Data Set: Dehydration and Fluid
Maintenance Triggers and Additional Risk factors for Dehydration
Among Residents of Long Term Care Facilities

Dehydration / fluid maintenance triggers.
  Deterioration in cognitive status, skills, or abilities in last 90 days.
  Failure to eat or take medications.
  Urinary tract infection in last 30 days.
  Current diagnosis of dehydration (ICD-9 code 276-5)
  Diarrhoea
  Dizziness / vertigo.
  Fever
  Internal bleeding
  Vomiting.
  Weight loss (> 5% in 30 days or 10% in 180 days).
  Insufficient fluid intake.
  > 25% of food uneaten at most meals.
  Requirement for parenteral fluids.
Additional potential risk factors.
  Hand dexterity / body control problems.
  Diuretic use
  Laxative abuse.
  Uncontrolled diabetes mellitus.
  Swallowing problems.
  Purposeful fluid restriction.
  Patients on enteral feeds.

Table 3

Complications of dehydration

Delirium
Renal Failure
Periodontal sepsis
Reduced skin viability / Pressure ulcers
Orthostatic symptoms
Falls
Constipation
Urge incontinence

III - CLINICAL FEATURES OF DEHYDRATION

The symptoms of dehydration in nursing home residents are very often absent or non-specific. Lethargy, easy fatiguability and reduced exercise tolerance may manifest as a result of reduced fluid intake. The hemodynamic effects of depleted intravascular volume may result in orthostatic symptoms, such as dizziness and recurrent falls. Delirium manifesting with confusion, agitation, disorientation and increasing somnolence can occur as clinical markers of compromised hydration status. Constipation, difficulty with mastication, periodontal sepsis and dental caries may also result from dehydration.

The clinical assessment of dehydration in older persons is subject to several pitfalls arising from age related changes. Loss of skin turgor, often relied upon as a valuable index of dehydration in younger persons, is unreliable in older adults. Age related changes in cutaneous elasticity and compressibility of subcutaneous fat independently reduce skin turgor, rendering this index relatively insensitive to changes in hydration status [34]. Sunken eyeballs resulting from reduced intraocular and episcleral pressure are also utilized as indices of dehydration in younger adults. However, data examining intraocular pressure in older persons failed to demonstrate a consistent relationship between intraocular pressure and hydration status [35]. The findings of Eaton and others indicate that axillary sweating is a reliable and easily reproducible sign of adequate hydration in older persons. They identified the sensitivity and positive predictive value of absent axillary moisture in detecting dehydration as 50% and 45% respectively. The specificity and negative predictive value of this clinical index was estimated to be 82% and 84% respectively [36]. It is pertinent to note that the clinical utility of this sign may be notably compromise by the co-existence of age related or diabetic autonomic neuropathy.

Abnormalities in orthostatic blood pressure and heart rates can result from moderate dehydration and are frequently used as parameters of hydration status in older persons. However, 20 - 30% of well hydrated community dwelling older persons have signifcant orthostatic changes. It is likely that age related changes in baroreceptor sensitivity, co-existing cardiovascular disease or the use of vasoactive drugs may interfere with the correlation between orthostasis and intravascular volume [37].

Gross and others examined clinical .indicators of dehydration severity among older persons presenting to the emergency room. The presence of dry mucus membranes in the mouth and nose, tongue furrowing and dryness correlated best with dehydration. Absence of saliva pooling and tongue coating were also relatively strong indices of dehydration. Upper body weakness, dysarthria and delirium were other signs found to be relatively reliable indices of dehydration severity. On the contrary, tachycardia, generalized lethargy and flat neck veins were relatively non-specific, correlating poorly with hydration status. The presence of orthostatic blood pressure changes and the absence of axillary sweating were unreliable signs of dehydration. This was attributed to age related autonomic changes and the common use of vasoactive agents in older persons. The finding that self reported symptoms, such as thirst and mouth dryness were the poorest indices of dehydration is in keeping with the general observation that older persons do not complain of thirst [38]. This is clinically important in the prevention and management of dehydration.

Review of weight measurements and fluid intake and output charts may assist in the detection of dehydration. However, within the long term care setting, the accuracy of such documentation is often questionable. Measurements may be significantly affected by inter observer variation. Additionally, the relatively high prevalence of incontinent residents and the difficulty encountered in tracking fluid intake and voiding volumes in relatively ambulant residents may preclude accurate measurement. Furthermore even when these measurements are recorded accurately, the frequency with which these are carried out in most facilities varies form weekly to monthly. This permits only a retrospective diagnosis of dehydration.

Within the long term care setting, the routine use of screening laboratory tests is discouraged as these have not been found cost effective, resulting in few treatable conditions [39]. However, laboratory tests still retain their value when used strictly for diagnostic purposes. The role of laboratory tests in the management of dehydration in the nursing home is even more specific as it assists not only with the diagnosis of this condition but also with the classification, which is mandatory to ensure appropriate treatment. The precise diagnostic definition of dehydration remains unclear. The term dehydration is usually considered to imply excess water loss resulting in a reduction in total body water content, usually due to pathological body fluid loss or decreased intake. A blood urea nitrogen : creatinine ratio exceeding 25 is considered indicative of dehydration. The correct diagnostic usage of the term dehydration mandates classification into hyponatremic or hypernatremic categories in order to effect appropriate therapy (see Table 4). Particularly in residents with moderate to severe dehydration, estimation of the serum osmolality and electrolyte profile is essential for this purpose.

Table 4
Classification of Dehydration

	Hypernatremic Dehydration	Hypotonic Dehydration
Causes	Free water loss Fever diarrhea Fluid deprivation	Extracellular fluid depletion Diuresis - drugs / osmotic Severe anorexia Third spacing, e.g. liver cirrhosis
Clinical features	Lethargy Delirium	Delirium Depression Anorexia Muscle cramps Hypothermia
Biochemistry	Serum sodium > 145 mmol / liter Serum osmolality > 300 mmol / kg	Serum sodium < 135 mmol / liter Serum osmolality < 280 mmol / kg
Treatment	*Hypotonic fluid replacement	Isotonic fluid replacement

* In persons with severe hypernatremia (> 160 mmol / liter) and evidence of intravascular volume depletion, isotonic saline should be used until hemodynamically stability is restored.

IV - MANAGEMENT OF DEHYDRATION IN THE NURSING HOME

Dehydration in nursing homes can be avoided. Effective therapeutic strategies should focus primarily on prevention. Nursing home residents at high risk for dehydration should be identified and appropriate preventive and intervention measures instituted.

All high risk nursing home residents should have their fluid consumption and voiding volumes monitored. The recommended daily fluid intake for a non-perspiring adult weighing approximately 70 kg is 1,500 mls [40]. An upward adjustment should be made for increased ambient temperature and febrile illness. A therapeutic goal of 1,500 - 2000 mls is recommended, which should account for daily fluid requirements and replace urine, fecal and insensible fluid loss.

Nursing staff and physicians in nursing homes must be pro-active in ensuring adequate fluid intake by residents of long term care facilities. Residents with urinary incontinence may be reluctant to consume fluids in an attempt to decrease urine output and thereby, perhaps reduce the frequency of incontinent episodes. However, data exists in support of the fact that dehydration may actually worsen incontinence as concentrated urine may increase bladder irritability. Restoring optimal hydration status in such persons has been shown to reduce urinary incontinence [41]. Education and counseling of residents by the staff may negate their reluctance to consume fluids. Similarly, reduced motivation in depressed or dysphoric persons may impair fluid consumption as the predominance of neurovegetative symptoms in depressed older persons often leads to hypodipsia and anorexia. The onus in such cases is entirely upon the staff to ensure adequate fluid intake by affected residents.

A review of drinking patterns in the nursing home revealed that few nursing home residents complained of thirst. Furthermore, 75% of fluid intake occurred between 6 a.m. and 6 p.m. The majority of fluid consumption occurred around mealtimes, underscoring the dependence of most institutionalized older persons on the staff for fluid consumption. An interesting observation is the fact that the majority of residents will drink exactly what is offered, regardless of quantity [42]. Semidependent residents, defined as residents with either impaired cognition or impaired mobility, are at highest risk of dehydration due to abnormal drinking patterns. This is attributed to the fact that independent persons are more likely to seek out staff and communicate their requests, while fully dependent residents appear to be the main focus of staff attention. Semi dependent residents, on the other hand, are likely to go unnoticed either due to lack of communication or the inability to seek out available resources [43].

Effective nursing interventions to prevent dehydration among residents must include risk stratification and recognition of the importance of individualized strategies tailored to suit the needs of each resident. The removal of environmental barriers to water access is a crucial component of such strategies. The ill-advised use of physical restraints within long term care facilities constitutes a perfect recipe for ensuring compromised hydration, by increasing agitation and severely restricting access to fluids. Most residents in whom restraints are used can be reasonably calmed by frequent re-orientation and close supervision. Occupational therapists should be involved in assessing the manual dexterity of each resident and providing pitchers and cups, where applicable, that can be easily manipulated without assistance. Residents who are incapable of pouring fluids should be provided with large cups which can hold quantities of fluid in excess of their immediate needs. Wheelchair accessible fountains should be provided at convenient distances, such that they are easily accessible to mobile patients. The institution of snack carts and the convenient location of vending machines within the facility may also serve to enhance fluid consumption. Social interaction significantly improves the quality of meal times and food ingestion. Recreational therapists may be helpful in incorporating liquid refreshments into daily scheduled activities. Family members should also be educated about the importance of fluid consumption and should be encouraged to offer residents drinks during visits. The assistance of nutritional services within the facility should also be utilized to ensure a wide variety of liquid refreshments to compensate for differences in liquid preference and palatability among residents. Staff must be cognizant of the fact that inhibitory oropharyngeal reflexes are more easily stimulated by cold liquids. The consumption of iced drinks may therefore curtail thirst and limit fluid intake more readily than other fluids.

Residents at high risk for dehydration should be offered fluids frequently during the day, at mealtimes and with snacks. Accurate documentation of fluid consumption and urine output should be maintained. Daily clinical assessments and measurements of blood pressure and heart rate to exclude orthostasis should be carried out. Visual inspection of the urine to assess concentration and measurement of specific gravity, where possible, should be done. The daily urine output in a well hydrated patient should range from 1000 - 1,500 mls with a specific gravity ranging between 1.003 - 1.035. Bowel habits should be monitored closely as constipation may herald dehydration and prompt increased fluid intake. The residents weight should be monitored two or three times each week to evaluate for rapid weight decreases suggestive of fluid depletion. Accurate measurements are best ensured by utilizing the same observer and the same set of weighing scales. Accuracy may be further enhanced by weighing the resident in minimal clothing and at the same time of day.

Effective intervention mandates close communication between the nursing staff and physicians. Inadequate fluid intake should prompt the physician to prescribe fluids as a written order. The daily fluid requirement for the individual resident is best prescribed in split doses administered during each shift. Residents should be screened for risk factors and an attempt should be made to identify possible causes or precipitants of undernutrition. A review of medications is essential. Diuretics and laxatives are common contributory causes of impaired hydration status. Sedatives, hypnotics, antipsychotics and anticholinergic agents may impair cognitive function and mental status, thus compromising fluid intake.

Residents fed through gastrostomy or jejunostomy tubes are at especially high risk for dehydration, as the commercial formulas in common use rarely provide enough free water for the resident's daily needs. Additional water should be administered in split doses at 3 - 4 hourly intervals through the enteral tube to ensure that the total free water requirement is met. As a general rule, the total water intake provided by the enteral feeding formula and additional supplemental water should be approximately 30 mls / kg body weight of the resident [40]. Involvement of a dietitian is mandatory to ensure effective maintenance of hydration status in residents receiving enteral tube feeds.

V - ENTERAL REHYDRATION

In all residents with established rehydration and a functioning gastrointestinal tract, enteral rehydration is preferred , where tolerated. Classification of dehydration as either hypo- or hypernatremic is helpful in deciding the fluid of choice . The required volume of fluid to restore normal hydration status is determined by calculating the free water deficit, as follows:–Weight (kg) X 0.45 - (140/Serum Na X Weight (kg) X 0.45). The recommended rate of fluid replacement is usually 20 - 30% of the calculated free water deficit each day [43]. Appropriate additions should be made for ongoing fluid losses and daily fluid requirements (check).

In order to encourage fluid intake, a wide variety of drinks should be offered. Several commercial preparations and "sports drinks" are available which serve as effective hydrating fluids and residents may find these more palatable [44]. These are usually carbohydrate and electrolyte solutions. Studies in young adults show that these fluids are just as effective as water in restoring hemodynamic stability [45]. Broths and fruit juices may also be offered to the resident. However, the osmolarity of such fluids should be considered when making a choice. Hyponatremic fluid is best corrected with normal saline or fluids of similar osmolarity (150mEq). Water and fluids of lower osmolarity are more effective for hypernatremic dehydration.

Oral rehydration therapy (ORT) preparations are being used with increasing frequency in children There is a striking paucity of information regarding its clinical utility and efficacy in other age groups. Formulas for ORT range from simple preparations comprising water, sugar and salt to the more expensive preparations containing varying proportions of sodium, potassium, acetate and lactate [46]. The possibility of the availability of ready-made inexpensive hydrating solutions for the treatment of dehydration within the long term care setting seems attractive. However, the clinical utility of this therapeutic modality in dehydrated older persons remains to be explored.

VI - PARENTERAL REHYDRATION

For persons who are unable to tolerate enteral fluids, intravenous rehydration is very often the only alternative option. A major drawback to intravenous therapy is undoubtedly the higher risk of complications associated with the venous access. Very few long term care facilities have well established and active intravenous programs and a significant proportion contract this service out to other agencies. Residents on intravenous fluids require close clinical and laboratory monitoring, often best carried out in a skilled nursing facility. Likewise, residents with severe dehydration and hemodynamic instability, requiring intravenous rehydration, are best managed in an acute care facility.

VII - HYPODERMOCLYSIS

A common scenario within the long term care setting is the dehydrated resident with poor venous access, who is unwilling or unable to drink fluids. Even in the absence of an underlying acute medical condition, this often results in the transfer of the resident to an acute care setting for effective rehydration. With the re-emergence of hypodermoclysis as an acceptable therapeutic option, parenteral rehydration may be accomplished with greater ease within nursing homes. Hypodermoclysis refers to parenteral fluid administration using the subcutaneous route. This therapeutic modality gained popularity during the 1950's but rapidly fell into disuse due to the unacceptably high complication rate. It is now evident that the majority of these complications were associated with inappropriate fluid prescription and poor technique.

Hypodermoclysis is based on the theoretical principle that fluid infused slowly into the subcutaneous tissue can be transferred into the circulation by the combined effect of the forces of diffusion and tissue perfusion without resulting in tissue edema [47,48]. In clinical practice, subcutaneous infusion of fluid at a rate not exceeding 1 ml / minute is advised [49]. The equipment required for hypodermoclysis is essentially the same as that used for intravenous infusions. However, available infusion sets terminate in two arms enabling infusion at two separate sites. At an infusion rate of 1 ml / minute, fluid volumes as large as 3000 mls may be delivered over 24 hour period. Small gauge needles such as the 21 gauge butterfly needles are recommended. Areas with loose subcutaneous tissue such as the inner and outer aspects of the thighs, the lateral abdominal wall and the chest wall lateral to the breast are preferred for clysis needle placement. Following insertion of the subcutaneous line, it must be ensured that the infused fluid flows freely at 1 ml / min without pain or swelling. One ml (150 units) of hyaluronidase solution should be injected into each liter of fluid and 75 units injected subcutaneously directly into clysis site. Hyaluronidase is an enzyme that hydrolyzes hyaluronic acid, a polysaccharide component of the intracellular ground substance connective tissue. Hyaluronidase thus serves to decrease the viscosity of connective tissue and facilitate diffusion of infused fluid. The needles and clysis tubing must be changed daily. In order to prevent significant fluid compartment shifts isotonic fluid is preferred for clysis infusions. However, when large volumes are being used the relatively high sodium load of normal saline may precipitate pulmonary edema. Gluck recommends an isotonic clysis solution comprising 0.45% sodium chloride and 2.5% glucose, which notably reduces the sodium load [50]. Several commercial clysis solutions are readily available.

Within the long term care setting, hypodermoclysis is an acceptable option for non emergent parenteral rehydration when daily fluid requirements do not exceed 3000 mls. The advantages and relatively low complication rate of hypodermoclysis enhance it's clinical acceptability. (see Table 5) [49,51]. Complications such as severe soft tissue infection and gas gangrene reported in the 1950's have been attributed to poor aseptic technique [52]. A review of the current literature indicates a virtual absence of these complications in recent times. Furthermore, available data shows that hypodermoclysis has a much lower incidence of infection than intravenous infusions. Early complications also included reports of soft tissue sloughing. This complication can be completely prevented by the use of isotonic fluids only and limiting the rate of fluid infusion to 1 ml / minute.

Table 5
Hypodermoclysis: advantages and disadvantages

Advantages
    Safe and simple procedure
    Limited skilled training required
    Clysis site may be used for weeks
    Infusion may be discontinued and restarted without clotting
    Clysis site sepsis occurs rarely
    Can be monitored easily within nursing home
    Reduces necessity for transfer to acute hospital for rehydration
    Lower risk of fluid overload compared to intravenous infusion
Disadvantages
    Precludes the infusion of large volumes of fluids
    Precludes the delivery of hypo- or hypertonic fluids
    Hypersensitivity reactions to subcutaneous hyaluronidase

VIII - PALLIATIVE CARE

Available data indicate that about 75% of the population die outside the home setting, either in an acute care or long term care facility (53%). Thus, it is not surprising that end-of-life decisions frequently need to be made in the nursing home. In the terminally ill resident, the preservation of patient comfort, dignity and autonomy should be the prime determining factor in deciding management strategies. Issue regarding the continuation of hydration often arise and the decision to withhold hydration or permit only patient endorsed intake is often met with considerable resistance by some family members and health professionals alike. It is crucial to ensure that the resident, relevant family members and involved staff are fully informed of the medical, ethical and legal issues surrounding hydration in such circumstances. Family and staff members must be fully informed of the expected outcome of the resident's condition and the prognosis should then serve as the basis for the definition of therapeutic goals and outcomes. It must also be emphasized that the definition of extraordinary measures must be tailored to suit the individual patient's clinical condition. Thus, intravenous hydration under certain circumstances may constitute futile and extraordinary intervention. The involvement of a hospice team is invaluable in the care of the terminally ill resident and often expedites the resolution of palliative care issues. Studies have shown that hospice staff have the most positive perception of dehydration in terminally ill patients. This difference in perception has been attributed to greater experience and education in this field.

Contrary to popular perception, dehydration is not painful and dehydrated terminally ill persons experience less discomfort than persons receiving optimal hydration. Several studies have identified real benefits resulting from dehydration in the terminally ill patient (see Table 6) [53,54,55,56,57,58,59]. The only significant side effect associated with dehydration is oral discomfort resulting from dry mucosal membranes and thirst. Reduced thirst perception may render the latter symptom of lesser significance in older persons. Furthermore, mucosal dryness responds satisfactorily to the use of saliva substitutes and good mouth care.

Table 6
Benefits of dehydration in the terminally ill.

	Mechanism of action
* Analgesia	Increased secretion of hypothalamic opioid peptides
* Anesthesia	Ketone generation and acidosis resulting from starvation
* Decreased pulmonary distress	Reduction in pulmonary and tracheal secretions
* Decreased vomiting	Reduction in gastrointestinal fluids
* Lower incidence of urinary incontinence / catheterization	Decreased urine output

Ethically, utilizing the principle of patient autonomy and, where this is lacking due to impaired decision making ability, substituted judgement on the part of family members, withholding dehydration is acceptable if this is in line with the resident's wishes. It should be emphasized that dehydration in terminally ill patients has not been shown to hasten death, thus alleviating the fears of family members who are often concerned that withholding dehydration may render them accomplices in the death of their loved one.

It is significant to note that several professional bodies have issued statements in support of sound legal, ethical and medical decisions to withhold nutritional support and hydration in the terminally ill, under appropriate circumstances. The council on Ethical and Judicial Affairs of the American Medical Association stated in 1986 that "Life-prolonging medical treatment and artificially or technologically supplied respiration, nutrition and hydration may be withheld from a patient in an irreversible coma even if death is not imminent" [60]. The American Dietetic Association also contends that discontinuing nutritional support may be an option when a competent patient has expressed an informed preference not to receive aggressive nutritional support [61]. In a position paper in 1992, The American Nurse's Association stated that the refusal of fluid by competent patients is morally and legally permissible for nurses to honor [62]. It is likely that an increase in the understanding of the relevant legal and ethical issues and education regarding the benefits of appropriate terminal dehydration will notably alleviate the moral discomfort associated with this issue and improve the quality of holistic care administered to terminally ill nursing home residents.

The prevalence of dehydration among nursing home residents is a cause for grave concern, in view of the significant morbidity and mortality attached to this syndrome. Health professionals involved in the care of older adults in the long term care setting must cultivate a heightened sensitivity to the potential dangers of this problem. The development of educational and training programs focused on the prevention, detection and treatment of dehydration will be invaluable in this regard. Critical care pathway protocols used in nursing homes must permit effective continued surveillance of hydration status and fluid maintenance. Current preventive and therapeutic strategies used in the management of dehydration are effective in the majority of cases. However, the elucidation of the precise mechanisms involved in the genesis of age related hypodipsia will notably expand the available therapeutic options.

REFERENCES

1. Health Care Financing Review, Medicare and Medicaid Statistical Supplement, 1992 Annual Supplement, Washington, DC: US Dept. Of Health and Human Services, Health care Financing Administration, Office of Research and Demonstrations; October 1993, vol 63. Health Care Financing Administration publication 0334.

2. Warren JL, Bacon E, Harris T, McBean AM, Foley DJ, Phillips C. The burden and outcomes associated with dehydration among US elderly, 1991. Am J Pub Health. 1994;84(8):1265 - 69.

3. Lavizzo-Mourey R, Johnson J, Stolley P. Risk factors for dehydration among elderly nursing home residents. J Am Geriatr Soc. 1988;36:213 - 18.

4. Himmelstein DU, Jones AA, Woolhandler S. Hypernatremic dehydration in nursing home patients: an indicator of neglect. J Am Geriatr Soc 1983;31:466 - 71.

5. McKinley MJ. Osmoreceptors for thirst. In Ramsay DJ, Booth DA eds. Thirst: physiological and psychological aspects. Springer - Verlag: London, 1991.

6. Phillips PA, Johnston CI, Gray L. Disturbed fluid and electrolyte homeostasis following dehydration in elderly people. Age and Ageing. 1993; 22:26 - 33.

7. Phillips PA, Bretherton M, Johnston CI, Gray L. Reduced osmotic thirst in healthy elderly men. Am J Physiol. 1991;261: R166 - R171.

8. Geelen G, Keil LC, Kravik SE, et al. Inhibition of plasma vasopressin after drinking in dehydrated humans. Am J Physiol. 1984;247:R968 - R971.

9. Januszewicz P, Thibault J, Gutkowska R. et al. Atrial natriuretic factor and vasopressin during dehydration and rehydration in rats. Am J Physiol. 1986;251:E497 - E501.

10. Rolls B, Wood RJ, Rolls ET, Lind H, Lind W, Ledingham JGG. Thirst following water deprivation in humans. Am J Physiol. 1980;239:R476 - R482.

11. Seckl JR, Williams TDM, Lightman SL. Oral hypertonic saline causes transient fall of vasopressin in humans. Am J Physiol. 1986;251:R214 - R217.

12. Dontas AS, Marketos SG, Papanayiotou P. Mechanisms of renal tubular defects in old age. Postgrad Med J. 1972;48:295-303.

13. Rowe JW, Andres R, Tobin J et al. The effect of age on creatinine clearance in men: a cross sectional and longitudinal study. J Gerontol 1976;31:155 - 163.

14. Geelen G, Corman B. Relationship between vasopressin and renal concentrating ability in aging rats. Am J Physiol. 1992;262:R826 - R833.

15. Phillips PA, Rolls BJ, Ledingham JGG, et al. Reduced thirst after water deprivation in healthy elderly men. NEJM 1984;311(12): 753 - 59.

16. Phillips PA, Johnston CI, Gray L. Thirst and fluid intake in the elderly. In: Ramsay DJ, Booth DA eds. Thirst: Physiological and psychological aspects. London; Springer Verlag, 1991.

17. Gribben B, Pickering Tg, Sleight P, Peto R. Effects of age and high blood pressure on baroreflex sensitivity in man. Circ. Res. 1971;29:424 - 431.

18. Cleroux J, Giannattasio C, Grassi G, et al. Effects of aging on the cardiopulmonary receptor reflex in normotensive humans. J Hypertens 1989:6, Suppl4:S141 - S144.

19. Ohashi M, Fujio M, Nawata H, et al. High plasma concentrations of human atrial natriuretic polypeptide in aged men. J Clin Endocrinol Metab 1987;64:81 - 5.

20. Silver AJ, Morley JE. J Am Gerontol Soc. 1992;40:556 - 560.

21. Cooper SJ, Holtzman SG. Pattern of drinking in the rat following the administration of opiate antagonists. Pharmacol Biochem Behav. 1983;19:505 - 511.
22. Reid LD. Endogenous opioid peptides and regulation of drinking and feeding. Am J Clin Nutr 1985;42:1099 - 1132.
23. Gosnell BA, Levine AS, Morley JE. The effects of aging on opioid modulation of feeding in rats. Life Sci1983;32:2793 - 2799.
24. Silver AJ, Flood JF, Morley JE. J Gerontol 1991;46:B117 - B121.
25. Morley JE. Behavioral pharmacology for eating and drinking. In: Metzer KY, ed. Psychopharmacology, The third generation of progress. New York, Raven Press, 1987,pp1267 - 1272.
26. Lalonde R, Badescu R. Exploratory drive, Frontal lobe function and adipsia in aging. Gerontology. 1995;41:134-144.
27. Miller PD, Krebs RA, Neal BJ, McIntyre DO. Hypodipsia in geriatric patients. Am J Med 1983;73:354 - 356.
28. Phillips PA, Bretherton M, Risvanis J, Casley D, Johnston C, Gray L. Effects of drinking on thirst and vasopressin in dehydrated elderly men. Am J Physiol 1993;264:R877 R881.
29. FransonTR, Schnicker JM, LeClair SM et al. Documentation and evaluation of fevers in hospital based and community based nursing homes. Infect Control Hosp Epidemiol 1988;9447 - 50.
30. Weiberg DA, Pals JK, Levesque PG et al. Dehydration and death during febrile episodes in the nursing home. J Am Geriatr Soc. 1994;42:968 - 971.
31. Morley JE, Kraenzle D. Causes of weight loss in a community nursing home. J Am Geriatr Soc. 1994;42:583 - 585.
32. Restraints.
33. Omnibus Budget Reconciliation Act of 1987 and 1990(federal). 6.2 CFR # 483.25.
34. Shuster S, Black MM, McVitie E. Influence of age and sex on skin thickness, skin collagen and density. Br J Dermatol 1975;93:639 - 643.
35. Rhodes KM. Can the measurement of intraocular pressure be useful in assessing dehydration and rehydration? J Am Geriatr Soc.1995; 43:589 - 593.
36. Eaton D, Bannister P, Mulley GP, Connolly MJ. Axillary sweating in clinical assessment of dehydration in ill elderly patients. BMJ 1994;308:1271 - 1272.
37. Wandel JC. The use of postural vital signs in the assessment of fluid volume status. J Prof Nursing 1990;6(1):46 - 54.
38. Gross CR, Lindquist RD, Woolley AC, Granieri R, Allard K, Webster B. Clinical indicators of dehydration severity in elderly patients. J Emer Med. 1992;10:267 - 274.
39. Kim DE, Berlowitz DR. The limited value of routine laboratory assessments in severely impaired nursing home residents. JAMA 1994;272:1447 - 1452.
40. National Academy of Sciences, Food and Nutrition Board. Recommended Dietary allowances. 9th ed. Rev. Washington, DC., The Academy, 1980.
41. Spangler Pf, Risley TR, Bilyew DD. The management of dehydration and incontinence in non ambulatory geriatric patients. J Appl Behav Anal 1984;17:397 - 401.
42. Adams F. How much do elders drink? Geriatric Nursing. 1988; July / August: 218 - 221.
43. Gaspar PM. What determines how much patients drink? Geriatric Nursing. 1988 July / August: 221 - 223.
44. Luft FC, Weiberger MH, Grim CE et al. Sodium sensitivity in normotensive human subjects. Ann Intern Med. 1983;98:758 - 762.
45. Campbell SM. Maintaining hydration status in elderly persons. Support Line 1992;14:7 10.
46. Rice KH. Oral rehydration therapy: A simple, effective solution. J Paed Nurs 1994;9 (6):349 - 356.
47. Starling EH. The fluids of the body. Lecture VIII. Chicago. WT Keener & Co.,1909.
48. Perl W, Chinard FP. A convection-diffusion model of indicator transport through an organ. Circ Res 1968;22:273.
49. Berger EY. Nutrition by hypodermoclysis. J Am Geriatr Soc. 1984;32:199 - 203.
50. Gluck SM. Hypodermoclysis revisited. JAMA 1982;248:1311.
51. Molloy DW, Cunje A. Hypodermoclysis in the care of older adults. Can Fam Physician 1992;38:2038 - 2043.
52. Tenopyr J, Shapiroff BJP. Gas infection after hypodermoclysis. JAMA 1936;106:779-780.
53. National Center for health statistics. Vital Statistics of the United States, 1987, II: Mortality, Part A. Washington, DC: US Public Health Service; 1990.
54. Dolan MB. Another hospice nurse says. Nursing 1983; 1:51.
55. Elliot J, Haydon D, Hendry B. Anesthetic action esters and ketones. Evidence for an interaction with the sodium channel protein in squid axons. Journal of Physiology. 1984;354:407 - 418.
56. Majeed N, Lason N, Przewlocka B. Brain and peripheral opioid peptides after changes in ingestive behavior. Neuroendocrinology. 1986;42:267 - 276.
57. Printz LA. Withholding hydration in the terminally ill. Is it valid? Geriatric Medicine. 1989;43 (11): 84 - 88.
58. Takahashi M, Motomatsu T, Nobunage M. Influence of water deprivation and fasting on

hypothalamic, pituitary and plasma opioid peptides and prolactin in rats. Physiology and Behavior. 1986;37:603 - 608.

59. Zerwekh JV. The dehydration question. Nursing. 1983;1:47 - 51.
60. O'Rourke K. The AMA statement on tube feeding: an ethical analysis. America. 1986; Nov: 321 - 324.
61. King DG, Maillet JO. Position of the American Dietetic Association: issues in feeding the terminally ill adult. J Am Diet Assoc 1991;92:996 - 1005.
62. American Nurses Association. Position statement on foregoing artificial nutrition and hydration. Washington: American Nurses Association, 1992.

SUBCUTANEOUS HYDRATION IN THE ELDERLY

A. SALIM, M. CROWE, S. O'KEEFFE

Department of Geriatric Medicine, St Columcille's Hospital, Loughlinstown, Co Dublin, Ireland.
Correspondence to Dr S O'Keeffe, Consultant Physician, St Michael's Hospital, Dun Laoghaire, Co
Dublin Ireland. Telephone 00353-1-2806901. Fax 00353-1-28844651.

Abstract : In recent years there has been a resurgence in the popularity of the subcutaneous route for administering fluids, particularly in the treatment of elderly people. In general, subcutaneous fluid administration is appropriate as a short-term measure to restore or to maintain hydration in patients who are mildly dehydrated or who are at risk of dehydration because of poor fluid intake or excessive fluid losses. In such patients, subcutaneous infusions are as effective as intravenous infusions in restoring and maintaining hydration. Subcutaneous infusions are particularly valuable in patients with difficult venous access, confused patients and patients requiring rehabilitation. Complications are rare with subcutaneous infusions when modern guidelines regarding the type of fluid and the rate of infusion are used.

Key Words : Subcutaneous infusions, Dehydration.

INTRODUCTION

Use of the subcutaneous route for administering fluids fell into disuse about forty years ago because of concerns about safety and because of improvements in the technology for giving fluids intravenously. In recent years there has been a resurgence in the popularity of the subcutaneous approach, particularly in the treatment of elderly people. Schen and Singer-Edelstein reviewed 1,850 subcutaneous infusions given to 270 patients in acute and long-stay geriatric beds and concluded that the subcutaneous route was the method of choice for administering fluid to elderly patients in non-urgent situations [1]. Other writers have reached similar conclusions [2-5].

I - BENEFITS OF SUBCUTANEOUS FLUID ADMINISTRATION

In general, subcutaneous fluid administration is appropriate as a short-term measure to restore or to maintain hydration in patients who are mildly dehydrated or who are at risk of dehydration because of poor fluid intake or excessive fluid losses. In such patients, subcutaneous infusions are as effective as intravenous infusions in restoring and maintaining hydration [3-5]. Subcutaneous infusions are less likely than intravenous infusions to produce fluid overload or pulmonary oedema. Subcutaneous fluid administration is particularly useful in the following circumstances:

1.1. Difficult venous access

The most common complication of intravenous infusions is thrombophlebitis [6]. It is common in hospitals to see patients with multiple thrombosed veins and extensive bruises on the arms as a consequence of repeated intravenous infusions. All physicians will be familiar with the frustration and distress for patients and for staff of fruitless attempts to cannulate veins in such patients. In contrast, it is easy to gain subcutaneous access. Furthermore, subcutaneous infusions can be stopped and started at will without worrying about the possibility of thrombosis [7].

1.2. Confusional states

Dehydration in the elderly can precipitate or worsen acute confusion [8], and effective rehydration can shorten the duration of acute confusional states [9]. Nursing staff are often asked to 'push oral fluids' in patients whose intake is inadequate, but this makes significant demands on nursing time and is often ineffective [10]. Patients with cognitive impairment may be unable to comply with requests to increase fluid intake and may resist physical help from nursing staff. Intravenous cannulation can be very difficult if a patient is unable to cooperate because of cognitive impairment. Subsequently, close supervision is often needed to maintain the drip. It is relatively easy to obtain and maintain subcutaneous access in the restless or agitated patients [3]. There are a number of likely explanations for this finding: it is easier to insert the subcutaneous cannula; relatively pain-insensitive areas can be used for subcutaneous infusions; finally, subcutaneous lines can be sited in relatively discreet locations, where they may not impinge on the awareness of a confused patient. O'Keeffe and Lavan randomized 60 elderly patients with cognitive impairment who required parenteral fluids to receive either intravenous or subcutaneous fluids [3]. There was no significant difference in the volume of fluid prescribed or in the proportion of prescribed fluids actually administered over a 48 hour period. Also, after adjusting for baseline differences, there was no difference between serum urea or creatinine levels in the two groups at 48 hours. Agitation related to the infusion was reported in 11 (37%) patients receiving subcutaneous fluids and 24 (80%) patients receiving intravenous fluids (p<0.005). The cost of the cannulae used during the study for the subcutaneous group was less than a quarter that for the intravenous group.

1.3. Stroke and other rehabilitation patients

Subcutaneous infusions are very useful in patients requiring rehabilitation, since the limbs are spared from encumbrance. Overnight infusions leave the patient free from any restrictions by day and are particularly useful in such patients [1]. Challiner and colleagues conducted a randomized comparison of subcutaneous and intravenous fluids in 34 elderly stroke patients who required parenteral fluids because of impaired consciousness or dysphagia [4]. They found no difference in serum osmolality levels between the two groups at 48 hours. The cost of cannulas was greatly reduced in the subcutaneous group.

1.4. Long-term care institutions

Subcutaneous infusions can be used in institutions without facilities or staff for initiation and maintenance of intravenous infusions. Hence, it may be possible to avoid hospitalization of patients who have a poor oral intake during acute illness [7,11]. Subcutaneous administration of fluids, with or without added analgesics and anti-emetics, is also suitable for domiciliary use, thereby allowing terminally ill patients to be nursed in their own home [12].

II - LIMITATIONS OF SUBCUTANEOUS FLUID ADMINISTRATION

Subcutaneous administration of fluids is not suitable in emergencies or for patients who are severely dehydrated [2,7]. The volume of fluid which can be given at a single site is limited and usually no more than 3 litres can be given subcutaneously over a 24 hour period. Absorption is more erratic for fluid given subcutaneously than for intravenous fluid. Hence, the intravenous route should be used when precise control of the volume and rate of infusion is essential, as for example in patients with cardiac or renal failure. In general, subcutaneous fluid administration should only be used as a short-term measure [2]. In patients with prolonged difficulties with oral intake, it is necessary to consider the need for nutritional supplements. Although subcutaneous fluids have a valuable role in terminal care [12], parenteral hydration is usually only necessary in terminally ill patients who are distressed by symptoms of dehydration and in whom other more simple measures have failed.

III - PRACTICAL ASPECTS OF SUBCUTANEOUS FLUID ADMINISTRATION

There are a wide variety of techniques for administering subcutaneous fluids, and there have been no studies reported comparing the efficacy or safety of different approaches.

3.1. What fluids can be administered by the subcutaneous route?

Normal and half normal saline and dextrose/saline combinations are commonly used solutions. Concern has been expressed in the past that rapid subcutaneous infusion of electrolyte-free solution can cause hypotension [7]. Shock has been reported with subcutaneous infusion of 5% dextrose at rates of 8ml/minute or greater to children [13] and with infusion of dextrose 10% at rates of 10ml/minute or greater in adults [14]. However, Schen and Singer-Edelstein reported giving 721 infusions of 1 to 2 litres of isotonic glucose a day without any adverse effects [1] ; in their practice, half-litre containers were given over 1 to 2 hours (infusion rate 4-8 ml/minute). Similarly, Berger has reported giving 5% dextrose at 1ml/minute (1.5L per day) without adverse effects [7]. We also have experienced no problems with the administration of up to 2 litres of 5% dextrose over 24 hours [3]. Thus, careful administration of relatively small amounts of dextrose 5% subcutaneously is safe. This is important because hypertonic dehydration is common in elderly people in hospitals and in long-stay institutions [11,15]. Colloid and hyperosmolar solutions should not be given via the subcutaneous route [16]. Potassium chloride, up to 40 mEq, can be added to each litre of solution [3,12,17,18]. A variety of medications can be administered via the subcutaneous route [12]. However, this subject is outside the scope of the present review.

3.2. Amount and Rate of Infusion

Fluid can be administered as a continuous infusion throughout a 24 hour period [3,4], as an overnight infusion [2] or a rapid intermittent infusion of up to 500ml fluid over 20 minutes [19] to 2 hours [1] several times a day. (In its most extreme form, the last technique has been termed the 'camel's hump' method [18]).

Lipschitz and colleagues demonstrated using radioisotope tracers that 500 ml normal saline (with hyaluronidase) given subcutaneously over 3 hours was rapidly and fully absorbed into the blood stream [5]. In general, no more than 3 litres should be administered by hypodermoclysis over a 24-hour period. It is usually difficult to give more than 2 litres and sometimes difficult to give more than 1.5 litres of fluid over 24 hours at a single site without using hyaluronidase. Rapid infusion of fluids (>500ml/hour) causes swelling of the infusion area, and, although this subsides with time and is harmless, in our experience it often provokes patient discomfort and staff anxiety. Hence, we do not use this approach. Because of the possible risk of hypotension discussed earlier, we administer no more than 2 litres of dextrose 5% in a 24 hour period and we restrict the rate of administering dextrose 5% to a maximum at any time of 2ml/minute.

3.3. Use of hyaluronidase

Hyaluronidase is a mixture of enzymes which break down hyaluronic acid, the main constituent of the connective tissue barrier. Hyaluronidase increases the speed of absorption of subcutaneous fluids by increasing the size of the absorptive area exposed to the fluid [20]. Although hyaluronidase is not necessary in most cases, it is useful when one wishes to administer a relatively large volume of fluid at a single site or to give fluid quickly. Hypersensitivity reactions have been reported to hyaluronidase in the past; in 1957, Kendall reported 3 cases of urticaria, one case of purpura and one of bronchospasm with oedema of the eyelids following 4,800 injections of hyaluronidase 1000 iu [21]. Such reactions are much less likely with the highly purified and standardized hyaluronidase preparations now available. For example, Schen and Singer-Edelstein noted no allergic reactions in a series of 4500 infusions using hyaluronidase [22]. Minor local irritation does occasionally occur at the site of the infusion; this can be prevented by adding 1-2ml of 1% lignocaine to the hyaluronidase [2]. Our current practice is to use hyaluronidase if more than 2 L are to be infused at a single site over a 24 hour period or if the planned infusion rate during a particular period is more than 2ml/min. Also, we consider hyaluronidase if a drip is running slowly or there is swelling of the infusion site. In these circumstances, we give 1500 iu hyaluronidase dissolved in 1ml water for injection as a bolus directly through the infusion cannula. Some authors have described adding hyaluronidase to the infusion bag [19]. However, hyaluronidase loses potency with time in solution, and this approach means that the concentration of hyaluronidase at the infusion site is lower (personal communication, Dr EA Wickham, CP Pharmaceutical Ltd).

IV - SETTING UP SUBCUTANEOUS INFUSIONS

Subcutaneous infusions should only be sited in healthy, clean, oedema free areas. The site chosen will depend upon patient comfort, convenience and the need for mobilisation of the patient. Possible sites include the lateral lower abdomen, thighs, scapular areas, axilla and infraclavicular areas. The scapular area is particularly useful in confused patients [3]. A 21-25G 'butterfly' cannula or paediatric teflon cannula is inserted into the skin at an angle of about 45 degrees. If the needle is in the subcutaneous space, it should be possible to wiggle it from side to side without difficulty or patient discomfort. If required, hyaluronidase is now injected through the cannula. The infusion fluid is connected via a standard, gravity-fed giving set and the rate adjusted as required. The fluid should flow easily without pain or immediate swelling. The needle and tubing should be secured using a clear occlusive dressing.The infusion site (and patient) should be inspected periodically. The needle should be resited if the patient complains of pain at the administration site, if the skin is hard, red or inflamed or if there is leakage. Minor degrees of oedema usually respond to slowing of the infusion rate or the use of hyaluronidase. Farrand and Cambell recommend changing the infusion site with each litre of fluid administered [2]. Our preference, if no problems have been experienced, is to change the infusion site every 48 hours. Other authors have reported a similar practice [4].

V - COMPLICATIONS OF SUBCUTANEOUS FLUID ADMINISTRATION

Complications attributed to subcutaneous fluid administration in the past include tissue necrosis at the infusion site, cellulitis and abscess formation and even gas gangrene. However, as Schen and Singer-Edelstein have noted [1], these reports are based primarily on the experiences during an era when infusion sets were sterilized and re-used many times and the risks of sepsis were greater. These authors reported infection at the site of the infusion in only 1 of 634 patients who received approximately 4500 subcutaneous infusions [22]; 2 patients in this series developed an ecchymosis at the infusion site. The risk of shock if large quantities of electrolyte-free solutions are infused subcutaneously have been described earlier. No such problems have reported using modern guidelines for administration of electrolyte-free fluids. The most common complication noted in the modern literature is local oedema at the infusion site [1,3,22]. Schen and Singer-Edelstein reported 5 cases of subcutaneous oedema in their series of 634 patients receiving subcutaneous infusions [22]. Alarming oedema of the genitals and the gluteal regions can occur with abdominal infusions, especially if the patient is hypoalbuminaemic [1]. This usually responds promptly to diuretics. Less dramatic oedema responds to a change in infusion site or a reduction in infusion rate.

CONCLUSIONS

Subcutaneous fluid administration is a safe and effective means of treating and preventing mild dehydration in patients with an inadequate oral intake. Compared with intravenous fluids, subcutaneous fluids are particularly valuable in patients with difficult veins, those with cognitive impairment and those undergoing active rehabilitation.

REFERENCES

1. Schen RJ, Singer-Edelstein M. Subcutaneous infusions in the elderly. J Am Geriatr Soc 1981; 29:583-585.
2. Farrand S, Cambell AJ. Safe, simple subcutaneous fluid administration. Br J Hosp Med 1996; 55:690-692.
3. O'Keeffe ST, Lavan JN. Subcutaneous fluids in elderly hospital patients with cognitive impairment. Gerontology 1996; 42:36-39.
4. Challiner YC, Jarrett D, Hayward MJ, Al-Jubouri MA, Julious SA. A comparison of intravenous and subcutaneous hydration in elderly acute stroke patients. Postgrad Med J 1994; 70:195-197.
5. Lipschitz S, Cambell AJ, Roberts MS, et al. Subcutaneous fluid administration in elderly subjects: validation of an under-used technique. J Am Geriatr Soc 1991; 39:6-9.

6. Hecker JF. Potential for extending survival of peripheral intravenous infusions. Br Med J 1992; 304:619-624.
7. Berger EY. Nutrition by hypodermoclysis. J Am Geriatr Soc 1984; 32:199-203.
8. Seymour DG, Henscheke PJ, Cape RDT, Cambell AJ. Acute confusional states and dementia in the elderly: the role of dehydration/volume depletion, physical illness and age. Age Ageing 1980; 9:137-146.
9. Koizumi J, Shiraishi H, Ofuku K, Suzuki T. Duration of delirium shortened by the correction of electrolyte imbalance. Jpn J Psychiatr Neurol 1988; 42:81-88.
10. Turner J, Brown A, Russell P, Scott P, Browne M. 'Pushing fluids' - can current practices of maintaining hydration in hospital patients be improved? J Royal Coll Phys Lond 1987; 21:196-198.
11. Weinberg AD, Minaker KL. Dehydration. Evaluation and management in older adults. J Am Med Assoc 1995; 274:1552-1556.
12. Hays H. Hypodermoclysis for symptom control in terminal care. Can Fam Physician 1985; 31:1253-1256.
13. Mateer FM. Hyaluronidase and the subcutaneous administration of electrolyte-êfree glucose solutions. Am J Med Sci 1953; 226:139-143.
14. Abbott WE, Levey S, Foreman R, et al. The danger of administering parenteral fluids by hypodermoclysis. Surgery 1952; 32:305-315.
15. Palevsky PM, Bhagrath R, Greenberg A. Hypernatremia in hospitalized patients. Ann Intern Med 1996; 124:197-203.
16. Butler J. Peripheral vascular collapse after the subcutaneous use of hypertonic non-electrolyte solution. N Engl J Med 1953; 249:990-999.
17. Bruere E, Legris MA, Kuehn N, Miller MJ. Hypodermoclysis for the administration of fluids and narcotic analgesics in patients with advanced cancer. J Pain Symptom Manage 1990; 5:218-220.
18. Schen RJ, Arieli S. Administration of potassium by subcutaneous infusion in elderly patients. BMJ 1982; 285:1167-1168.
19. Simpson RG. Hyaluronidase in geriatric therapy. Practitioner 1977; 219:361-363.
20. Hechter O. Mechanism of spreading factor action. Ann N Y Acad Sci 1950; 52:1028-1040.
21. Kendall PH. Allergic response to hyaluronidase. Br Med J 1957; 1:1419-1420.
22. Schen RJ, Singer-Edelstein M. Hypodermoclysis. J Am Med Assoc 1983; 250:1694.

HYPEROSMOLAR COMA IN OLDER PERSONS

A. E. BERNARDO, J. E. MORLEY

Geriatric Research, Education and Clinical Center, St. Louis VA Medical Center and Division of Geriatric Medicine, St. Louis University Health Center

Abstract : *Hyperosmolar coma (HC) is a life threatening hyperglycemic emergency mostly affecting the older person who has either diagnosed or undiagnosed Type II diabetes mellitus. Elderly people tend to be hypodipsic or do not recognize the need to ingest water but are able to maintain body water homeostasis. The physiological hypodipsia of aging increases the propensity to develop a pathological hemodynamical state of disequilibrium when older persons encounter physiologic stressors or during illnesses that leads further to dehydration. A serious outcome of this disequilibrum is HC. Impaired neurotransmitters such as opioid peptides, neuropeptide Y and angiotensin II have been implicated and play a role in the failure of the drinking system with advancing age. The working knowledge about the pathophysiology of HC is based on three proposed major mechanisms which include 1) higher levels of endogenous insulin reserve, 2) lower levels of counter regulatory hormones and free fatty acids, and 3) inhibition of lipolysis thereby decreasing ketogenesis. Recent studies showed that 1) vasopressin is markedly elevated because of severe dehydration and hyperosmolality and it may play an important role in the supression of ketosis, and 2) enhanced concentration of GABA at pre- and postsynaptic inhibitory GABA receptors on neighboring neurons probably caused a decrease in neuronal excitability and release of other neurotransmitters. These recent findings contributes further in our understanding about the pathogenesis of HC. Further studies revealed that serious depletion of body water produces hypernatremia instead of hyponatremia in older persons with HC. Mental impairment in hyperglycemic condition correlates strongly with hypernatremia and hyperosmolality. A variety of illnesses and physiological stressors can lead to HC. Obtaining a concise history and performing a thorough physical examination are critical to the appropriate management.*

Laboratory data and essential diagnostic modalities in particular stressors should be obtained as well for clearer picture of the clinical senario in its entirety. Housestaffs should be equipped with important calculations such as plasma osmolality or an 'effective' osmolality and 'corrected' plasma sodium. Mortality rate remains high. The role of particular stressors in the mortality rate should not be overlooked. The complications of therapy of HC should be avoided. Fluid replacement and insulin are still the cornerstone in the management of HC. The approach to the elderly person requires a perspective different from that of younger individuals. The use of hypotonic solutions has been suggested for the management of older persons with hypernatremic and hyperglycemic dehydration. Its judicious use is extremely important.

INTRODUCTION

Diabetes mellitus has been reported to be present in approximately 18% of those aged between 65 and 75 years and up to 40% aged over 80 years [38,40]. Nearly 50% of individuals with type II diabetes mellitus are over the age of 65 years [37]. Of the 6.5 million diabetics with Type II diabetes mellitus in the United States, nearly 3.1 million are over the age of 65 years [41], and 63% of the 7 billion dollars spent on patients with Type II diabetes was spent on this group [42].

Institutionalization is more common among diabetic patients over 65 than among other older persons, and the relative risk of mortality for diabetics aged 65 to 74 years is 1.7, while for those 75 and older it is 1 [43].

HC is a serious and acute complication of Type II diabetes mellitus [1,2,76]. The rate of hospital admissions accounts for less than 1% of all diabetic-related admissions [77,78]. It represents only 5-15% [85] of all hyperglycemic emergencies mostly affecting elderly patients with Type II diabetes mellitus. More expensive hospitalizations are associated with intercurrent medical problems or chronic complications of diabetes [87].

The mortality rate in patients with Hyperosmolar Syndrome is considerably higher than with Diabetic Ketoacidosis, with recently reported mortality rates of 12-70% [85,86] compared to 15-35% [79,80,81]

The pathogenesis, etiology, and risk factors of hyperosmolar coma in older individuals are not completely understood. Basic knowledge of this disorder is very essential in achieving the rational systematic approach to therapy in older persons [16].

Despite major advances in the understanding of their pathogenesis and a more uniform and best agreement on the diagnosis and treatment of hyperosmolar syndrome, hyperosmolar coma continue to be important cause of morbidity and mortality among patients with Type II diabetes mellitus. Thus in this article, the investigators will attempt to broaden the paradigm in discussing the pathogenesis and the management of hyperosmolar coma, particularly in the older persons.

I - DEFINITION

Although Diabetic Ketoacidosis (DKA) and Hyperosmolar Coma (HC) are often discussed as separate entities, many investigators [28,30,76,94,97] believe that there is a clinical spectrum of severe hyperglycemic disorders that ranges from hyperosmolar coma to full-blown diabetic ketoacidosis, with a significant degree of overlap in the middle.

This particular acute diabetic complication has surprisingly adopted a great variety of names in medical literature that can lead to further confusion in understanding the disease. (See Table 1) From this myriad of names, several modifiers could be avoided and three terms in its simplest form could be utilized for this purpose, namely: hyperosmolar syndrome, hyperosmolar state and hyperosmolar coma.

1.1. Hyperosmolar syndrome

Hyperosmolar syndrome (HS) covers a spectrum from minor degrees of hyperosmolality to severe degrees with central nervous system (CNS) symptoms including coma [26]. It is also characterized by severe hyperglycemia, hypernatremia and mild to severe dehydration in the absence of or trace of ketoacidosis [83].

1.1.1. Hyperosmolar state

Hyperosmolar state (HT) comprises all the characteristics of HS except coma. The level of consciousness ranges from alert, obtunded and stupor, but not frank coma. Trace of ketoacidosis could be found in patients with this type of condition. Patient in this condition has a good chance of recovery and the mean age is <65 years old.

1.1.2. Hyperosmolar coma

Hyperosmolar coma (HC) is the extreme end of the spectrum in which the mortality and morbidity are very high and the mean age is >65 years old. Severe hyperosmolality, profound dehydration, severe hypernatremia in hyperglycemic comatose elderly in the absence of ketoacidosis are the hallmarks of this clinical entity.

Table 1
Myriad of Names in Medical Literature

Diabetic collapse [33]
Diabetic Hyperosmolar State [30]
Diabetic with Hyperosmolality
Diabetic Nonketotic Hyperosmolar State (DNKHS) [84]

Hyperglycemic Hyperosmolar Coma [99]
Hyperglycemic Hyperosmolar Nonketotic Coma [30]
Hyperglycemic Hyperosmolar Nonketotic State (HHNS) [31]
Hyperglycemic Hyperosmolar Nonketotic Syndrome (HHNS) [33,76]
Hyperglycemic Hyperosmolar Syndrome (HHS) [13,28,29]
Hyperglycemic Nonketotic Hyperosmolar Syndrome [6]
Hyperglycemic Nonketotic Hyperosmolar Coma [6,34]

Hyperosmolar-Hyperglycemic Coma [32,37,38]
Hyperosmolar Hyperglycemic Nonketotic Coma (HHNC) [29] or (HHNKC) [3,7]
Hyperosmolar Hyperglycemic Nonketotic States [17]
Hyperosmolar Hyperglycemic Nonketotic Syndrome (HHNS) [35]
Hyperosmolar Coma, [1,9,30,39]
Hyperosmolar Diabetic Coma [72]
Hyperosmolar Nonacidotic Uncontrolled Diabetes [30]
Hyperosmolar Nonacidotic Diabetes (HNAD) [30]
Hyperosmolar Nonketotic Diabetic Coma (HNDC) [5,20]
Hyperosmolar Nonketotic Diabetic Decompensation [2]
Hyperosmolar Nonketotic Uncontrolled Diabetes
Hyperosmolar Non-ketotic Coma (HNC) [30,95]
Hyperosmolar Non-ketotic State [17]
Hyperosmolar State [10]

Nonketotic Hyperglycemic Coma [34]
Nonketotic Hyperglycemic Hyperosmolality [28]
Nonketotic Hyperglycemic-Hyperosmolar Coma (NKHHC) [36]
Non-ketotic Hyperosmolar coma [4,14,15,18,26,27]
Non-ketotic Hyperosmolar diabetic coma
Nonketotic Hyperosmolar Syndrome [26]
Nonketotic Hypertonicity (NKH) [33]

II - OVERVIEW OF THIRST REGULATION

Release of plasma arginine vasopressin (AVP) and thirst are closely coordinated. When plasma osmolality is greater than 292 mosmol/kg thirst is perceived. When water is lost hypernatremia leads to increase fluid intake. This is due in part to angiotensin II release [1]. With age AVP release is increased in response to a rising plasma osmolality [1]. Fluid intake is terminated in part by gastric distension [50].

Older persons maintain body water homeostasis [51], but often they do not recognize the need to ingest fluids [45]. The exact prevalence of dehydration in community-dwelling elderly is unknown. In nursing home patients up to 25% have been found to be dehydrated [61].

However, with stressors such as fever, diarrhea, infection, water deprivation, heat [62,63], or exercise, the disruption in homeostasis is more severe, the time needed to return to baseline is prolonged compared to younger individuals, thus producing the potential for severe dehydration [45,51] with subsequent morbidity and mortality [51]. Polyuria and lack of thirst perception can also lead to dehydration [17]. Thus, dehydration represents a major problem in older individuals [48].

Miller [53] studied six patients (ages 68-91) who had suffered previous cerebrovascular accidents and had a history of recurrent dehydration and hypernatremia. Despite the ability to obtain water, none of the patients complained of thirst. It was concluded that the deficits in thirst perception were due to a cortical lesion.

Some specific age-related declines in renal function are decline in renal, basement membrane thickens, number and length of tubules decline and decreased glomerular filtration rate. Its functional implications were reduction in maximal concentrating and diluting capacity and less responsiveness to volume depletion [16]. Older subjects tended to have lower urine osmolality and lower urine/plasma osmolality ratios [51]. Hence, aging impairs renal concentrating ability [54].

Physiological factors accompanying aging which place the elderly at a high risk for dehydration include a decrease in the concentrating capacity by the kidney [54], impaired angiotensin II production [52], and alterations in vasopressin sensitivity [55,56] as well as hypodipsia. Despite higher serum sodium and osmolality levels in older persons they do not show alterations in thirst or mouth dryness following fluid deprivation [57,58,59,60].

III - PATHOPHYSIOLOGY OF HYPEROSMOLAR COMA

Impaired insulin secretion and tissue resistance to the action of insulin produce the glucose intolerance of Type II diabetes [17]. Some evidence suggests that hyperglycemia results in accelerated atherosclerosis and possibly accelerated aging [44]. A remarkable increase in plasma glucose accompanies marked glucosuria and osmotic diuresis [4].

Elderly that have hypodipsia interacts with the hyperosmolar diuresis. Thus, the patient suffer from serious dehydration [37]. Hypodipsia, commonly interferes with the management of older persons with diabetes mellitus, leading to dehydration and HC [37].

3.1. Current perspective

HC occurs without the development of ketoacidosis [1]. This occurs because the higher circulating insulin levels prevent lipolysis (possibly by preventing full activation of the carnitine palmitoyltransferase system [1]) but cannot stimulate glucose utilization or inhibit its hepatic production [17,76]. Hyperosmolality per se appears to inhibit lipolysis resulting in a decrease in ketogenesis [76] Persons with HC also have lower levels of fatty acids than seen in those who develop ketoacidosis.

3.2. New perspective

3.2.1. Vasopressin

In HC there is an increase in AVP, plasma renin levels and aldosterone concentration [18,19]. In animal studies AVP suppresses ketone body formation when given in high doses [20]. This may be, in part, because of decreased blood flow to adipose tissue [22,23]. The AVP effect appears to be specific for long chain fatty acids [24,27]. AVP appears also to inhibit ketogenesis in the liver by shifting oleate metabolism towards oxidation instead of ketogenesis [24,25,26,27].

3.2.2. GABA

In high concentrations glucose modulates [^{3}H]GABA release from cortical slices [74]. This increase in GABA release is associated with inhibition of norepinephrine and serotonin release [72]. GABA is the major inhibitory neurotransmitter in the central nervous system [75]. It is possible that the increase in GABA in HC is responsible for the central nervous system symptoms associated with HC.

3.2.3. Hyperglycemia versus Hypernatremia in Hyperosmolar coma

A marked increase in plasma glucose is common in DKA and HC. Serum sodium levels are expected to decrease at the rate of 1.6 mEq/l per 100 mg/dl increase in plasma glucose using a corrected serum sodium Roscoe et al [8] found.

Two subgroups of the patients with HC, namely, the hypernatremic group of 162.5 ± 1.8 mEq/l and the hyponatremic group of 125.8 ± 4.3 mEq/l. There was an inverse change in serum sodium (Na) and potassium (K) levels [4]. The two opposing constellations of disordered serum electrolytes at the time of hospitalization in the patients in diabetic coma were demonstrated by Ishikawa et al [4]. The changes in serum Na and K levels were studied in seventeen patients in DKA and nine patients in HC, who had marked hyperglycemia and dehydration. The disorder characterized two types of alteration. Hyponatremia with hyperkalemia was found in the patients in DKA and HC, and hypernatremia with hypokalemia in HC. Aging and volume contraction (fluid loss) were both factors involved in predicting whether the subjects were hypo- or hypernatremic. Aged persons were more likely to be hyponatremic and when the loss of circulatory volume was greater than 20% persons tended to be hypernatremic [4]. Hypernatremic patients took longer to normalize their sodium and potassium levels than hyponatremic individuals.

3.2.4. Hyperglycemia and Hypernatremia in Hyperosmolar coma

Cerebral dehydration leads to neurologic manifestations in patients with hypernatremic HC. Persons with hyponatremic HC do not have as many neurological complications presumably because of the absence of hypernatremic-induced cerebral cellular dehydration. A slower onset of hyperglycemia appears to be associated with greater accumulation of "idiogenic osmoles" in the brain cells [10-12].

Elevated Na levels are more important than hyperglycemia in producing brain dysfunction [6-9]. In contrast, in the study of Miller et al [53] on the elderly patients aged 68 to 91 years, the striking observation was that despite hypernatremia, hyperosmolality, volume depletion and without hyperglycemia, all of the subjects' mental status was normal as assessed by standard neurologic and psychologic evaluation and confirmed by neurologic consultation. Mental alterations on hyperglycemic states correlate better with hypernatremia and hyperosmolality than with elevated glucose levels [13]. Hyponatremia is a favorable sign usually associated with a lack of CNS manifestations and cerebral dehydration [6].

IV - CLINICAL PRESENTATION

Since HC is a hyperglycemic emergency and should opt for immediate management, obtaining a brief history and performing a thorough physical examination is critical. In most cases, little or no history is available because older persons present in a comatose state [80]. Most of the time, the history is obtained from nursing home staffs or from relatives and friends [76].

4.1 History

Middle-aged to elderly patients whose ages range from 55 to 70 years old [32,33,76,92] with type II diabetes suffering from symptoms due to severe hyperosmolality and profound dehydration typically present HC [26,89]. 15-60% of these patients have no history or are undiagnosed to have diabetes at the time of onset of this condition [15,32,33,86,87,88,90]. Previously diagnosed type II diabetics usually present with mild decompensation [32] and noncompliance of medication is a contributing cause in up to 25% [87]. In addition, HC is often seen in previously diabetics well controlled by diet and small doses of an oral hypoglycemic agent [2]. Elderly females living in nursing homes [81,84] are very prone to this acute complication.

The duration of gradual progression of symptoms of increasing dehydration and hyperglycemia can take from days to weeks [32,33,81,87]. Occassionally this as seen to occur within 24 hours.

Several factors could lead to the precipitation of HC whether in acute or chronic condition. Precipitating factors need always to be diligently sought [92]. These factors need to be treated for optimal outcomes.(See Table 2)

Table 2
Precipitating Illnesses

ACUTE SITUATIONS
    Acute Trauma [6]
    Extensive severe burns [35,6,29,91]
    Gastrointestinal hemorrhage [35,29]
    Heat stroke [91,29]
    Hypothermia [29]
    Infection [35,26,29]
        Diabetic gangrene [35]
        Gram-negative pneumonia [91]
        Septicemia [35]
            Gram-negative septicemia [91]
        Urinary tract infection [35]
    Massive Vascular Accident [91]
        Cerebrovascular accident [35,26,29,91]
        Gastrointestinal hemorrhage [91]
        Mesenteric vascular accidents [91]
        Myocardial infarction [35,91,29]
        Pulmonary emboli [91]
        Subdural hematoma [91]
    Pancreatitis [35,6,29,91]
    Severe acute hyponatremia [29]
    Thyrotoxicosis [29]

CHRONIC ILLNESSES
    Alcoholism [35]
    Dementia [39]
    Heart disease [35]
    Hypertension [35]
    Loss of thirst [35]
    Malignant hyperthermia [90,93]
    Old stroke [35]
    Psychiatric [35]
    Renal disease[35]
        Chronic renal insufficiency [91]
    Severe water restriction [29]

MISCELLANEOUS
    Excess sugar-containing beverages [29]

Several drugs have also been reported and have been implicated to initiate the disorder. HC also has been precipitated by several therapeutic procedures. (See Table 3)

Table 3
Iatrogenic Causes

THERAPEUTIC AGENTS
    b-Adrenergic-blocking agents [33,35]
        Propranolol [91,29]
    Antipsychotic agents
        Chlorpromazine [35,29,91]
        Loxapine [91]
    L-Asparaginase [35,29,91]
    Cimetidine [91,29,33]
    Diazoxide [35,91,29,33]
    Didanosine [96]
    Diuretic agents [35,1,2,26,29]
        Ethacrynic acid [91]
        Furosemide [91,33]
        Thiazide diuretics [91,33]
    Encainide [33]
    Immunosuppressive agents [35,1,91]
    Osmotic agents
        Mannitol [1]
        Urea [1]
    Phenytoin [1,26,29,35,91,33]
    Steroids [1,26,91,33]
        Glucocorticoids [35,29]

THERAPEUTIC PROCEDURES
    Dialysis [6,29]
        Hemodialysis [35,1,91]
        Peritoneal dialysis [35,1,26,91,33]
    Parenteral or Enteral Hyperalimentation [35,6,26,33,91,29]
        Glucose administration [29]
        High-carbohydrate infusion loads [1]
        Tube feeding of high-protein formulas [1]
    Surgical stress [35,29]
        Cardiac Surgery [90,93,33]

4.2. Physical Examination

Hypovolemia and neurologic function are the major clinical presentations [27,29]. Clinical examination includes evaluation of the level of consciousness alert, obtunded, stupor and coma [84]. State of hydration is evaluated and is classified as mild, moderate or severe, according to different gradings based on the persistence of the skinfold tenting, dry skin and mucous membranes and the presence of a soft and sunken eyeballs [84,91]. Orthostatic changes in blood pressure, and, in severe cases, hypotension and shock are also noted [91]. Fever can be due to infection, myocardial infarction or cerebral dehydration [29].

4.3. Neurologic Manifestation

CNS symptoms are the major manifestation of HC [27]. Seizures occur in 10 to 15% of patients with HC [91]. Neurological symptoms can involve any area of the brain from the cortex to the brain stem [103]. Besides dehydration these symptoms are thought to be due to neurotrasmitter abnormalities and microvascular ischemia [88].

Focal neurologic findings are common in patients with HS [12,103,104]. Stroke is a common misdiagnosis [105]. Table 4 shows the reported focal neurologic findings that are related to HS.

Table 4
Focal Neurologic Findings in Hyperosmolar Syndrome [33,105]

Acute urinary retention
Aphasia
Autonomic dysfunction
    Hyperpnea
    Hypertension
Babinski sign
Eye deviation
Fasciculations
Focal increased or decreased muscle tone
Hemianopsia
    Homonymous
Hemiparesis
Hemisensory defects
Hyperreflexia
    Bilateral

Unilateral
Hyperthermia
Nystagmus
Quadriplegia
Seizures
> grand mal
> Jacksonian [1]
> myoclonus
Severe dysphagia
Vestibulobasal dysfunction
Visual hallucinations
Visual loss

4.4. Laboratory Findings

There is a large vanity in the reported laboratory findings in HC. Pertinent initial laboratory findings in HC in persons over the age of 65 years is presented in Table 5.

Table 5
Laboratory findings in hyperosmolar coma

	Spain [84] (n=132)	South Africa [109] (n=16)	Japan [4] (n=5)
Age, years	75±8	66.2±11.3	65.0±7.1
Glucose, mg/dL	750	925	707
Sodium, mmol/L	153±11	139.4±14.5	162.5±1.8
BUN, mg/dL	138±57	118.2±70.2	75.0±11.8
Osmolality, mOsm/kg	380±23	356±24	355.3±7.2
pH	7.4±0.06	---	7.34±0.02

Base on the above data, the laboratory findings that are essential for diagnosis in older persons with pure HC can be derived. (Table 6) When serum sodium is elevated there is severe hyperosmolality and water depletion [28].

Table 6
Laboratory findings essential for diagnosis of HC in older persons

• Hyperglycemia:	>750 mg/dL
• Hypernatremia:	>150 mmol/L
• Serum osmolality:	>350 mOsm/kg
• Serum ketones:	absent

Coma is always present when serum osmolality is greater than 400 mOsm/kg and rare when under 350 mOsm/kg [28]. Ketoacidosis should be absent in HC but some patients actually exhibit trace ketoacidosis. Older persons may have a mixed ketoacidotic/HC presentation.

Other basic laboratory findings should include complete blood count, urinalysis, arterial blood gas, x-ray and an electrocardiogram. Other work up will depend upon the possible precipitating factor the patient has. It is worth mentioning that in HC, perenal azotemia with marked elevation of blood urea nitrogen (BUN) and creatinine is also characteristic [1,26]. In addition the hemoglobin levels are elevated and the central venous pressure is low [2].

V- IMPORTANT COMPUTATIONS

There are two important computations that are useful in an elderly patient who is dehydrated, with changes in sensorium and with hyperglycemia. These are "the corrected sodium" and "the serum osmolality".

Corrected Sodium

An elderly person who presents with extreme hyperglycemia and is at risk for neurologic disturbance must have a careful analysis of the plasma sodium. A corrected plasma sodium level should be calculated [91]. The serum sodium, when corrected for the prevailing degree of hyperglycemia, should be normal or elevated. If the uncorrected serum sodium is elevated, the degree of dehydration is enormous [106].

$$\text{corrected Na} = \text{measured Na} + 1.6 \times \frac{(\underline{\text{plasma glucose in mg/dl} - 100})}{100}$$

or

corrected Na = measured Na + 1.6 x (plasma glucose in mmol/1 - 5.5)
$$5.5$$

Serum osmolality

Serum osmolality (Osm) or the effective serum osmolality (Osm$_E$) must be computed for an elderly patient with changes in mental state. This can be approximated by the formula:

Osm = 2 x [Na$^+$ + K$^+$ (mmol/L)]+ plasma glucose (mg/dl) + BUN (mg/dl)
$$18 \qquad\qquad 2.8$$

Since urea is freely diffusible across cell membranes, it does not alter the effective serum osmolality, which is the clinically important factor to consider in this hyperosmolar condition. Most experts [33,82] do not consider BUN levels in this calculation and prefer to estimate effective serum osmolality as:

OsmE = 2 x [Na$^+$ + K$^+$ (mmol/L)] + plasma glucose (mg/dl)
$$18$$

Any value greater than 300 mOsm per liter is abnormal and when values are above 320 mOsm per liter, they are clinically significant [26]. The importance of total serum osmolality in causing HC has been emphasized by several authors [15,84,88,108]. In the study of Piniés et al [84] of 132 patients with HC, blood urea nitrogen was the factor most influential in predicting the risk of mortality by multiple logistic regression analysis.

VI - MORTALITY AND MORBIDITY

Age, high plasma osmolality, and nursing home residence are well-known factors associated with nonsurvival [86,91]. Death is usually due to underlying illnesses such as myocardial infarction or stroke [76]. Depression is also highly correlated with mortality in older diabetic patients [37].

Despite even the best therapy, morbidity and mortality are high in this conditon. Thrombosis and embolic events [2,26] (occurring probably as a consequence of the hyperviscous, hypercoagulable state induced by the metabolic derangements) as well as infections, result in poor outcomes.

In one study, septic shock was the most frequent cause of death [84]. Myocardial infarction or stroke increased mortality. Increasing age, low sodium and bicarbonate levels and hypotension are also related to mortality. Urea was the most significant risk factor. This justifies why several investigators still prefer the total serum osmolality over the effective osmolality. In addition, non-survivors received higher doses of insulin than survivors [84].

The estimated mortality rate has varied from 12 to 60% in past studies [15,86,96,98,100]. However, recently a downward trend has been noted from the 1970s onward [84]. In these recent reports the mortality approximates 14 - 18% [86,101,102]. This is in agreement with the study of Piniés et al [84] in which the overall mortality from HC in their series was 16.9%. The reason for this finding is not completely clear, but may be related to the different case definition by various authors, increased knowledge disseminated concerning the disease, the immediate application of 'therapy' and decreased usage of extremely high doses of insulin.

VII - TREATMENT

Immediate treatment is indicated once the diagnosis has been established. Rigorous but carefully monitored hydration and reestablishment of circulatory integrity are critical for successful therapy. Precipitating factors should be carefully sought [26]. The hemodynamic state of the patient should be carefully monitored in view of its role in prognosis [84].

7.1. Goals of Therapy

Patients with HC require insulin and volume repletion. Intravascular volume expansion is a key to management [26]. In general, the goals of therapy should be focused on the restoration of hemodynamic stability by correcting serum osmolality, electrolytes and glucose through judicious usage of fluids and insulin and treating the underlying disease.

7.2. Fluid Replacement

Although we know that fluid replacement is the treatment of choice for the HS, various authors present different approaches. The art of fluid therapy is a major challenge to the clinicians. Avoidance of excessive or improper use of normal saline is key to the appropriate management.

Elderly individuals thus have wider variations in fluid and electrolyte balance and other homeostatic mechanisms [16] but a common goal should be pursued. Undertreatment or overtreatment can lead to complications such as cerebral edema and the less common rhabdomyolysis [5,110].

In general, severely hypergylcemic elderly patient who present with normal or elevated uncorrected serum sodium concentration have severe hyperosmolality and water depletion [28]. Optimum treatment is given with hypotonic (0.45%) saline [110]. Fluid deficits range from 10 to 20 percent of total body water [28]. Central venous pressure must be monitored in all patients [28,84].

In the hypotensive patient isotonic saline is used to initially replace fluid but after the first 2 liters switching to 0.45% saline is preferred [109,111]. While this is theoretically sound one study failed to show any significant difference in outcome based on the fluid given [107].

7.3. Insulin

Continuous intravenous administration of insulin is preferred in the management of an elderly with HC as volume depletion impedes absorption from muscle or subcutaneous tissue [28]. Treatment consists of a bolus of 5 to 10 units of regular insulin followed by 2 to 5 units per hour intravenously. Plastic tubing needs to be coated with insulin before the infusion starts. Persons with HC who die receive more insulin (115.2 units) compared to survivors (98 units) [84] When serum glucose falls below 250 mg/dl the fluid infused should be changed to 5% dextrose.

7.4. Electrolyte Replacement

Severe hyperglycemia results to osmotic diuresis. This diuresis leads to tremendous losses of potassium and phosphorus. Five to 10 meq/kg body weight of potassium is lost in HC. Potassium needs to be replaced with fluid in HC.

There is a loss of 70 to 100 mmol of phosphate in patients with HS. Phosphate can be conveniently replaced by utilizing potassium phosphate to replace potassium.

7.5. Other Medications

Prophylactic use of low-molecular weight heparin appeared to be of benefit in the study of Rolfe et al [109] though it has been reported not to reduce mortality in HC by others [111] In view of the high risk of thrombosis of major vessels in HC, prophylactic low-molecular weight heparin should be contemplated.

VIII - PREVENTION

Accessibility to water and adequate intake of it daily by the elderly is important to prevent this serious outcome. Older persons should have a good exercise program to avoid sedentary activity that leads to obesity and hyperglycemia [37]. However excessive exercise in hot weather can lead to dehyration and care must be taken to ingest adequate fluids at these times. Glucose-rich carbonated drinks taken to alleviate thirst by the older persons must be discouraged [109].

Elderly found unconscious with no history at hand should have a rapid glucose estimation by reagent strips to avoid the practice of indiscriminate administration of dextrose to comatose patients [3]. In addition, for known type II diabetic elderly, blood glucose monitoring is very important.

CONCLUSION

Elderly patients and physicians must be aware that type II diabetes is not a static condition and that changes in symptomatology should be taken seriously. To render optimum quality care, HS must be clearly defined and understood. Severe hyperosmolality, profound dehydration and severe hypernatremia in a hyperglycemic comatose elderly in the absence of ketoacidosis are the hallmarks in formulating the diagnosis of hyperosmolar coma in older persons. The management of HC in older persons presents a considerable challenge to clinicians. We may not dramatically reduce the mortality rate especially the older persons, moreso, with advanced age and intercurrent disease, but optimum care is achievable.

REFERENCES

1. Isselbacher KJ, E. Braunwald, et al. Harrison's Principles of Internal Medicine. 13th ed. New York:McGraw-Hill, Inc.;1994.
2. Paterson KR and Quin JD.Hyperosmolar non-ketotic Diabetic Decompensation (comment).Br J Hosp Med. February;43(2):107; 1990
3. Soni A, Rao SV, Bajaj R and Treser G. Extreme Hyperglycemia and hyperosmolarity (letter) Diabetes Care. February; 13(2):181-2; 1990
4. Ishikawa S, Sakuma N, Fujisawa G, Tsuboi Y, Okada K and Saito T. Opposite changes in serum sodium and potassium in patients in diabetic coma. Endocrine Journal Feb;41(1):37-43;1994

5. Trump D, O'Hanlon S, Rinsler M and Sharp P. Hyperosmolar non-ketotic diabetic coma and rhabdomyolysis. Postgrad Med J 70:44-46; 1994
6. Popli S, Leehey DJ, Daugirdas JT, Bansal VK, Ho DS, Hano JE and Ing TS Asymptomatic, nonketotic, severe hyperglycemia withhyponatremia. Arch Intern Med Sep;150(9):1962-4; 1990
7. Purnell L Triage decisions. A 68-year-old unconscious woman with a history of urinary tract infection treated with oral antibiotics. J Emerg Nurs Jul-Aug;16(4):303-4; 1990
8. Roscoe JM, Halperin ML, Rolleston FS, Goldstein MB. Hyperglycemia-induced hyponatremia:metabolic considerations in calculation of serum sodium depression. Can Med Assoc J. 12:452-453; 1975
9. Daugirdas Jt, Kronfol NO, Tzamaloukas AH, Ing TS. Hyperosmolar coma:cellular dehydration and the serum sodium concentration. Ann Intern Med. 110:855-857; 1989
10. Arieff AI, Guisado R, Lararowitz VC. Pathophysiology of hyperosmolar states. In: Andreoli TE, Grantham JJ, Rector FC Jr, eds. Disturbances in Body Fluid Osmolality. Bethesda, Md: AmericanPhysiological Society. 227-250; 1977
11. Pollock AS, Arieff AI. Abnormalities of cell volumes regulation and their functional consequences. Am J Physiol. 239:F195-F205; 1980
12. Guisado R, Arieff AI. Neurological manifestations of diabetic comas: correlation with biochemical alterations in the brain. Metabolism. 24:665-679; 1975
13. Leehey DJ, Manahan FJ, Daugirdas JT, Ing TS. Predictors of mental status in the hyperglycemic hyperosmolar syndrome (HHS). In: Programs and abstracts of the 22nd annual meeting of the American Society of Nephrology; December 3-6; Washington, DC; 1989
14. Arieff AI. Cerebral edema complicating nonketotic hyperosmolar coma. Miner Electrolyte Metab. 12:383-389; 1986
15. Arieff AI, Carroll HJ. Nonketotic hyperosmolar coma with hyperglycemia: clinical features, pathophysiology, renal function, acid-base balance, plasma-cerebrospinal fluid equilibria and the effects of therapy in 37 cases. Medicine (Baltimore). 51:73-94; 1972
16. Goldman L. editor. MKSAP 10 - Geriatrics. American College of Physicians. 1994
17. Goldman L. editor. MKSAP 10 - Endocrinology and Metabolism. American College of Physicians; 1995
18. Ishikawa S, Saito T, Okada K, Nagasaka S, Kuzuya T. Prompt recovery of plasma arginine vasopressin in diabetic coma after intravenous infusion of a small dose of insulin and a large amount of fluid. Acta Endocrinol 122:455-461; 1990
19. Christlieb AR, Assal JP, Katsilambros N, Williams GH, Kozak GP, Suzuki T Plasma renin activity and blood volume in uncontrolled diabetics:Ketoacidosis, a state of secondary aldosteronism. Diabetes 24:190-193; 1975
20. Harano A, Hidaka H, Kojima H, Harano Y and Shigeta Y. Suppressive effect of vasopressin on ketosis in diabetic rats. Horm Metab Res Jan;24(1):5-9; 1992
21. Harano Y, K Kosugi, A Kashiwagi, T Nakano, H Hidaka, Y Shigeta Regulatory mechanism of ketogenesis by glucagon and insulin in isolated and cultured hepatocytes. J. Biochem. (Tokyo) 91:1739-1748; 1982
22. Rofe, AM, DH Williamson Metabolic effects of vasopressin infusion in the starved rat. Reversal of ketonemia. Biochem J. 212:231-239; 1983a
23. Rofe, AM, DH Williamson Mechanism for the 'antilipolytic' action of vasopressin in the starved rat. Biochem J. 212:899-902; 1983b
24. Williamson, DH, V Ilic, AFC Tordoff, EV EllingtonInteractions between vasopressin and glucagon on ketogenesis and oleate metabolism in isolated hepatocytes from fed rats. Biochem J.186:621-624; 1980
25. Sugden, MC, AJ Ball, V Ilic, DH Williamson Stimulation of (1-14C)oleate oxidation to 14CO2 in isolated rat hepatocytes by vasopressin: Effect of Ca2. FEBS Lett. 116:37-39; 1980
26. Wyngaarden JB, Smith LH and Bennett C. eds. Cecil Textbook of Medicine. 19th ed.; 1992
27. DeGroot LJ, et al. eds. Endocrinology. Vol. 2. 3rd ed. Pennsylvania:W. B. Saunders Company; 1995
28. Kassirer JP, Hricik DE and Cohen JJ. Repairing Body Fluids Principles and Practice. Philadelphia:W.B. Saunders Company; 1989
29. Narins RG. ed. Clinical Disorders of Fluid and Electrolyte Metabolism. 5th ed. New York:McGraw-Hill, Inc.; 1994
30. Matz R. Hyperosmolar nonacidotic diabetes (HNAD). In Rifkin H, Porte D; eds. Diabetes Mellitus, Theory and Practice, 4th ed. New York:Elsevier pp 604-16; 1990
31. Kitabchi AE, Fisher JN, Murphy MB, Rumbak MJ. Diabetic ketoacidosis and the hyperglycemic hyperosmolar nonketotic state. In Kahn CR, Weir GC; eds. Joslin's Diabetes Mellitus, 13th ed. Philadelphia:Lea & Febiger pp 738-70; 1994
32. Olson OC. Diagnosis and Management of Diabetes Mellitus. 2nd ed. New York:Raven Press. pp 296-299; 1988

33. Lorber D. Nonketotic Hypertonicity in Diabetes Mellitus. Med Clin North Am Jan;79(1):39-52; 1995
34. Tierney Jr LM, McPhee SJ and Papadakis MA. eds. Current Medical Diagnosis and Treatment. 34th ed. Connecticut:Appleton and Lange. pp 1033-1034; 1995
35. Medical Management of Non-Insulin-Dependent (Type II) Diabetes.3rd ed. American Diabetes Association, Inc., Alexandria,VA, 1994
36. Berkow R, Fletcher AJ, et al. The Merck Manual of Diagnosis and Therapy. 16th ed. New Jersey:Merk and Co., Inc.; 1992
37. Morley JE , Perry HM 3d. The management of diabetes mellitus in older individuals. Drugs Apr;41(4):548-65; 1991
38. Morley JE, Mooradian AD, Rosenthal MJ, Kaiser FK. Diabetes in elderly patients: is it different? American Journal of Medicine 83: 533-544; 1987
39. Rosenthal MJ, Hartnell JM, Morley JE, et al. Diabetes in the elderly. Journal of the American Geriatrics Society 35:435-447; 1987
40. Harris MI, Hadden WC, Knowlen WC, et al. Prevalence of diabetes and impaired glucose tolerance and plasma glucose levels in US population ages 20-74 years. Diabetes 136:523-534; 1987
41. Center for Economic Studies in Medicine: Direct and indirect costs of diabetes in the United States in 1987, p.9, American Diabetes Association Inc., Washington, DC, 1988
42. Huse DM, Oster G, Kellen AR, et al. The economic costs of non-insulin-dependent diabetes mellitus. Journal of the American Medical Association 262: 2708-2713; 1989
43. Waugh NR, Dallas JM, Jung RT, Newton RW. Mortality in a cohort of diabetic patients. Diabetologia 32:103-104; 1989
44. Brownlee M, Cerami A, Vlassarci M. Advanced glycosylation end products in tissue and the biochemical bases of diabetic complications. New England Journal of Medicine 318:1315-1321; 1988
45. Phillips PA, Rolls BJ, Ledingham JG, et al. Reduced thirst after water deprivation in healthy elderly men. New England Journal of Medicine 311:753-758; 1984
46. Silver AJ, Morley JE. The role of the opioid system in hypodipsia of aging. Clinical Research 37:90A; 1989
47. Morley JE, Hernandez EN and Flood JF. Neuropeptide Y increases food intake in mice. Am J Physiol. 253:R516-522; 1987
48. Morley, JE. Nutritional status of the elderly. Am. J. Med.81:679-695; 1986
49. Morley, JE and Flood JF. The effect of neuropeptide Y on drinking in mice. Brain Res. Aug 7;494(1):129-37; 1989
50. Rolls BJ, Wood RJ, Rolls ET et al. Thirst following water deprivation in humans. Am J Physiol. 239:R476-R482; 1980
51. Silver AJ and Morley JE. Role of the opioid system in the hypodipisia associated with aging. J Am Geriatr Soc. Jun;40(6):556-60; 1992
52. Yamamoto T, Harada H, Fukuyama J et al. Impaired arginine-vasopressin secretion associated with hypoangiotensinemia inhypernatremic dehydrated elderly patients. JAMA. 259;1039-1042; 1988
53. Miller PD, Krebs RA, Neal BJ, McIntyre DO. Hypodipisia in Geriatric Patients. Am J Med. 73:354-356; 1982
54. Rowe JW, Shock NW, De Fronzo RA. The influence of age on the renal response to water deprivation in man. Nephron. 17:270-278; 1976
55. Helderman JH, Vestal RE, Rowe JW, Shock NW. The response of arginine vasopressin to intravenous ethanol and hypertonic saline in man: The impact of aging. J Gerontol 33:39-47; 1978
56. Kirkland J, Lye M, Goddard G et al. Plasma arginine vasopressin in dehydrated elderly patients. Clin Endocrinol. 20:451-456; 1984
57. Phillips PA, Rolls BJ, Ledingham JG et al. Reduced thirst after water deprivation in healthy elderly men. N Engl J Med. 311:753-759; 1984
58. Li CH, Hsieh SM, Nagai I. The response of plasma arginine vasopressin to 14h water deprivation in the elderly. Acta Endocrinol. 105:314-317; 1984
59. Crowe MJ, Forsling ML, Rolls BJ et al. Altered water excretion in healthy elderly men. Age Ageing 16:285-293; 1987
60. Epstein A. The physiology of thirst. In: Pfaff DW, ed. ThePhysiological Mechanisms of Motivation. New York, Springer-Verlag, pp 162-214; 1982
61. Lavisso-Mourey R, Johnson J, Stolley P. Risk factors for dehydration among elderly nursing home residents. J Am Geriatr Soc. 36:213-218; 1988
62. Fortney S, Miescher E, Rolls B. Body hydration and aging. Prog Biometeorol. 7:105-112; 1989
63. Miescher E, Fortney S. Responses to dehydration and rehydration during heat exposure in young and older men. Am J Physiol. 257:1050-1056; 1989
64. Morley JE, Levine AS, Yim GK, Lowry MT. Opioid modulation of appetite. Neurosci Biobehav Rev. 7:281-305; 1983
65. Brown DR, Holtzman SG. Evidence that opiate receptors mediate suppression of hypertonic saline-

induced drinking in the mouse by narcotic antagonists. Life Sci 26:1543-1550; 1980

66. Ostrowski NL, Rowland N, Foley TL et al. Morphine antagonists and consummatory behaviors. Pharmacol Biochem Behav. 14:549-559; 1981

67. Rowland N. Comparison of the suppression by naloxone of water intake induced in rats by hyperosmolarity, hypovolemia, and angiotensin. Pharmacol Biochem Behav. 16:87-91; 1982

68. Fishman SM, Carr DB. Naloxone blocks exercise-stimulated water intake in the rat. Life Sci. 32:2523-2527; 1983

69. Siviy SM, Calcagretti DJ, Reid LD. Opioids and palatability. In: Hoebel BG, Novin D, eds. The Neural Basis of Feeding and Reward. Brunswick:Haer Institute, pp 517-530; 1982

70. Holtzman SG. Effects of narcotic antagonists on fluid intake in the rat. Life Sci. 16:1465-1470; 1975

71. Rolls BJ, Phillips PA. Aging and disturbances of thirst and fluid balance. Nutr Rev. 48:137-144; 1990

72. Fink K, Zentner J, and Göthert M. Increased GABA Release in the Human Brain Cortex as a Potential Pathogenetic Basis of Hyperosmolar Diabetic Coma. J Neurochem. Apr;62(4):1476-81; 1994

73. Rosen AS and Andrew RD Glucose concentration inversely alters neocortical slice excitability through an osmotic effect. Brain Res. 555,58-64; 1991

74. Fink K and Göthert M High D-glucose concentration increase GABA release but inhibit release of norepinephrine and 5-hydroxytryptamine in rat cerebral cortex. Brain Res. 618,220-226; 1993

75. Olsen RW. Drug interactions at the GABA receptor-ionophore complex. Annu. Rev. Pharmacol. Toxicol. 22,245-277; 1982

76. Umpierrez GE, Khajavi M, Kitabchi AE. Review: Diabetic Ketoacidosis and Hyperglycemic Hyperosmolar Nonketotic Syndrome. Am J Med Sci 311(5):225-233; 1996

77. Munshi MN, Martin RE, Fonseca VA. Hyperosmolar Nonketotic Diabetic Syndrome Following Treatment of Human Immunodeficiency Virus Infection With Didanosine. Diabetes Care Apr;17(4):316-7; 1994

78. Fishbein HA. Diabetic ketoacidosis, hyperosmolar coma, lactic acidosis and hypoglycemia. In Harris MI, Hamman RF; eds. Diabetes in America (National Diabetes Group). Washington, DC:Department of Health and Human Services pp 1-22; 1985

79. Schade DS, Eaton RP, Alberti KGGM, Johnston DG. Diabetic Coma:Ketoacidosis and Hyperosmolar, 1st ed. Albuquerque: University of New Mexico Press pp 3-9; 1981

80. Kitabchi AE, Ayyagari V, Guerra SMO, Medical House Staff. The efficacy of low dose versus conventional therapy of insulin for treatment of diabetic ketoacidosis. Ann Intern Med. 84:633-8; 1976

81. Gonzalez-Campoy JM, Robertson RP Diabetic ketoacidosis and hyperosmolar nonketotic state: gaining control over extreme hyperglycemic complications. Postgrad Med Jun;99(6):143-52; 1996

82. Ennis ED, Stahl EJVB, Kreisberg RA. The hyperosmolar hyperglycemic syndrome. Diabetes Review. 2:115-26; 1994

83. Sament S, Schwartz SA. Severe diabetic stupor without Ketosis. S. Afr. Med. J. 31,893-4; 1957

84. Piniés JA, Cairo G, Gaztambide S, Vazquez JA. Course and prognosis of 132 patients with diabetic non ketotic hyperosmolar state. Diabete Metab Jan-Feb;20(1):43-8; 1994

85. Gill GV, Alberti KG. Hyperosmolar nonketotic coma. Pract. diabetes 2,30-5; 1985

86. Wachtel TJ, Tetu-Mourddjian LM, Goldman DL. Hyperosmolarity and acidosis in diabetes mellitus: a three-year experience in Rhode Island. J. Gen. Intern. Med. 6,495-502; 1991

87. Wilson BE, Sharma A. Public cost and access to primary care for hyperglycemic emergencies, Clark County, Nevada. J Community Health Jun;20(3):249-56; 1995

88. Gerich JE, Martin MM, Recant L Clinical and metabolic characteristics of hyperosmolar nonketotic coma. Diabetes 20:228-238; 1971

89. Wachtel TJ, Silliman RA, Lamberton P Predisposing factors for the diabetic hyperosmolar state. Arch Intern Med 147:499-501; 1987

90. Pope DW, Dansky D Hyperosmolar hyperglycemic nonketotic coma. Emerg Med Clin North Am 7:849-857; 1989

91. Cruz-Caudillo JC, Sabatini S Diabetic hyperosmolar syndrome Nephron 69(3):201-10; 1995

92. Wachtel TJ. The diabetic hyperosmolar state. Clin GeriatrMed. 6:797-806; 1990

93. Balzan M, Cocciottolo JM Neuroleptic malignant syndrome presenting as hyperosmolar non-ketotic diabetic coma. Br J Psychiatry 161:257-258; 1992

94. Kitabchi AE, Murphy MB Diabetic ketoacidosis and hyperosmolar hyperglycemic nonketotic coma. Med Clin North Am 72:1545-1563; 1988

95. Podolsky S. Hyperosmolar nonketotic coma: Death can be prevented. Geriatrics. 34:207-208; 1979

96. Durr F. Beitrag zum hyperosmolaren nichtacidotischen koma bei Diabetes Mellitus. Dtsch Med. Wsch. 89,76; 1964

97. Siperstein MD. Diabetic ketoacidosis and hyperosmolar coma. Endocrinol Metab Clin North Am. Jun;21(2):415-32; 1992

98. Plauchu MM, Arnaud PH, Pousset G.Le coma par hyperosmolarite chez les diabetiques. A propos de cinquante observations dont deux personnelles. J. Méd. Lyon 47,1413-29; 1996
99. Cahill GF. Hyperglycemic hyperosmolar coma: A syndrome almost unique to the elderly. J. Am Geriatr Soc 31:103-105; 1983
100. Mc Cardy D. Hyperosmolar hyperglycemic non-ketotic diabetic coma. Med Clin North Am 54:683-699; 1970
101. Carrol P, Matz R. Uncontrolled diabetes mellitus in adults: Experience in treating diabetic ketoacidosis and hyperosmolar nonketotic coma with low-dose insulin and a uniform treatment regimen. Diabetes Care 6:579-585; 1983
102. Levine SN, Sanson TH. Treatment of hyperglycemic hyperosmolar non-ketotic syndrome. Drugs 38:462-472; 1989
103. Maccario M Neurological dysfunction associated with nonketotic hyperglycemia. Arch Neurol 19:525-534; 1968
104. Podolsky S. Hyperosmolar nonketotic coma in the elderly diabetic. Med Clin North Am 62:815-828; 1978.
105. Asplund K, Eriksson S, Hagg E, Lithner F, Strand T, Wester PO. Hyperosmolar nonketotic coma in diabetic stroke patients. Acta Med Scand 212:407-411; 1982
106. Genuth SM. Diabetic ketoacidosis and hyperglycemic hyperosmolar coma. Curr Ther Endocrinol Metab 5:400-6; 1994
107. Khardori R, Soler NG. Hyperosmolar hyperglycaemic nonketotic syndrome. Report of 22 cases and brief review. Am J Med. 77:899-904; 1984
108. Fulop M, Tannenbaum H, Dreyer N Ketotic hyperosmolar coma. Lancet ii:635-639; 1973
109. Rolfe M, Ephraim GG, Lincoln DC, Huddle KR. Hyperosmolar non-ketotic diabetic coma as a cause of emergency hyperglycaemic admission to Baragwanath Hospital. S Afr Med J. Mar;85(3):173-6; 1995
110. Wang L, Tsai S, Ho L, Hu S and Lee C. Rhabdomyolysis in diabetic emergencies. Diabetes Res. Clin. Pract. 26:209-214; 1994
111. Krentz AJ, Nattrass M. Diabetic ketoacidosis, non-ketotic hyperosmolar coma and lactic acidosis. In: Pickup J. Williams G. eds. Textbook of Diabetes. Vol. 1. Oxford:Blackwell Scientific 479-494; 1991

HYDRATION AND CRITICAL ILLNESS IN THE ELDERLY

A. T. H. CHENG, L. D. PLANK, G. L. HILL

University Department of Surgery, Auckland Hospital, Park Road, Grafton, Auckland. New Zealand. Correspondence to : Prof. G. L. Hill University Department of Surgery Auckland Hospital Private Bag 92024 Park Road, Grafton, Auckland 3 New Zealand. Funding Sources L.D.P. was supported by the Health Research Council of New Zealand.

Abstract : *Critical illness is accompanied by profound derangements in body composition including massive proteolysis and expansion of body water. We have examined the changes in total body water (TBW), total body protein (TBP) and fat-free body mass (FFM) in a group of ten elderly patients (median age 72, range 68 to 84 years) over a three-week period following admission to intensive care with severe sepsis. TBP decreased by 12 percent over this period while hydration of the FFM, represented by the ratio of TBW to FFM, remained elevated throughout. This prolonged overhydration is in contrast to our earlier findings in young critically injured patients who more rapidly restore hydration to normal levels. The results highlight the importance of careful attention to fluid and electrolyte status in the critically ill, elderly patient in order to hasten normalisation of hydration.*

Key Words : *critical illness, sepsis, body composition, total body water, fat-free mass, elderly*

INTRODUCTION

Critical illness is invariably associated with profound derangements in body composition and this is particularly apparent when the changes in hydration are examined. Following major injury or sepsis, the characteristic compositional changes are massive proteolysis and lipolysis associated with expansion of body water [1, 2]. Changes in hydration therefore reflect on the one hand the wasting of body cell mass with reduction in both intracellular water and protein, and on the other an expansion of extracellular water. The balance between these processes is implicitly expressed by the ratio of total body water to fat-free body mass (TBW/FFM), known as the hydration of fat-free mass, and it is this balance which reflects the clinical picture so readily observed in critical illness [3].

Aging is also accompanied by predictable changes in body composition, reflecting the changes associated with alterations in metabolic and endocrine function [4]. Lean body mass, or the fat-free mass of the body, tends to decline progressively with age [5], due primarily to a reduction in muscle mass (up to 50 percent between the ages of 20 and 80) [6], and, with it, a corresponding decrease in total body water is seen, as demonstrated by extensive cross-sectional studies as well as a few longitudinal studies [7-11]. Available data suggests that there is a small increase in hydration of the fat-free mass with age in healthy individuals, due to a relative increase in the proportion of total body water that is in the extracellular space [12].

How these age-related changes in body composition and hydration are affected in critical illness have been little studied to date [13]. Until now, our knowledge of the metabolic response to critical illness in the elderly has been limited, and much of our understanding of these changes has been based on the responses of younger and generally healthier adults [14, 15]. We present our experience with studies of hydration in critical illness, drawing upon our observations in elderly patients who present with severe surgical sepsis.

PATIENTS AND METHODS

Our department has developed a highly specialised metabolic laboratory designed to carry out body composition studies on critically ill patients under the care of the intensive care unit (Department of Critical Care Medicine, DCCM). In recent years, we have carried out a number of extensive studies examining the sequential changes in metabolic response in critically ill patients to either major trauma or severe sepsis using methodology especially adapted for use in critically ill, intensive care patients [16].

Patients

Criteria for entry to our studies of severe sepsis were those of the ACCP/SCCM Consensus Conference [17]. These studies were approved by the North Health Ethics Committee and informed consent was obtained for each patient from their nominated next-of-kin prior to entry into the study.

Clinical Management of Patients with Severe Sepsis in Intensive Care

Patients were managed in consensus fashion by a group of five full-time Intensivists, according to standard clinical guidelines and a series of protocols. Patients were ventilated to normoxaemia and normocarbia, and positive end expiratory pressure (PEEP) was limited to 15 cm H_2O or less, unless required for alveolar flooding or hypoxaemia despite an inspiratory oxygen fraction (FiO2) of more than 0.8. Patients were sedated with morphine and pancuronium, with intermittent diazepam added when neuromuscular blockade was desired [18]. Tracheostomy (percutaneous) was performed before ventilatory weaning in some cases.

Circulatory resuscitation was guided by clinical assessment, including continuous monitoring of thoracic compliance, core temperature, pulse oximetry, intra-arterial blood pressure and electrocardiography (ECG). For plasma volume expansion, colloid (4% albumin, fresh frozen plasma, polygelatin or pentastarch) or physiological saline were used with transfusion of packed red cells to maintain the haematocrit between 0.30 and 0.40. All patients received inotropic support with dopamine and, in the majority of patients, noradrenaline [19]. In addition, some patients received infusions of adrenaline, dobutamine, milrinone or angiotensin [20]. All patients without contraindications received digoxin [21]. Amiodarone and/or DC cardioversion were used to control cardiac rhythm when required [22]. Pulmonary artery catheters were inserted only if shock, respiratory failure and renal function were simultaneously worsening. Resuscitation was considered optimal when mean arterial pressure was between 90 and 110 mmHg, the heart rate between 80 and 120 beats per minute and in sinus rhythm, acid-base status was corrected to normal, and urine output above 2 mL/kg/hr. Where necessary, intermittent veno-venous haemodialysis was utilised.

Antibiotics were given according to pre-determined protocol and were modified according to specific microbiological identification of definitive pathogens. No patient received selective decontamination of the gut, non-steroidal anti-inflammatory drugs or steroids. Only patients with blood found on nasogastric aspiration were given sucralfate, or famotidine was used instead if there was massive gastric fluid loss. Famotidine was also given for enterocutaneous fistula.

In all cases, patients were given either enteral or parenteral nutrition as soon as clinically indicated [23, 24]. Enteral feeding (via nasogastric or nasojejunal tubes) using a polymeric formula (Osmolite, Ross Laboratories, Columbus, Ohio, USA), with a caloric distribution of 15% protein, 32% fat and 53% carbohydrate, or a parenteral formula (Baxter Healthcare New Zealand Ltd, Auckland, NZ), with a caloric distribution of 20% protein, 40% fat and 40% carbohydrate, was administered as clinically determined. Parenteral nutrition was administered via dedicated single-lumen central venous catheters.

Survivors were transferred from intensive care in the DCCM when endotracheal intubation, ventilatory support (including continuous positive airway pressure) and titrated inotropic support were no longer required. Tracheostomy, haemodialysis, intravenous nutrition, or low-dose dopamine infusion did not preclude ward care, but patients receiving several such therapies at once often remained in intensive care.

Study Design

Patients underwent measurements of body weight, total body fat (TBF), total body protein (TBP) and total body water (TBW) as soon as haemodynamic stability (defined by no escalation of inotropic support or resuscitation fluids) was achieved (day 0), and these were repeated 5, 10 and 21 days later. Body weight, obtained from a hoist-weighing system used to transfer the patients from bed to scanners, was recorded to the nearest 0.1 kg.

Measurement of Total Body Fat and Fat-free Mass

Measurement of TBF was carried out using dual-energy x-ray absorptiometry (DEXA) (Model DPX+, software version 3.6y, Lunar Radiation Corp., Madison, Wisconsin, USA). This technique is based on the differential absorption of two photons with energies of 38 and 70 keV through soft tissue and bone. In areas where bone is not present, suitable calibration allows fat and lean fractions to be resolved from soft tissue. The composition of these areas of soft tissue is extrapolated to the soft tissue overlying bone to produce TBF. Using anthropometric phantoms of known fat content, and with different levels of hydration, we have found short-term precision for TBF measurements to be 1.3% and with an accuracy within 5% [16].

Fat-free mass (FFM) was calculated from the difference between measured body weight and TBF.

Measurement of Total Body Protein

Measurement of TBP was carried out using prompt gamma in vivo neutron activation analysis whereby total body nitrogen (TBN) is obtained independently of total body hydrogen using a method previously described [25]. Whole-body scans were performed twice. We have found this method has a precision of 2.5% and an accuracy of within 4% compared with chemical analysis of anthropometric phantoms [16]. Total body protein was calculated as follows:
$$TBP = TBN \times 6.25.$$

Measurement of Total Body Water

TBW was measured by dilution of tritiated water according to previously published methods [26]. Each patient received 10 mL of 3.7 MBq tritiated water intravenously at the time of each body composition measurement. Venous blood was sampled at 4, 5 and 6 hours after administration and analysed for tritium content. TBW obtained by this method approaches a precision of 0.9% as compared to 1.5% when only a single sample is obtained. No correction was made for non-aqueous exchangeable hydrogen.

Hydration of the Fat-free Mass

The ratio of TBW/FFM for each patient was calculated on days 0, 5, 10 and 21 of the study. Normal values were obtained from the measurements of TBW and FFM on healthy volunteers performed in our laboratory using the same techniques. This was carried out in 104 males (aged 17 to 80 years) and 154 females (aged 19 to 74 years).

Statistical Analysis

Changes over time were assessed by repeated measures analysis of variance with correction made for asphericity (SAS Institute, Cary, North Carolina, USA). For comparison of two samples of paired data between study days, Student's t-test was used. In all cases, a 5% level of significance was chosen. All numerical values are expressed as mean ± standard error of the mean (SEM).

RESULTS

Over a 28 month period, 56 patients entered our studies of severe sepsis. Nineteen of these patients were over the age of 65 years and, of these, a total of ten patients (median 72 years, range 68 to 84 years) completed the study protocol. Of the other nine patients, three died within the first 5 days, one withdrew after 10 days, while the remaining five (of whom two died beyond 21 days) failed to complete the study protocol.

Table 1 summarises the clinical details of the ten patients who completed the study protocol. It can be seen that eight of the patients had peritonitis secondary to perforation of an intraabdominal viscus, one patient had an ischaemic bowel complicating a ruptured abdominal aortic aneurysm and one patient had empyema thoracis complicating a traumatic pneumothorax. The acute physiology score (APS) for these patients, which is determined from the most deranged values of 12 physiologic variables during the first 24 hours after admission into intensive care and forms the major component of the APACHE II score [27-29], ranged from 10 to 30 with a median of 17.5 (APACHE II = 22.5). Whilst 8 of the 10 patients had some form of pre-existing comorbidity, only one had a history of congestive heart failure and none had a history of clinically significant renal failure. No patient had a prior health status class above B (class C being the presence of chronic disease producing serious restriction of activity).

One patient, a 70 year old man with peritonitis secondary to a perforated infarcted small bowel, died 26 days after admission to the intensive care unit. His clinical course was affected by high intraabdominal pressures necessitating staged abdominal repair, complicated further by fistula formation, small bowel obstruction on day 15 and intraabdominal bleeding on day 16 of admission, both requiring repeat laparotomies. He was the only patient requiring surgery beyond 7 days after admission to critical care. Of the other nine patients, four had to return to the operating rooms on at least one further occasion, and all bar two had a percutaneous tracheostomy performed in the DCCM prior to ventilatory weaning.

The median interval from time of admission to the DCCM to the time of the first study (period of haemodynamic instability) was 2 days (range 1 to 5 days). Median duration of stay in the critical care unit and hospital were 12 and 30 days, respectively.

Table 1

Clinical data of 10 elderly patients who underwent sequential metabolic studies over 21 days after onset of severe sepsis

Patient	Sex	Age	A II	Diagnosis (Bacteriology)	Surgical Procedures*	Clinical events*	Comorbidity*	PHS
JA	M	70	30	Peritonitis due to perforated obstructed small bowel (E. faecalis)	Small bowel resection (0) Staged abdominal repair (4,11,15) Tracheostomy (12) Laparotomy (16)	Acute renal failure (4) Small bowel obstruction (15) Abdominal hematoma (16) Death (26)	Ulcerative colitis with past total colectomy and ileostomy	A
RB	F	71	19	Peritonitis due to perforated sigmoid diverticulum (No organism isolated)	Hartmann's operation (0)	Septic shock (0)	Hypertension Past repair of ventricular septal defect	B
AC	M	73	34	Ischaemia of sigmoid colon complicating ruptured abdominal aneurysm (No organism isolated)	Repair of aortic aneurysm and incarcerated inguinal hernia (0) Tracheostomy (6)	Septic shock, Adult Respiratory Distress Syndrome (0) Acute renal failure, inferior myocardial infarction (1)	Chronic obstructive respiratory disease	B
BC	M	84	23	Peritonitis due to perforated gallbladder (Mixed gram negative bacilli)	Cholecystectomy (0) Pleural drainage (3) Tracheostomy (3)	Acute renal failure (1) Pleural effusion (3)	Anterior myocardial infarction (-11)	B
FC	F	76	19	Peritonitis due to perforated sigmoid carcinoma (No organism isolated)	Hartmann's operation (0) Pleural drainage (0)	Septic shock (0) Pneumothorax (0)	Hypertension Rheumatoid arthritis	B
SG	F	68	15	Peritonitis due to perforated sigmoid diverticular abscess (E.coli, P. aeruginosa)	Hartmann's operation (0) Staged abdominal repair (3,5) Tracheostomy (4)	Acute renal failure (0) Adult Respiratory Distress Syndrome (4) Respiratory failure (23)	Fracture neck of femur (-2) Past radiotherapy for carcinoma of cervix	A
MN	F	72	29	Peritonitis due to perforated ischaemic sigmoid colon (Mixed gram negative flora)	Hartmann's operation (0) Staged abdominal repair (4,7) Tracheostomy (4)	Septic shock (0) Coagulopathy (0) Stomal infarction (7)	Hypertension Previous transient cerebral ischaemic attacks	B
DT	F	73	19	Empyema thoracis (posttraumatic pneumothorax) (S. aureus)	Pleural drainage (-6) Pleural drainage/lavage (0-3) Tracheostomy (5)	Rapid atrial fibrillation (0)	Nil	A
LT	F	70	24	Peritonitis due to infarcted small bowel volvulus (No organism isolated)	Small bowel resection (0) Tracheostomy (4) Right hemicolectomy (7)	Septic shock (0) Acute renal failure (4) Intestinal haemorrhage (7)	Hypertension Ischaemic heart disease Congestive heart failure	B
JW	F	70	22	Peritonitis due to gallstone ileus with small bowel perforation (No organism isolated)	Small bowel resection (0) Tracheostomy (5) Small bowel repair (6)	Septic shock (0) Coagulopathy (0) Small bowel leak (6)	Nil	A

A II = APACHE II score; PHS = Prior health status (class A, B, C or D).
*Parenthetical figures refer to days of admission to the Department of Critical Care.

Table 2 lists the mean (± SEM) data for the measurements of body weight, TBF, TBP and TBW on each of the four study days. It can be seen that, on average, these elderly patients had lost 1.02 ± 0.19 kg of protein (p=0.005) over the 21-day study period, corresponding to a mean loss of 11.5 percent of protein stores from day 0. This compares with an overall loss of 9.32 ± 1.55 kg or an average of 16.3 percent of fat-free mass (p=0.001). There was no significant change in fat mass over the study period (p=0.35).

Table 2

Sequential body composition measurements over 21 days in 10 elderly patients with severe sepsis.

	Day 0	Day 5	Day 10	Day 21	p value*
BWt (kg)	79.9±4.6	79.1±5.3	78.7±5.4	69.8±4.6‡	0.005
TBF (kg)	22.78±2.40	22.03±2.30	21.86±2.26	22.07±2.21	0.35
TBP (kg)	8.89±0.45	8.67±0.44	8.26±0.41	7.87±0.39†	<0.0001
TBW (L)	44.45±2.71	43.81±3.38	42.00±3.46	36.84±2.70‡	0.007

BWt = body weight; TBF = total body fat; TBP = total body protein; TBW = total body water.
Values are shown as: mean ± standard error of the mean.
* p value determined using repeated measures analysis of variance.
† p<0.05 for paired t-test vs. preceding measurement.
‡ p<0.01 for paired t-test vs. preceding measurement.

Figure 1 shows the changes in TBW that occurred in these ten patients. Over the period of haemodynamic instability before the first study day (day 0), during which time the patients had received over 21.60 ± 5.43 litres of crystalloids and colloids for resuscitation, there was a positive fluid balance of 10.87 ± 2.79 litres. By day 10, the patients had lost an average of 2.46 ± 2.77 litres of this excess body water. By day 21, this loss had increased to 7.61 ± 1.56 litres. When measured at day 0, the average hydration of the fat-free mass was 0.781 ± 0.011, compared with a value of 0.773 ± 0.011 obtained on day 21 (p=0.53 over the 21 days) (Figure 2). Values for TBW/FFM obtained in the group of healthy volunteers measured in our laboratory were 0.709 ± 0.004 and 0.751 ± 0.003 for males and females, respectively.

Figure 1
Total body water (TBW) in 10 elderly patients with severe sepsis over
a 21-day study period. TBW at the time of admission to the intensive care
unit was estimated (shown by dotted line) from the fluid balance over
the period of haemodynamic instability (median of 2 days). Bars indicate
SEM. *Significant change from preceding measurement.

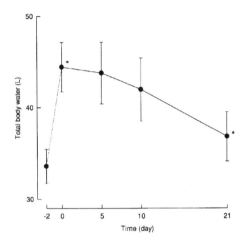

Figure 2
Hydration of the fat-free body mass (TBW/FFM) in 10 elderly patients
with severe sepsis over a 21-day study period. The mean value for
TBW/FFM based on measurements performed in our laboratory of 258
healthy volunteers, weighted for sex distribution, is shown (dotted line).
Bars indicate SEM.

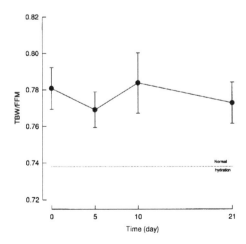

DISCUSSION

Severe sepsis produces a characteristic metabolic response in which there is massive proteolysis associated with an increased hydration of the fat-free body mass. The body compositional changes that ensue can be considered in distinct, sequential phases. Like the traumatic or haemorrhagic insult, the septic insult is associated with a sequestration phase and a mobilisation phase [30]. In the early response to shock and resuscitation, pathophysiologic and homeostatic changes lead to expansion of total body water, especially of the interstitial space, a process which occurs at the expense of the intravascular volume [31]. This phenomenon of extravascular sequestration is obligatory, occurs independent of organ function, and is due largely to an increase in capillary permeability [32] but is also associated with structural and functional changes in the interstitial matrix and cell membrane [33]. The volume of fluid sequestered in the extravascular space may be massive in the case of a severe septic insult, particularly with peritonitis where massive soilage in the peritoneal cavity occurs. In addition, severe sepsis often leads to a hyperdynamic state associated with peripheral vasodilatation, which increases the capacitance of the circulatory system. Consequently, large volumes of resuscitation fluids are required to achieve haemodynamic stability.

Our results have shown the magnitude of the volume of fluid required for resuscitation and its effects on the hydration of the fat-free body in a group of elderly, critically ill patients. In these ten patients presenting with severe surgical sepsis, an average of over 21 litres of resuscitation fluids was required to achieve haemodynamic stability. A large volume of this resuscitative infusate was retained (a net fluid accumulation of over 10 litres) and gross expansion of TBW occurred. At day 0, there was major overhydration of the fat-free mass with a ratio of TBW to FFM of 0.78, which is well above the average value obtained for normal adults in our own series, weighted according to sex distribution (shown in Figure 2), and outside generally accepted biological limits for normal hydration of the fat-free mass (0.69 to 0.75) [34-37]. More importantly, from the clinician's point of view, this state of relative overhydration persisted throughout the 21 day study, despite the loss of over 70 percent of the retained resuscitative fluid over this period, as indicated by the fall in TBW from day 0 and especially after day 10.

We have previously examined the effects of blunt trauma on the sequential changes in water, fat and protein metabolism in ten critically injured patients (median age 33 years), defined by an injury severity score of 16 or greater [14]. In this study, it was shown that these patients had retained nearly five litres of resuscitative fluids by the time they were haemodynamically stable (a median period of 3 days in the intensive care unit) but, by day 10, an average of over four-and-a-half litres, or 90 percent of the retained resuscitative fluids, had already been excreted, with mean TBW and hydration (TBW/FFM of 0.74) having returned to pre-trauma levels. By contrast, in the elderly septic patients, less than 30 percent of the retained resuscitation fluids had been dissipated after the first 10 days. Moreover, after three weeks, it is apparent from Figure 1 that mean TBW levels had yet to return to pre-illness levels and not until after the second week of illness, or the last 10 days of the study period, had mobilisation of body water occurred to a significant extent.

Mobilisation of total body water occurs principally due to loss of extracellular water, but we have shown elsewhere that loss of intracellular water occurs as well [15]. Whilst intracellular water is lost in similar proportion to loss of body cell mass, as measured by total body potassium, we have shown that cells lose water in quantities greater than would be expected from protein losses, indicating that cellular dehydration occurs over the course of critical illness. It has been suggested that cellular hydration state is an important determinant of protein catabolism and that this process is triggered and maintained by cell shrinkage secondary to cellular dehydration [38 39].

What are the clinical implications of these findings, particularly as they relate to elderly, critically ill patients? As already pointed out, aging is accompanied by a number of important changes in protein and fat metabolism, reflected by the changes in body composition so clearly demonstrated by Forbes and others [4-6]. Elderly people tend to have proportionately less body cell mass, and therefore less total body protein and more body fat, than younger subjects, which in turn reflects their diminished physiologic reserve. What is evident from the present study is that elderly, critically ill patients are no less prone to significant and major losses of body protein than younger subjects [14], but as a consequence of their lower initial protein mass, are more at risk of important losses of protein, a manifestation of their diminished 'metabolic reserve'. As a corollary, associated with this catabolic proteolysis, there may also be cellular dehydration, a process masked by the gross TBW expansion and concomitant overhydration of the fat-free body mass that occurs.

A profound increase in hydration of the fat-free mass of the body is therefore a hallmark of critical illness in the elderly, arising from the combination of loss of body cell mass and expansion of extracellular water, and hence total body water. Assessment of the ratio of TBW/FFM provides a useful index of illness in protein-losing, critically ill patients. That this hydration index remains so profoundly elevated even after mobilisation of body water has occurred raises concern about the effects of resuscitation in elderly patients and the time taken to normalise the hydration state. Transition from the sequestration phase to the mobilisation phase is often prolonged in the severely septic patient and may last several days [30]. Prolongation of this 'transitional phase' decreases the likelihood of recovery from the septic insult as the risk of a further septic insult increases, but once mobilisation and diuresis occur, the probability for recovery increases and survival then becomes more predictable. Thus, the important implication of delayed mobilisation of body water accumulation is one of ultimate survival and the reduced probability thereof.

What is evident is that the state of metabolic derangement is altogether more prolonged in the elderly, critically ill patient, as shown by the sequential changes in water and protein metabolism in these patients. The importance of careful support over this period between sequestration and mobilisation phases becomes even more critical in the elderly patient whose physiologic and metabolic reserves are frequently compromised [40]. Our findings are of importance to clinicians who are called to manage critically ill elderly patients. Once haemodynamic stability has been achieved, the septic or traumatic insult treated and renal function restored, special attention to sodium and water restriction and efforts to facilitate the mobilisation of sequestered fluid are required to hasten normalisation of the hydration state.

Acknowledgements : The authors wish to acknowledge the support and cooperation of the medical and nursing staff of the Department of Critical Care Medicine.

REFERENCES

1. MOORE F.D., OLSEN K.H., MCMURRAY J.D., et al. : The Body Cell Mass and Its Supporting Environment. Body Composition in Health and Disease. Philadelphia: W.B. Saunders, 1963.
2. MOORE F.D. : Metabolic care of the surgical patient. Philadelphia: W.B. Saunders, 1959.
3. MOORE F.D., BOYDEN C.M. : Body cell mass and limits of hydration of the fat-free body: their relation to estimated skeletal weight. Ann. N.Y. Acad. Sci. 1963, 110, 62-71.
4. FORBES G.B. : Human Body Composition. Growth, Aging, Nutrition, and Activity. Berlin: Springer-Verlag, 1987.
5. FORBES G.B. : The adult decline in lean body mass. Hum. Biol., 1976, 48, 161-173.
6. COHN S.H., VARTSKY D., YASUMURA S., et al. : Compartmental body composition based on total body nitrogen, potassium and calcium. Am. J. Physiol., 1980, 239, E524-530.
7. WATSON P.E., WATSON R.D., BATT R.D. : Total body water volumes for adult males and females estimated from simple anthropometric measurements. Am. J. Clin. Nutr., 1980, 33, 27-39.
8. SHOCK N.W., WATKIN D.M., YIENGST M.J. : Age differences in the water content of the body as related to basal oxygen consumption in males. J. Gerontol., 1963, 18, 1-8.

9. FULOP T. Jr., WORUM I., CSONGOR J., FORIS G., LEOVEY A. : Body composition in elderly people. I. Determination of body composition by multiisotope methods and the elimination kinetics of these isotopes in healthy elderly subjects. Gerontol., 1985, 31, 6-14.
10. LESSER G.T., MARKOVSKY J. : Body water compartments with human aging using fat-free mass as the reference standard. Am. J. Physiol., 1979, 236, R215-220.
11. STEEN B., ISAKSSON B., SVANBERG A. : Body composition at 70 and 75 years of age: some longitudinal observations. J. Clin. Exp. Gerontol., 1979, 1, 185-200.
12. SCHOELLER D.A. : Changes in total body water with age. Am. J. Clin. Nutr., 1989, 50, 1176-1181.
13. WATTERS J.M., WILMORE D.W. : Physiology of aging: the response to injury. In: Meakins J.L., McLaran J.C., eds. Surgical care of the elderly. Chicago: Year Book Publishers, 1988, 76-87.
14. MONK D.N., PLANK L.D., FRANCH-ARCAS G., et al. : Sequential changes in the metabolic response in critically injured patients during the first 25 days after blunt trauma. Ann. Surg., 1996, 223(4), 395-405.
15. FINN P.J., PLANK L.D., CLARK M.A., et al. : Progressive cellular dehydration and proteolysis in critically ill patients. Lancet, 1996, 347, 654-656.
16. HILL G.L., MONK D.N., PLANK L.D. : Measuring body composition in intensive care patients. In: Wilmore D.W., Carpentier Y.A., eds. Metabolic support of the critically ill patient. Berlin: Springer-Verlag, 1993, 3-18.
17. Members of the American College of Chest Physicians/Society of Critical Care Medicine Consensus Conference Committee. Definitions for sepsis and organ failure and guidelines for the use of innovative therapies in sepsis. Crit. Care Med., 1992, 20, 864–874.
18. ARMSTRONG D.K., CRISP C.B. : Pharmacoeconomic issues of sedation, analgesia, and neuromuscular blockade in critical care. New Horiz., 1994, 2, 85–93.
19. VINCENT J.L. : Do we need a dopaminergic agent in the management of the critically ill? J. Autonomic Pharmacology, 1990, 10, 123–127.
20. THOMAS V.L., NIELSEN M.S. : Administration of angiotensin II in refractory septic shock. Crit. Care Med., 1991, 19, 1084–1086.
21. NASRAWAY S.A., RACKOW E.C., ASTIZ M.E., CARRAS F., WEIL H. : Inotropic response to digoxin and dopamine in patients with severe sepsis, cardiac failure and systemic hypoperfusion. Chest, 1989, 95, 612–615.
22. CHAPMAN M.J., MORAN J.L., O'FATHARTAIGH M.S., PEISACH A.R., CUNNINGHAM D.N. : Management of atrial tachyarrhythmias in the critically ill: a comparison of intravenous procainamide and amiodarone. Inten. Care Med., 1993, 19, 48–52.
23. GRANT J.P. : Nutritional support in critically ill patients. Ann. Surg., 1994, 220, 610–616.
24. STREAT S.J., HILL G.L. : Nutritional support in the management of critically ill patients in surgical intensive care. World J. Surg., 1987, 11, 194–210.
25. MITRA S., PLANK L.D., HILL G.L. : Calibration of a prompt gamma in vivo neutron activation facility for direct measurement of total body protein in intensive care patients. Phys. Med. Biol., 1993, 38, 1971-1975.
26. STREAT S.J., BEDDOE A.H., HILL G.L. : Measurement of total body water in intensive care patients with fluid overload. Metabolism, 1985, 34, 688-694.
27. KNAUS W.A., ZIMMERMAN J.E., WAGNER D.P., et al. : APACHE—acute physiology and chronic health evaluation: a physiologically based classification system. Crit. Care Med., 1981, 9(8), 591-597.
28. KNAUS W.A., DRAPER E.A., WAGNER D.P., et al. : APACHE II—a severity of disease classification. Crit. Care Med., 1985, 13, 818-829.
29. MARGULIES D.R., LEKAWA M.E., BJERKE S. et al. : Surgical intensive care in the nonagenarian. No basis for age discrimination. Arch. Surg., 1993, 128, 753-758.
30. LUCAS C.E., LEDGERWOOD A.M. : Cardiovascular and renal response to hemorrhagic and septic shock. In: Clowes G. H. A., Jr., ed. Trauma, sepsis, and shock. The physiological basis of therapy. New York: Marcel Dekker, 1988, 187-215.
31. LUCAS C.E., LEDGERWOOD A.M. : The fluid problem in the critically ill. Surg. Clin. North Am., 1983, 63, 439-454.
32. PETRAKOS A., MYERS M.L., HOLLIDAY R.L., et al. : A systemic increase in capillary permeability in septicemia. Crit. Care Med., 1981, 9, 214.
33. DAWSON C.W., LUCAS C.E., LEDGERWOOD A.M. : Altered interstitial fluid space dynamics and post-resuscitation hypertension. Arch. Surg., 1981, 116, 657.
34. SHENG H.P., HUGGINS R.A. : A review of body composition studies with emphasis on total body water and fat. Am. J. Clin. Nutr., 1979, 32, 630-647.
35. BROZEK J., GRANDE F., ANDERSON T., et al. : Densitometric analysis of body composition: revisions of some quantitative assumptions. Ann. N.Y. Acad. Sci., 1963, 110, 113-140.

36. STREAT S.J., BEDDOE A.H., HILL G.L. : Measurement of body fat and hydration of the fat-free body in health and disease. Metabolism, 1985, 34(6), 509-518.
37. BEDDOE A.H., STREAT S.J., HILL G.L. : Hydration of fat free body mass in protein-depleted patients. Am. J. Physiol., 1985, 249(12), E227-233.
38. HÄUSSINGER D., ROTH E., LANG F., et al. : Cellular hydration state: an important determinant of protein catabolism in health and disease. Lancet, 1993, 341, 1330-1332.
39. HÄUSSINGER D. : The Wretlind Lecture. Regulation of metabolism by changes in cellular hydration. Clin. Nutr., 1995, 14, 4-12.
40. WATTERS J.M., BESSEY P.Q. : Critical care of the elderly patient. Surg. Clin. North Am., 1994, 74(1), 187-197.

Société d'Exploitation de l'Imprimerie ESPIC - 13, rue Gonzales - 31200 TOULOUSE
Dépôt légal n° 9712.65 - Décembre 1997